Europe and Ethnicity

Europe and Ethnicity examines the impact of the First World War on the ethnic map of Europe as it exists today. Specialist contributors present case studies of regions of conflict, each of which has its mixed legacy. Ranging from Yugoslavia, Czechoslovakia, the South Tyrol and Hungary to the Ukraine, the Baltic States, Ireland and the Middle East, *Europe and Ethnicity* presents a comprehensive picture of ethnic tensions in Europe.

While taking into account the Second World War and the ending of the Cold War, this collection presents and emphasises the enduring significance of decisions made during the Great War and the subsequent Peace Settlement. It points to the various ways in which ethnic conflicts have been, or might be, managed. Its conclusions bring fresh perspectives to issues of vital contemporary concern.

Seamus Dunn is Professor of Conflict Studies and Director of the Centre for the Study of Conflict at the University of Ulster.
T.G. Fraser is Professor of History and Head of the School of History, Philosophy and Politics at the University of Ulster.

Europe and Ethnicity

The First World War and
contemporary ethnic conflict

Edited by Seamus Dunn
and T.G. Fraser
With a Foreword by Dr Otto von Habsburg

London and New York

First published 1996
by Routledge
11 New Fetter Lane, London EC4P 4EE

Simultaneously published in the USA and Canada
by Routledge
29 West 35th Street, New York, NY 10001

Typeset in Palatino by Routledge
Printed and bound in Great Britain by Redwood Books, Trowbridge,
Wiltshire

British Library Cataloguing in Publication Data
A catalogue record for this book is available from the British Library

Library of Congress Cataloguing in Publication Data
A catalogue record for this book has been requested

ISBN 0–415–11995–2 (hbk)
ISBN 0–415–11996–0 (pbk)

Contents

Contributors

Antony Alcock is Professor of European Studies at the University of Ulster, specialising in the problems of minorities. He is author of *History of the South Tyrol Question* and *Sudtirol seit dem Paket*.

Seamus Dunn is Professor of Conflict Studies and Director of the Centre for the Study of Conflict at the University of Ulster. He is author and editor of a number of studies, including *Managing Divided Cities* and *Facets of the Northern Ireland Conflict*.

T.G. Fraser is Professor of History and Head of the School of History, Philosophy and Politics at the University of Ulster, formerly Fulbright Scholar-in-Residence, Indiana University South Bend. His books include *Partition in Ireland, India and Palestine: theory and practice* and *The Arab-Israeli Conflict*.

A.M. Gallagher is Reader in Education at The Queen's University of Belfast and formerly Research Fellow in the Centre for the Study of Conflict at the University of Ulster. He has written extensively on the Northern Ireland problem, including the *Majority–Minority Reports*.

Otto von Habsburg represents Bavaria in the European Parliament. He is the eldest son of the Archduke Charles, later Emperor of Austria and King of Hungary, and the Archduchess Zita, Princess of Bourbon-Parma. Sentenced to death in absentia by the National Socialists, he later worked for the independence of eastern Europe. He is the author of thirty-four books.

T. Hennessey is Research Officer in the Centre for the Study of Conflict at the University of Ulster where he specialises in modern Irish history and politics.

Ann Lane is Lecturer in Politics at The Queen's University of Belfast and formerly worked for the Historical Branch of the Foreign and Commonwealth Office. She specialises in the history of Yugoslavia on which she has published widely.

Raymond Pearson is Professor of European History at the University of Ulster, specialising in the ethnic history of eastern Europe. He is author of *Problems of Nationality in Eastern Europe* and *The Longman Companion to European Nationalism*.

Alan Sharp is Professor of International Studies at the University of Ulster. He is an authority on the Peace Settlement on which he has published *The Versailles Settlement*.

W.V. Wallace was Professor of History at The New University of Ulster and then Director of the Centre of Soviet and East European Studies at the University of Glasgow. A specialist in the history of eastern Europe, he is the author of *Czechoslovakia*.

Ken Ward is Senior Lecturer in History at the University of Ulster where he specialises in European history and the history of the mass media, on which he has published *The Mass Media and Modern Society*.

Andrew Wilson works in the Research Programme on Post-Soviet States in Transition at Sidney Sussex College, University of Cambridge. He is the author of *Ukrainian Nationalism in the 1990s: a minority faith*.

Foreword

Otto von Habsburg, MEP

The sequence of events in our century has much logic. There are laws of history, which cannot be violated without dire punishment. The sequence is uninterrupted: cause and effect.

Seen from this perspective, one can say that there is a common denominator between the Paris peace treaties at the end of the First World War, the crises which followed in the years between 1921 and 1938 and finally Yalta and its consequences down to the present. These events were predictable, but were generally not understood by those politicians who assumed responsibility for deciding the fate of the nations.

We have important witnesses who show that what happened was foreseeable. Already in 1921 the great Jacques Bainville published a book with the title *Les conséquences politiques de la paix* – 'The political consequences of the peace treaty'. Today anyone reading this text written more than seven decades ago will be deeply impressed by the clarity of Bainville's vision and the exact predictions he made. He had certainly understood that the politicians who dictated the conditions in Versailles, St-Germain and Trianon had acted in a highly irresponsible manner, because they did not accept the lessons of history.

In the year 1939, at the beginning of the Second World War, another great European intellectual, the Italian Guglielmo Ferrero, in his masterly book on the congress of Vienna had clearly determined the conditions for a genuine peace. He foresaw what would happen and consequently wanted, using history as an example, to show to those who would be responsible for a new order how they could accomplish a truly lasting peace. There were two main principles for achieving this end. It would be indispensable to include the vanquished in the peace negotiations just as Talleyrand had been permitted to sit at the table of the mighty in Vienna after the Napoleonic wars. Second, Ferrero emphasised that a first task would be to elaborate principles of peace that would be equally applicable to the victors and the vanquished. In other words, the great Italian anti-Fascist was determinedly opposed to dictating a treaty. Unfortunately nobody listened to him.

Indeed, one can say that Yalta was just a worse edition of Versailles, St Germain and Trianon. In the 1920s the defeated were barred from the negotiations. In Yalta even the allies of the winners were silenced. Only three men decided the fate of the world and of these one, Winston Churchill, was no longer speaking for a real power. He was the only one who saw what would happen, but his words were no longer listened to by the two representatives of the superpowers.

Since the collapse of the Soviet Union, that is the non-bloody end of the Cold War, a new peace treaty and a new peaceful order have to be established. So far, unfortunately, one does not perceive whether those in responsible positions have understood what this means. They do not seem to have realised yet that a new Congress of Vienna is necessary, if we want to find a solution to the world's problems. We have today, since the end of the Soviet superpower, not only a renascent Russian hegemonialism, but also many wars, which the existing powers are obviously unable to control.

The reason for this sad state of affairs is not only the ignorance of the rulers, but also the fact that, subsequent to the collapse of the former Soviet Union, for the first time a potential monopoly of power exists. The United States is reluctantly the last superpower. In any case it would be unable to fulfil this global task. It is an old historic experience that such a task needs the input of a wide partnership, that is, it is beyond the means of a single country. This is unfortunately lacking, because Europe has not yet found its unity and hence its capability to cope with the multiple problems of the Continent and of its surrounding areas.

This lack of partnership applies to the resurgent elements of national strife. The events in Bosnia herald what may come, for, seeing what is happening in Russia, one must say that national tensions are far from over. The question of ethnic minorities and nationalities is thus turning out once more to be one of the paramount problems that beset the world. Here the study of past events can provide valuable insights. It is a mistake to assume that these problems are insoluble. What man made, man can resolve. To that end they need the right information with adequate historical, geographical and ethnographical data. The study of ethnic conflicts is hence most important.

It is thus very fortunate that under the direction of Professor T.G. Fraser and Professor Seamus Dunn the University of Ulster, itself located in an area of old national tensions, has decided to turn its attention to the twentieth century's ethnic conflicts. This is a timely study, which should be read by those who are in responsible positions. One can but wish Professors Fraser and Dunn great success.

It would be in the interest of all European nations, if, this time at least, those who lead the destinies of the nations would take cognisance of the problems and not ignore them, like the contemporaries of Jacques Bainville, whose disregard for the advice of the great thinker made them responsible for one of humanity's greatest catastrophes.

Acknowledgements

The editors are grateful to Ruth McIlwaine, Pat Shortt and Joanne Taggart for their invaluable work on the manuscript. Crown copyright material is reproduced with the permission of the Controller of HMSO.

Chapter 1

Introduction

Seamus Dunn and T.G. Fraser

The intention of this book is to examine the proposition that – in simple terms – a number of the current political conflicts in the world are leftovers or unfinished business from the First World War. The currency of many of these conflicts – and the world-wide dangers created by the proliferation of small wars now at the end of the twentieth century – makes an understanding of their history and context important.

The structure of the book reflects this intention. It consists of this introduction, followed by a general scene-setting chapter; then, at the heart of the book, there are eight chapters, each written about a particular current political conflict or location; and, finally, there is a summary chapter based on the material presented in the rest of the book.

Obviously the set of conflicts or locations chosen for analysis cannot be seen as representative in any universal sense, mainly because any attempt at an exhaustive analysis of all the possible locations would have produced an impossibly large book. The eight examples, therefore, are intended to represent a sample of the range of possible, relevant locations, but chosen so as to reflect the complete spectrum of themes and issues. In each of the eight chapters the authors place the conflict in the context of the First World War, and reflect on the proposition that this war represents an important factor in current difficulties.

The two introductory chapters, along with the final chapter, elaborate on the central question addressed by the book. They deal with the impact and relevance of the war, and provide a general description and analysis with special reference to regions and states where the national and ethnic questions were particularly complex and intransigent. They also deal with the concepts of ethnicity and nationalism, and with the modern significance and ubiquity of ethnic conflict.

The Europe that emerged out of the aftermath of the First World War was barely recognisable as the continent whose statesmen, generals and peoples had rushed to war in 1914. Four powerful dynasties, as well as several minor German ones, had been cast aside by their peoples: the Ottomans who had led the Turks out of central Asia in the late Middle Ages to rule much of south-west Europe and the Arab civilisations of the Middle East; the Romanovs under whom the Russians had come to dominate much of the Eurasian land area; the Hohenzollerns who had welded most of the Germans into a Prussian-dominated empire in 1866–71; and the most venerable of them all, the Habsburgs, Catholic Europe's historic defender against Islam, protestantism, and latterly nationalism, whose possessions had once reached from central Europe to South America. Germany and Russia survived largely intact under new republican forms, the former being required to restore Alsace–Lorraine to France and the Polish Corridor to the reconstituted Poland, the latter conceding independence to Finland and the three small Baltic states of Estonia, Latvia and Lithuania. But the empires of the Ottomans and Habsburgs which for centuries had given coherence to the peoples of the Middle East and central Europe had been replaced by new states which had sprung to life, or in the case of the former been manufactured, in the name of 'self-determination'. The Ottoman empire had been succeeded by a new Turkish-dominated republic in Anatolia, its former Arab territories becoming the French Mandates of Syria and Lebanon and the British Mandates of Iraq, Palestine and Transjordan. Out of the Habsburg domains came the severely truncated nation states of Hungary and Austria, the latter denied its natural association with Germany, and the new countries of Czechoslovakia and the Kingdom of the Serbs, Croats and Slovenes, each of which reproduced in miniature the ethnic tensions of the old empire. The remaining parts of the earlier Habsburg possessions were distributed to Poland, Romania and Italy, with varying degrees of justice. While the far-reaching nature of these changes to the politico-ethnic map of Europe may in large measure be attributed to defeat, even the victors were not immune to the pace of change, for in the aftermath of the war Britain had to concede virtual independence to Ireland and to a partition of the island which rested to a considerable extent on the notion of 'self-determination'.

Such far-reaching changes to the structure of the continent could hardly have been imagined in the years prior to the outbreak of war. Imperial Germany had its ethnic groups, Danes, Poles and in Lorraine, which were described as *reichsfeindlich* ('hostile to the empire'), but otherwise only the United Kingdom, faced with the seemingly intractable Ulster question, appeared to have a major ethnic problem in western Europe. In the Middle East, Arab nationalism had only the most cautious presence. Zionism was still a minority sentiment among European Jews who either preferred assimilation or emigration to the United States. In eastern and central Europe the multinational empires of the Romanovs and Habsburgs seemed to present a very different prospect, but neither was on the verge of dissolution. The latter, in particular, had accommodated itself to the political ambitions of the Hungarians in the *Ausgleich* of 1867 which had created the Dual Monarchy with capitals in Vienna and Budapest. While tensions between the two parts of the empire could still be acute, Hungarian leaders had no wish to sever an arrangement which allowed them to dominate their half of the empire inside the protection of a larger unit. The major point at issue within the empire was how to reconcile the rising ambitions of some Slav groups, notably the Czechs. It was an empire held together by its army, an honest and efficient bureaucracy, respect for the venerable Emperor and King, Franz Josef, the Catholic church, and by a feeling among its peoples that their common home was a safer prospect than that offered by its fragmentation. Imperial sentiment was notably weakest among the non-Catholic sections of the population, though not the Jews who have sometimes been referred to as the truest Austrians of them all. It was certainly significant that the shot which killed the Archduke Franz Ferdinand and precipitated the war was fired by an Orthodox Serb. If the other states of Europe went to war for a variety of reasons too long to list here, ethnicity lay at the heart of the decisions taken in Vienna and Budapest.

Recalling the events of 1914, the empire's chief military figure, Field-Marshal Conrad von Hötzendorff was to write: 'Two principles were in sharp conflict, the maintenance of Austria as a conglomerate of various nationalities ... and the rise of independent national States claiming their ethnic territories from

Austria-Hungary'.[1] While Conrad's analysis certainly held true for the multi-national empire whose future he thus sought to safeguard by curbing Serb pretensions, the struggle in western Europe had very different origins in the competing rivalries of the powers, with their economic and imperial ambitions. Here ethnic tensions played little part in the outbreak of war, with two exceptions. In 1871, the new imperial Germany had taken control from France of the long-disputed provinces of Alsace and Lorraine. With its Germanic character and language, Alsace, it could plausibly be argued, had reverted to its natural home along the Rhine valley; but not so Lorraine which had been acquired in order that its raw materials might serve the developing industries of the Ruhr. Germany's disregard for the ethnic loyalties of Lorraine was one of the fundamental causes of the war, guaranteeing France's desire for *revanche*. In 1914, western Europe's other ethnic flashpoint was Ireland, or at least Ulster. From 1912, when the government introduced the Third Home Rule Bill in the House of Commons, the situation deteriorated alarmingly as the Ulster Unionists led by Sir Edward Carson mobilised to prevent its implementation. The formation of the Ulster Volunteer Force was followed in March 1914 by the so-called Curragh Mutiny when army officers indicated their unwillingness to act against the UVF. When the UVF succeeded in landing 20,000 rifles the following month, the prospect of a violent confrontation in Ulster had moved measurably closer. That these events were being clearly noted in Vienna and Berlin as the summer crisis of 1914 unfolded need not be doubted.

But it is to the Balkans that we must turn to see the full impact of ethnic tensions. In 1908, the Austro-Hungarian Foreign Minister Count Aerenthal sought to consolidate the empire's position by formally annexing Bosnia-Hercegovina, with its mixed Muslim, Croat and Serb population, which the empire had administered since 1878. However, his attempt to do this with the co-operation of his Russian counterpart, Alexander Izvolski, fell apart. The following year, the question of annexation brought Austria-Hungary and Serbia to the edge of war, setting in train the fateful rivalries which reached their climax on 28 June 1914 when the young Bosnian Serb, Gavrilo Princip, assassinated the heir to the Habsburg throne, the Archduke Franz Ferdinand, and his wife, the Countess Sophie. Vienna's ultimatum to Belgrade, where the outrage had been planned, led to the diplomatic breakdown of the old Europe. By 4 August, all the major powers of Europe, except Italy, were at war.

The struggle which resulted was not the war planned by the general staffs or imagined by the cheering crowds who thronged the capitals of Europe in the summer of 1914. By 1916, the war had settled into a relentless, and seemingly unending pattern of horror, the mass suicide of a generation. At Verdun the German and French armies bled each other to death, on the Somme the British sacrificed the volunteer armies of 1914, while on the Eastern Front the Brusilov offensive shattered the best of the Habsburg armies while exhausting the last strength of imperial Russia. The Rising in Dublin in Easter 1916 should have served as a warning to more than the British. Amid the slaughter the old Europe died. It remained to be seen what would emerge to take its place. The following year the collapse of the Russian monarchy and subsequent triumph of the Bolshevik Revolution seemed to herald one way forward, deeply disturbing to the propertied classes of Europe and the United States which by then had entered the struggle on the Allied side. An alternative to Lenin with his siren call of social revolution seemed to be the American President Woodrow Wilson with his ill-defined, but to many of the nationalities of Europe infinitely seductive, message of self-determination. With the defeat of the Central Empires in 1918, the victorious statesmen of the Allied and Associated Powers could address the task of reconstructing the continent along the principles Wilson had outlined. But too many men had been lost for the leaders of France and Britain to be totally swayed by 'Wilsonianism', and the ethnic map of Europe was so complex, that their success was partial. And lying temporarily blinded in a hospital at Pasewalk in Pomerania was a young German-Austrian soldier, in whom the most poisonous ethnic hatreds of central Europe had taken hold, who was to play with brilliant success on the inevitable shortcomings of the Allies' work and march the world to war twenty years later.

When the Great War came to an end, the central problems debated and pursued at the Paris Conference were to do with the boundaries and powers of the major national states, and with Germany and the successor states of Austria-Hungary in particular. However, the less than clear lines of the settlement were confounded by a host of less central, often geographically peripheral, matters to do with old boundary arguments, national identities, migration patterns and ownership of territories. Many of the new states created, and the lines of their borders, were at best crude compromises. 'Often there was no possibility of drawing any frontier which did not leave substantial minorities on either side.'[2]

This book reflects the view that many of the current flashpoints in the western and mid-eastern worlds – that is regions with continuing conflicts where political and sectarian violence is either real or incipient – can be traced back to the compromises and failures of that settlement.

The origins of ethnic disputes are usually connected with one or more of a set of fundamental forms of human association (and therefore separateness) such as religion, politics, race, ethnicity and culture. It is becoming customary for the word ethnic to be used as a general and inclusive word to describe all such forms of association. These associations and divisions are of great power and significance because they relate to the ways in which people identify themselves and their individual places in the world. The determination to remain distinctive and separate leads to drawing of boundaries or building of walls, to marking out territories and to a physical and emotional distancing from others. One consequence of this process is called nationalism.

There are currently about 160 nation-states in the international system, in contrast to several thousand cultural and ethnic groups.[3] For reasons that are not completely clear, the past two decades have witnessed a remarkable growth in political and economic awareness among a great many of these ethnic groups. Very often they are reacting to the status of being permanent minorities within existing states, and inevitably their new self-awareness leads to conflict with the authority of the state and, often, to violence both from and against the state. It would be a simple matter to list numerous examples, from all parts of the world, to illustrate these developments and there is now a growing literature which attempts to produce structured lists and analytical categories.[4]

One important reason for this awakening of ethnic awareness is the disappearance, at least for the moment, of the Great Power clash of ideologies and world-views that produced the bipolar, Cold War world. With it has gone the immediate fear of, although not the potential for, a world-destroying nuclear war. It was this singular focus, particularly after the Second World War, which succeeded in occluding from view the existence of a great many other conflicts, relatively small in scale, long-lived, ethnic in character, and internal rather than inter-state. Many of them, of course, remain hidden in that the media has not yet found a reason to bring them centre-stage. Currently much of the focus is on Africa with attention being given to Nigeria, Rwanda, Somalia and Ethiopia. However in East Timor, Georgia, Kurdistan, Colombia, Afghanistan, Kashmir, and many others, the violence continues with little or no attention from western media.

The collapse of the Soviet empire led to a dramatic redistribution of world power, and the removal of some previously resolute forms of centralised restraint. Almost inevitably – it now seems – the way was clear for the emergence, or re-emergence, of ethnic awareness and mobilisation, whether this was defined in terms of civic nationalism, that is as a response to the failure of the previous system, or as ethnic nationalism, that is as primordial, racial, and characterised by ethnic continuity. In either event, many of these ethnic awakenings led quickly to quarrels which became violent and war-like, or teetered (and continue to teeter) on the edge of violence. The cumulative effect of the many – often bloody – disputes associated with the break-up of Yugoslavia and the former Soviet Union is to suggest that ethnic loyalty is ineradicable, with a constant potential for mobilisation. Many such loyalties are of great age, and reflect long-standing fears, separations and hostilities; they did not just emerge suddenly, without a past. Their persistence and virulence suggest that they will not be transformed by any simple remedy. A substantial and important subset of internal conflicts, not all of which are violent but all with the potential to become violent, contains those states and regions where minority ethnic groups wish to secede and set up independent states. Very few modern conflicts are of the classical inter-state war kind:

> there were only four inter-state armed conflicts for the whole period 1988–93. Strikingly, not one inter-state armed conflict was going on in 1993. In all, 90 armed conflicts took place during the five years, 1989–93, in 61 locations around the world, and more than 60 governments participated in at least one armed conflict.[5]

The actual number of ethnic groups in the world, whether self-defined or defined by others, is not easy to compute but their involvement in and commitment to armed conflict all round the world is not in doubt. Wallenstein and Axell identify 175 'non-governmental forces' involved in the 90 conflicts described above, but argue that the actual number is considerably higher. 'For instance, the government of India estimated that there were 180 groups active in Kashmir in 1992.'[6]

For these reasons, ethnic conflicts and consequent violence are likely to have the greatest impact on world affairs during the next period of history. Already the structure, constitution and rationale of international institutions is being affected: the composition of the United Nations as a body representative of states, rather than nations; the reluctance of the UN to interfere in what are deemed to be within-state conflicts; the increasing difficulty in policing the world; the growth in regional UN-like organisations.

For many western Europeans after 1945, closer economic and then political unity seemed to offer the way forward from the ethnic and national tensions which had bedevilled the continent, but it seems fair to say that the hopes of the founders have been painfully slow to realise and that true European union is still some way off. Even so, the emergence of regional groupings within Europe may yet offer a mechanism for softening ethnic tensions and in the case of the Tyrol this book explores one of these in some depth.

Finally, since 1917 Europe and the Middle East cannot be viewed in isolation from the United States. In 1941 even Adolf Hitler acknowledged this with his declaration of war on America. The onset of the Cold War bound the United States firmly to Europe. The Gulf Crisis of 1990–91 confirmed America as the dominant power in the Middle East. Much of this book is concerned with the working out of President Wilson's support for self-determination. Yet it should not be forgotten that America's relationship to ethnicity is complex and has been increasingly under scrutiny since the publication in 1963 of Glazer and Moynihan's pioneering study *Beyond the Melting Pot*, which challenged established assumptions about the 'melting pot', at least in parts of the country.[7] Wilson's own missionary zeal to reconstitute Europe on new principles has been identified in his Scottish and Scotch-Irish Presbyterian ethnic roots. The Versailles Settlement, he observed in July 1919, had come into being 'by the hand of God'.[8] Be that as it may, what follows tries to put contemporary ethnic issues in the context set by the statesmen of the period as they attempted to come to terms with the death of the old order.

NOTES

1   Conrad von Hötzendorff, *Aus Meiner Dienstzeit*, Vienna, vol. IV, quoted in Lewis Namier, *Vanished Supremacies*, London, 1958, p.97.
2   Alan Sharp, *The Versailles Settlement: peacemaking in Paris 1919*, London: Macmillan, 1991.
3   Rodolfo Stavenhagen, *The Ethnic Question*, Tokyo: The United Nations University Press, 1990.
4   Minority Rights Group, *World Directory of Minorities*, Harlow, Essex: Longman, 1989; Ylva Nordlander, *States in Armed Conflict 1993* (report no. 38), Uppsala: Department of Peace and Conflict Research, Uppsala University, 1994.
5   Peter Wallenstein and Karin Axel in Nordlander, *op. cit..*, p.7.
6   Ibid.
7   Nathan Glazer and Daniel Patrick Moynihan, *Beyond the Melting Pot*, Cambridge, MA: MIT Press, 1963.
8   See Arthur S. Link, 'Woodrow Wilson and his Presbyterian inheritance' in E.R.R. Green (ed.), *Essays in Scotch-Irish History*, introduced by Steve Ickringill, Belfast: Ulster Historical Foundation, 1992.

Chapter 2

The genie that would not go back into the bottle
National self-determination and the legacy of the First World War and the Peace Settlement

Alan Sharp

Woodrow Wilson, the President of the United States, knew why Europe had erupted into war in 1914. On 11 February 1918 he declared, 'This war had its roots in the disregard of the rights of small nations and of nationalities which lacked the union and the force to make good their claim to determine their own allegiances and their own forms of political life.'[1] Whether or not Wilson's perception of the role of frustrated nationalisms accurately identified the causes of the First World War is irrelevant; his diagnosis came to dominate the Peace Conference agenda. There were many national minorities in 1914. About 60 per cent of the population of the Austro-Hungarian and Russian empires were not members of the dominant German, Magyar and Russian nationalities. Although the figure fell below 50 per cent in the new Balkan states carved from the declining Ottoman empire, the overall position in eastern Europe was that about half the population were minorities, a total of 60 million people, of whom nearly half (27.4 million) were in the Austro-Hungarian empire.[2] The position in the Ottoman empire was less clear; unreliable and partial though the pre-war figures produced by the multinational empires in Europe might be, there had been some attempt to calculate them. This did not happen in the Ottoman area but Arabs, Armenians and Kurds are obvious examples to add to the empire's remaining European subjects.

Believing that problems of nationality had poisoned the world's peace, Wilson in 1917 and 1918 outlined his revolutionary antidote. It was deliberately in opposition to the concept that had dominated European diplomacy for centuries, condemned by Wilson as 'the great game, now for ever discredited, of the Balance of Power'.[3] On 22 January 1917 Wilson expressed his vision of a world in which

> no nation should seek to extend its polity over any other nation or people, but...every people should be left free to determine its own polity, its own way of development, unhindered, unthreatened, unafraid, the little along with the great and powerful.[4]

His Fourteen Points speech on 8 January 1918 made no direct reference to national self-determination but many of the points implied it. On 11 February 1918 he asserted that ' "Self-determination" is not a mere phrase. It is an imperative principle of action which statesmen will henceforth ignore at their peril' and declared that

> all well-defined national aspirations shall be accorded the utmost satisfaction that can be accorded them without introducing new or perpetrating old elements of discord and antagonism that would be likely in time to break the peace of Europe, and consequently of the world.

On 6 April 1918 he spoke of 'the principle of the free self-determination of nations'.[5] Encapsulated here are the main tenets of Wilsonian philosophy; the right of people to choose their state and their government and his underlying faith that states so constituted and controlled would create a peaceful and just international society. All of this was founded in his fundamental belief in the inherent goodness and perfectibility of mankind; that if given the opportunity and suitable institutions, the collective will of the people would be an absolute force for good.

Both sides in the war played the opportunistic card of encouraging discontented groups within their enemies' ranks to indulge in a variety of activities ranging from internal disruption to revolt and secession, but it was Wilson whose pronouncements elevated the idea from a tactic to a strategic principle. In this he had a number of enthusiastic allies, particularly among the British intelligentsia propelled by wartime exigencies into the subordinate ranks of the decision-making process in Britain, most notably in the Political Intelligence Department of the Foreign Office, and among the promoters and subscribers to the *New Europe* movement associated with R.W. Seton-Watson.[6] When Wilson sought the views of all the belligerents as to their peace terms in an attempt to broker a peace in late 1916 the Entente reply of 10 January 1917 spoke cautiously of 'the reorganisation of Europe, guaranteed by a stable regime and based at once on respect for nationalities and on the right to full security and liberty of economic development possessed by all peoples small and great'.[7] The reply of the Central Powers on 11 January 1917 was an uncomfortable reminder that 'If the adversaries demand above all the restoration of invaded rights and liberties, the recognition of the principle of nationalities and of the free existence of small states, it will suffice to call to mind the tragic fate of the Irish and Finnish peoples, the obliteration of the freedom and independence of the Boer Republics. . .'.[8]

Also unwelcome was the endorsement of the principle by Lenin, whom Wilson regarded as his arch-rival in the battle for the soul of the post-war world.[9] When the German government approached Wilson about an armistice in October 1918 they sought an assurance that the eventual treaty would be based upon his Fourteen Points speech. Wilson expanded this to include the whole package of his 1918 pronouncements – the Fourteen Points, the Four Principles, the Four Ends, the Five Particulars ('God', remarked the cynical French premier, Georges Clemenceau, 'only needed Ten Points') – but there can be no doubt that the Lansing Note of 5 November 1918 constituted a contract which established the Wilsonian programme for the peace of the world as the agenda for the Peace Settlement.

Wilson's European partners resented this bitterly but their grudging acquiescence implied a recognition not only of the immense material power of the United States but also of his moral ascendancy. Furthermore, the incredible combination of events in 1917 and 1918 which had seen first the defeat of an Ally, Russia, and then the collapse of the Central Powers, thus creating a power vacuum in eastern and central Europe, left the Entente searching for a moral principle upon which to base the necessary reconstruction of order. The only realistic contender was Wilson's concept of national self-determination but what exactly did this mean?

The disconcerting answer is that no-one was quite sure. Setting aside the connected problem of the existing framework of international relations which he wished also to see amended, Wilson had two main objections to the Europe of 1914; the refusal of multinational empires to grant autonomy to national groups and the lack of democratic control within many states. He tended to confuse the two issues – not surprisingly when, as in the cases of Austria-Hungary, the Ottoman empire, the Russian empire and Germany, both problems were simultaneously present, but, as Alfred Cobban perceptively pointed out, in Wilson's mind national self-determination was essentially a synonym for popular sovereignty.[10] Thus Wilson, as was natural, given the ethnic hotch-potch of the United States, based his concept of national self-determination on the Western liberal tradition which tended not to distinguish between the concept of a person as a member of a racial group and as a citizen of a state – expressed more simply, the equation was national equals citizen equals national. What Wilson did now was to transform this null correlation in the West between personal and political nationality (in that the former was not affected by the latter) into a positive correlation in which personal nationality was thought to determine political allegiance. Thus the injection of nationality into the concept of self-government created the hybrid of national self-determination and this produced a series of complex and complicated problems for the peacemakers to disentangle; not least because Wilson never entirely committed himself to the principle that nationality should be the sole determining factor in the drawing up of new frontiers in the Peace Settlement. He had specified already the caveat about not 'introducing new or perpetuating old elements of discord and antagonism', while in his thoughts on the future of the Balkan states he stated that their relations should be 'determined by friendly counsel along established lines of allegiance and nationality' but also mentioned secure access to the sea for Serbia and economic independence. Wilson was groping to come to terms with the continuing relevance of wider concepts of power in his recognition that there were considerations of international stability, historical development, economics, defensible frontiers, security and communications in addition to the idea of nationality, which in itself was very difficult to define.[11]

Here lay the key to many of the problems that the Peace Conference faced, especially in eastern Europe where the ethnography of the region was enormously complex, reflecting the historical interminglings and the ebb and flow of population movements over centuries. If national self-determination was to legitimise the new frontiers which would replace the defunct dynastic empires (and, by the time the conference opened, it was at least clear that Austria-Hungary and the Russian empire had imploded) what criteria would determine nationality? Language (certainly the favoured yardstick of the Americans in Paris but soon shown to be inadequate), race, culture, religion, historical allegiances, geography – all had their supporters. If the Western liberal tradition emphasised choice as a legitimate criterion in establishing nationality, the Germanic and east European tradition did not. For this latter tradition nationality was determined, not self-determined, and the determining factors were race, language and religion. Hence the possibilities for misunderstanding were enormous but, as Wilson belatedly came to realise, even applying his own definitions, the idea of every state a nation and every nation a state simply could not work in eastern Europe. Thus the even more difficult and morally fraught question was posed – which peoples would not be able to enjoy self-determination and on what basis would (and could) such a choice be justified? In practice the answer was that the quickest and best organised prevailed: Poland, Czechoslovakia, the Baltic states and Yugoslavia (technically, until 1929, the Kingdom of the Serbs, Croats and Slovenes) succeeded; Georgia, Ruthenia, the Ukraine, Azerbaijan and Armenia did not, but this was hardly based upon principle. Even before the conference opened there were serious doubts in the American delegation. Secretary of State Robert Lansing asked himself on 20 December 1918: 'When the President talks of "self-determination" what unit has he in mind? Does he mean a race, a territorial area, or a community? Without a definite unit which is practical, application of this principle is dangerous to peace and stability.'[12] The problem with all these questions was that no-one had agreed or definitive answers.

Although it was the peculiar circumstances of 1917 and 1918 and the decisive influence of Wilson that finally brought the principle to the fore, both sides had dabbled earlier with nationalism as a weapon of war. Gilbert Murray wryly pointed out in 1922, 'In a war between two empires *selbstbestimmungsrecht* [the German concept which he held to be the origin of self-determination] was found by each side to be a convenient stick for beating the other.'[13] Yet both sides knew that the dangerous expedient of promoting national self-determination in an attempt to disrupt the internal cohesion of the states ranged against them was, like poison gas, a weapon which, once unleashed, could be as deadly to themselves as to the enemy. It is surely a mark of the desperation of the multinational states involved on both sides in the Great War that they should think of employing such a double-edged weapon in their efforts to gain victory, or to stave off defeat. British speeches about the rights of small nations and of national groups might be well received in Belgium, Poland and Washington, thus helping the war effort, but they had an equally receptive audience in Egypt, India and Ireland, often with less positive results. Germany's attempts to subvert Indian revolutionaries or Irish prisoners of war were similarly ambiguous in their implications. The Germans were the first to experiment with such a policy when, on 4 September 1914, Chancellor Bethmann Hollweg authorised a campaign of unrest in India and Egypt. The record of their subsequent ineptitude belies the more usual stereotype of German efficiency.[14] Britain hardly needed to create disorder in Germany's colonies since these all (with the notable exception of German East Africa) fell rapidly to British, Dominion or Allied forces but, once the Ottoman empire became a belligerent, Britain followed a similar path. Lord Cromer suggested in October 1914 that 'a few officers who could speak Arabic, if sent into Arabia, could raise the whole country against the Turks'. From such ideas, especially after the failure of more conventional expeditions such as Gallipoli, sprang the negotiations with Arab leaders which precipitated the great revolt in the desert, romantically associated with T.E. Lawrence – Lawrence of Arabia. But to what ends? The undermining of an enemy through internal subversion had great attractions in wartime but what was the longer term view?

In the Middle East it is clear from the understandings that Britain reached with its French ally (which were always of greater importance to it than any arrangements with its Arab friends) that Britain was not intending to leave the post-war government of the region to its indigenous peoples, despite the splendidly hypocritical Anglo-French declaration of 7 November 1918. This stated that the Allies were fighting for 'the complete and definite emancipation of the peoples so long oppressed by the Turks and the establishment of national governments and administrations deriving their authority from the initiative and free choice of the indigenous populations'. Precisely what this meant became clearer during the post-war negotiations. In Paris Lord Milner, the British Colonial Secretary, defined Arab independence thus:

> what we mean by it is that Arabia while being independent herself should be kept out of the sphere of European political

intrigue and within the British sphere of influence: in other words that her independent native rulers should have no foreign treaties except with us.

The concept was thus of a region that would still require a European presence, whether through direct rule or the filter of a League of Nations mandate, and even here the notion of free choice was distinctly limited. Acknowledging that the Syrians had the right to choose their mandatory power, Arthur Balfour, the British Foreign Secretary, pointed out that since the Americans were not prepared to accept the mandate, the French were the only candidates and the inhabitants could indeed 'freely choose; but it is Hobson's choice after all'.[15] The history of the Middle East during and after the First World War is a salutary reminder of the dangers of unleashing forces that cannot be contained later and of the perils of indulging in the process of what has been appositely described as selling 'the same horse, or at least parts of the same horse, twice'. Caught between the promises it made to its Arab friends, the French and the Zionists, Britain found itself enmeshed in a sordid imperial mess in the Middle East in the aftermath of the war.[16]

It is interesting to note that both sides were less inclined to adopt such tactics in Europe itself. It is clear from the deals struck with Russia over the Dardanelles, with Serbia and Romania over territorial gains in the Balkans and with Italy in the Treaty of London in April 1915, not to mention the Anglo-French agreements over the Middle East, that the Entente had no intention of allowing the wishes of local inhabitants to determine the future of frontiers in which its members had an interest. When, on 9 November 1914, the British Prime Minister Herbert Asquith had spoken of the rights of small nations to be free, he was thinking of established states like Belgium and Serbia, not espousing a revolutionary concept which might encompass the discontented Irish or Indian subjects of the British crown.[17] Equally the Central Powers were unlikely champions of an idea which had bedevilled recent Austro-Hungarian history and which ran counter to the ambitious German war aims outlined in Bethmann Hollweg's September Programme. This may explain what has been described as the 'curiously lukewarm' nature of Germany's relationship with Irish nationalism.[18]

Neither side could resist the temptation of Poland which, like

Ireland, was one of the great nineteenth-century romantic nationalist causes. Despite support from President Wilson in his 'peace without victory speech' of January 1917, the cause of complete Polish independence seemed an impossible dream but Poles on both sides found themselves the target of propaganda and promises from the other; the proclamation addressed by the Russian Grand Duke Nikolai Nikolaevich to all Poles on 16 August 1914 offering Polish unity was matched by the Austro-German Two Emperors' Manifesto of 5 November 1916 which promised an independent Poland, though without specifying its frontiers.[19] Poland's likely fate was to become part of the spoils of war with, at best, the possibility of some Polish autonomy in that part of Poland which the victors would carve from the territory of the vanquished. Even given the traditional French sympathy for the plight of the Poles, there could be no question of sacrificing the vital alliance with Russia for such a cause. As Clemenceau admitted 'We...started as allies of the Russian oppressors of Poland, with the Polish soldiers of Silesia and Galicia fighting against us'[20] but the Russian revolutions of 1917 together with the military disappointments of 1916 and 1917 created a new situation. It was no longer necessary to consider the susceptibilities of St Petersburg, while an increasingly difficult military position and the strains of a long war encouraged the Entente to think more positively about encouraging nationalist ambitions among the subject peoples of the Central Powers.

This placed the future of the Austro-Hungarian empire in jeopardy, yet it is clear from the events and discussions of 1917 and 1918 that there was no clear policy on what the place of the empire would be in a future settlement. Wilson might wish to see the concept of balanced power consigned to oblivion but his European partners were not anxious to abandon a familiar and well-tested formula. It would assuredly be to the Entente's advantage if the full force of their efforts could be directed against Germany alone by removing Austria-Hungary from the war but the question was how best this might be achieved. There was no doubt that the war was radicalising the demands of the national groupings within Austria-Hungary; before 1914 both Edvard Benes and Tomas Masaryk had argued only for Czech national autonomy within the empire but rapidly after the outbreak of war they were converted to the cause of Czech independence, for which they campaigned in exile in London, Paris and Washington.[21] Thus on the one hand was the prospect of using the discontented subjects of the empire to bring about its collapse, and hence its disappearance from the world stage, but on the other was the tempting possibility of detaching the Habsburgs from the Hohenzollerns by making a separate peace with the empire, an option which demanded the continued existence of the empire in a post-war world – and it was not clear that Palmerston's contention that Austria was a European necessity had yet lost its force. Both policies had attractions but neither commanded the complete adherence of all the main Entente decision-makers at any one time, and indeed most of those decision-makers remained ambivalent about the empire almost beyond the point at which it had effectively ceased to exist.

'It was quite late in the War', commented Gilbert Murray, 'when we discovered that we were fighting for the independence of the Czecho-Slovaks, and General Smuts [the South African defence minister who was a member of the British Imperial War Cabinet and a close adviser of Lloyd George] confessed that it came to him as a surprise.'[22] The European Allies had already flirted with a possible massive reduction of the empire in the various wartime promises they had made to Serbia and in the later (and often contradictory) pledges offered to attract the support of Italy and Romania in the Treaties of London (26 April 1915) and Bucharest (17 August 1916). Yet in 1917 and 1918 the Entente showed at least some willingness to explore a separate peace with the empire in the discussions in London with Prince Sixtus, brother-in-law of the Austrian emperor, and in the contacts in Switzerland between Smuts, acting for the British government, and the ex-Austrian ambassador to London, Count Mensdorff, both in 1917 and then the meetings between Smuts and the Austrian foreign minister, Czernin, again in Switzerland in March 1918.[23] In their important speeches in January 1918 both Lloyd George and Wilson denied that the obliteration of Austria-Hungary was one of their war aims. 'Nor are we fighting to destroy Austria-Hungary', said the prime minister, while Wilson spoke of 'Austria-Hungary, whose place among the nations we wish to see safeguarded and assured'.[24] And yet 1918 saw increasing encouragement for groups advocating independence for Poland and Czechoslovakia and the creation of a large South Slav state in Yugoslavia. The experts of the Inquiry, Wilson's semi-official team of advisers, pointed out the implications of these contradictory initiatives: 'Our policy must therefore consist first in a stirring up of nationalist discontent, and then in refusing to accept the extreme logic of this discontent which would be the dismemberment of Austria-Hungary.'[25]

The Entente was never quite prepared to commit itself. On 3 June 1918 the prime ministers of Britain, France and Italy stated that the creation of a united and independent Poland 'is one of the conditions of a durable and just peace' but only expressed 'their most earnest sympathy for the national aspirations for liberty of the Czecho-Slovak and Yugo-Slav nations'.[26] The ambiguities persisted – as late as 24 September Wilson's close adviser Edward House believed that the president 'had no idea of what should be done with Austria, or how the Empire should be broken up, if indeed, it was to be broken up at all' although, in his 18 October reply to the Austrian request for an armistice, Wilson withdrew his support for the continuation of the empire. In the British Foreign Office there was a clear division between the younger officials who favoured the break-up of the empire and the development of independent states in eastern and central Europe, while the senior officials and many of the political leaders leaned towards the maintenance of a reformed empire. In France President Raymond Poincaré wrote in despair that his premier, Clemenceau, had 'no plan for the future of Central Europe'.[27] In peace, as in war, it was apparent that, no matter what Wilson might believe, national self-determination was, for the European Allies, a question of necessity rather than conviction and a principle whose most dangerous implications had to be resisted.

Robert Lansing, Wilson's secretary of state, shared these European concerns.

> It is bound to be the basis of impossible demands on the Peace Congress and create trouble in many lands. What effect will it have on the Irish, the Indians, the Egyptians, and the nationalists among the Boers? Will it not breed discontent, disorder, and rebellion? . . . The phrase is simply loaded with dynamite. It will raise hopes which can never be realised. It will, I fear, cost thousands of lives. . . . What a calamity the phrase was ever uttered! What misery it will cause!'[28]

On his way to Paris in 1918 and gradually becoming aware of the complexities of the eastern European situation, Wilson began to realise that he had stirred far more hopes than he could possibly satisfy and he predicted gloomily that the outcome of the conference would be 'a tragedy of disappointment'.[29]

The old world had fallen apart and a new one had to be constructed. The only principle that had survived the war, apart from force and the right of conquest, was the revolutionary Wilsonian doctrine of self-determination. The problem was that, whereas for the European victors this principle was seen as a possible political expedient to be applied only to such areas whose fate was called into question by the exigencies of defeat or revolution, they were aware that they would inevitably offer any opponent the opportunity to question the way in which the principle had been applied in any particular case. The rival principle that possession is nine-tenths of the law was also pursued with vigour. Lansing underlined the seriousness and urgency of the problems facing the peacemakers: on 22 January 1919 his diary noted 'all the races of Central Europe and the Balkans in fact are actually fighting or about to fight with one another . . . the Great War seems to have split up into a lot of little wars' and by 4 April he was warning:

> Central Europe is aflame with anarchy; the people see no hope; the Red Armies of Russia are marching westward. Hungary is in the clutches of the revolutionists; Berlin, Vienna and Munich are turning towards the Bolsheviks. . . . It is time to stop fiddling while the world is on fire, while violence and bestiality consume society. Everyone is clamouring for peace, for an immediate peace.[30]

Many of the peacemakers shared Lansing's perception of a world engaged in a race between anarchy and the need for an ordered settlement, but it was proving impossible to base that settlement on the principle of national self-determination. Eastern and central Europe did not divide into neat national packages, it was a hotch-potch of racial, linguistic and religious groups and even these categories were subject to further subdivisions – a racial group could itself be divided by religion or language or both, and so on. Thus, even if other considerations like the ambitions of the local or the great powers had not come into play in certain instances, the peacemakers could not have solved the problems by an application of the principle of national self-determination, always supposing the definition of that principle to be accepted by all the parties to any dispute. A number of examples illustrate the difficulties.

The Banat of Temesvar, which had previously belonged to Hungary, was now claimed by both Romania and the emerging Yugoslav state. Both powers were Allies, each advanced ethnic, economic, strategic and historic arguments, while the Romanians asserted that the promises made to them by the Treaty of Bucharest in 1916 were not invalidated by their subsequent surrender to the Central Powers in 1917. The population of the region was hopelessly mixed and there was no prospect of drawing a frontier which would not leave substantial minorities on either side. The Italians, seeking a client state, and always opposed to any Yugoslav claim on principle, backed the Romanians, the other Allies favoured a division of the territory. Each party would only accept a plebiscite if its form was likely to produce a result favourable to them; each toyed with the idea of using force to resolve the dispute. Eventually the conference decided that Hungary should retain the area around Szeged, Romania should have the bulk of the rest but Yugoslavia was allowed some gains in the west. The solution left 75,000 Romanians in Yugoslavia and 65,000 Slavs in Romania. The arrangements made for the League of Nations to protect these minorities were resented by both states as an infringement of their sovereignty. The Banat is an apt example of the frustrations and resentments engendered by the negotiations of 1919.[31]

Wilson's thirteenth point had promised an independent Poland encompassing territories inhabited by indisputably Polish populations, with secure access to the sea. Unfortunately, Polish access to the Baltic could not be achieved without assigning territory inhabited by Germans to the new state and Danzig (Gdansk), the port which the conference considered to be necessary to Poland, was unquestionably, in 1919, a German city. Largely thanks to the persistence of Lloyd George and his advisers the original French-inspired proposals to grant Poland much of the territory that it sought were whittled down. Danzig became a free city, self-governing under the League of Nations but economically linked to Poland. Poland was granted 260 square miles of German territory, to form a corridor to the sea that split East and West Prussia and the conference left 2.5 million people to decide their own fates in a series of plebiscites, the largest of which was to be held in Upper Silesia.

To the Germans none of this seemed fair. Even if they accepted defeat in the west – and the 'stab in the back' myth was already winning support – Germans considered that they had won the war in the east. The Poles had failed historically to sustain their state, now Germans were being assigned the rule. Was self-determination a principle which worked only in favour of the winners?[32] And were the German inhabitants of Austria and the Sudetenland to be denied their wish to merge with Germany? In the west the loss of Alsace–Lorraine was inevitable (though French officials resisted any attempt to legitimise this transfer by a plebiscite, fearing that population movements since 1871 might render the result unconvincing), but a stout Anglo-American resistance defeated French attempts to detach the Rhineland from Germany. Instead the Rhineland was demilitarised and occupied but remained German. On the other hand the Saar, whose coal assets were assigned to France to compensate it for the deliberate German destruction of mines in the north-east of France, became another League of Nations responsibility until the people could choose their subsequent destiny in 1935.[33] Thus the settlement was not based solely upon self-determination but such factors as economics, justice, communications and historic allegiances also came into play, along with geopolitical considerations, not least of which was the question of whether Germany, having lost the war, should actually emerge from the peace with a greater territory and population than in 1914. Such an outcome was unlikely but the Germans certainly did not accept the Allied claim that 'Every territorial settlement of the Treaty of Peace has been determined upon after most careful and laboured consideration of all the religious, racial and linguistic factors in each particular country.'[34]

Given the gains that it made in the South Tyrol, the Trentino, Trieste and Dalmatia, Italy had few reasons to complain about the outcome of the conference although its perception was that the peace was 'mutilated' because the issue of Fiume had not been resolved and it had not made the expected imperial gains in Dalmatia, the Near East and Africa. Wilson had accepted the Italian strategic argument for a frontier on the Brenner, even though this assigned some 250,000 Germans to Italy and was hardly a 'readjustment of the frontiers of Italy along clearly recognisable lines of nationality'. As he later admitted 'It was on the basis of insufficient study that I promised Orlando the Brenner frontier.' As with so many of the other disputed boundaries, 1919 was not the final word on the subject.[35]

Wilson came to regret his commitment to national self-determination. He admitted to the Senate

> When I gave utterance to those words ('that all nations had a right to self-determination'), I said them without the knowledge that nationalities existed, which are coming to us day after day. . . . You do not know and cannot appreciate the anxieties that I have experienced as a result of many millions of people having their hopes raised by what I have said.[36]

His colleagues in Paris shared his anxieties and fears for the future international stability of eastern Europe where disaffected minorities would create the perfect lever for would-be disturbers of the peace. None of the aspiring nationalities inhabited exclusive blocks of territory that could neatly be delimited on a map and it was inimicable to the liberal philosophies of the victors to try to make the people fit the maps by forcible transfers of population. Only in the later and distinctly unpleasant episode between the Greeks and Turks in Asia Minor did the conference endorse such an expedient, though some of the new states initiated their own policies of 'ethnic cleansing'. Aware that their decisions must disappoint and frustrate those who would be consigned to states other than those they would have chosen, the peacemakers resorted to two devices in an attempt to minimise the damage.

The first was the plebiscite. In a number of instances where the line of the new frontier was uncertain and sensitive the conference sought to discover the views of the local inhabitants. James Headlam-Morley, one of the British advisers in Paris believed this method should have been used more often:

> I sometimes ask whether the people on the spot are ever to be consulted, but I am always told that this is out of the question. Self-determination is quite *démodé*. Leeper and Nicolson determine for them what they ought to wish, but they do it very well.[37]

This is, at first sight, surprising since it seems a sensible way of resolving disputes to seek the preference of the inhabitants. The problem was that the style of the questioning and especially the manner of judging the result of any poll were often crucial factors in the outcome. Hence, as the case of the Banat, disputing parties might well accept the idea of a plebiscite in principle but would then insist upon a certain format which they believed would produce the required result. In the end five decisive plebiscites were held, in Schleswig, Klagenfurt, Allenstein, Marienwerder and Oedenburg. The Upper Silesian plebiscite produced an over-all majority for Germany but engendered a major dispute between Britain and France as to how the results should be interpreted and the settlement made. The various treaties also made provision for plebiscites to be held in fifteen years' time in the Saar Valley, Smyrna and East Galicia, although in the event only that in the Saar was held, giving Hitler his first major foreign policy triumph in 1935.[38]

The results often cast doubts on the assumptions made about the political importance of language or race. In Allenstein 46 per cent of the population spoke Polish according to the 1910 census, yet only 2 per cent voted to join Poland. In Upper Silesia 65 per cent were Polish speakers, but Germany received an overall majority. In Klagenfurt 68 per cent of the population were Slovenes, but only 40 per cent voted for secession from Austria. The principle of the plebiscite was, like national self-determination, double-edged and potentially disruptive to the internal security of the victors. Lord Hardinge, the Permanent Under Secretary at the Foreign Office, noted with some alarm: 'Obviously the conference has nothing to do with territories owned by the allies before the war . . . plebiscites taken in countries in our possession . . . might be very inconvenient and certainly should not be encouraged.' It is perhaps not surprising that, as Temperley noted, 'On the whole, plebiscites were more talked about than conceded.'[39]

The second device worked on the premise that minorities were inevitable but that, where the responsibility for creating the minority depended upon decisions taken by the conference, then there was a moral responsibility for offering some form of protection – although only in the case of the new or enlarged smaller powers. There was also the practical consideration that discontented minorities represented a dangerous threat to the stability of the settlement. The concept of minority protection owed much to earlier precedents, and was an expansion the religious toleration theoretically demanded of the new Balkan states created in the late nineteenth century. Indeed it was pressure from Jewish groups in the United States, Britain and France that played an important part in making sure that the conference did not neglect its responsibilities to their co-religionists scattered throughout eastern Europe. The language of the treaties, which referred not to national minorities but to minorities of 'language, race and religion', was designed to make sure that the Jews were covered by its provisions. As Macartney commented, 'if you can prevent a Jew from being persecuted on the score of his race, his language, or his religion, you will have made it humanly impossible to get at him at all'. By offering a modest package of rights guaranteed by the League of Nations the peacemakers hoped that these involuntary minorities would become reconciled to, and ultimately assimilated into, their host states. As Sir Austen Chamberlain confirmed at the League of Nations Council in April 1926, 'the purpose of the Treaties was to make conditions in the minority countries such that the minorities could be and were loyal members of the nations to which they belonged'. It was not to be. The minorities remained unassimilated, and both they, and the restrictions placed upon their sovereignty by the great powers, were resented by the majorities. Hitler's use of the Sudetenlanders in 1938 was a tragic example of what the peacemakers had feared and had unsuccessfully sought to avoid with the minority protection treaties.[40]

The settlement left some 30 million people as inhabitants of states in which they were not the majority nationality; the figure in 1914 had been about 60 million. National minorities in eastern and central Europe had been reduced from 50 to 25 per cent of the total population and, in the circumstances of the time and given the moral and practical constraints on the peacemakers, this was probably the maximum achievable.[41] Did the reduction in overall numbers outweigh the dangers of distilled discontent among disappointed people, not least 13 million Germans, whose expectations of freedom and power had been raised by a principle of whose inadequacies they were living proof?

The settlement of the Second World War, which was not in practice based upon the principle of self-determination, ironically produced a much more homogeneous eastern Europe. Poland, moved bodily 150 miles west, reduced by one-fifth in size, with its population cut from 35 to 24 million, had only 2 per cent of Germans (although the 1950 figure of 900,000 was remarkably similar to the 1921 total of 1,059,000) and only a few hundred thousand Ukranians and Belorussians while the Holocaust reduced the Jewish population to 0.03 per cent, a figure also valid for

Czechoslovakia. There the German minority of 50,000 represented 0.5 per cent, following the forcible expulsion of 3 million Sudetenlanders and the Hungarians in Slovakia constituted the only sizeable minority. The revived Trianon Hungary of 1945 was 92.1 per cent Magyar and Austria was even more clearly German.[42]

The basis of both settlements was the concept that the sovereign state was the foundation of the international system – neither the League nor the United Nations was designed as a super-state – but the expectation in 1919 and by implication in the UN Charter, despite the actuality of 1945, was that the legitimacy of the state rested on self-determination. Did this concept legitimise the right in all states of discontented groups to secede? As a Southerner Wilson would be painfully aware of the disruptive consequences of such an interpretation.[43] According to the Helsinki Final Act 1975 'all peoples always have the right . . . when and as they wish' to exercise self-determination, while Professor Brownlie declared in 1990 'The present position is that self-determination is a legal principle' and possibly has the special status as a law of overriding force.[44] If sovereignty was not secure, wherein lay the stability of the international system, yet if states were perceived as unjust in their treatment of their inhabitants wherein lay the security of the state?

There were, and are, no easy answers. Boutros Boutros-Ghali in *An Agenda for Peace* wrote in June 1992:

> The United Nations has not closed its door. Yet if every ethnic, religious or linguistic group claimed statehood, there would be no limit to fragmentation, and peace, security and economic well-being for all would become ever more difficult to achieve.

And perhaps more in hope than in realistic expectation he added

> The sovereignty, territorial integrity and independence of States within the established international system, and the principle of self-determination for peoples, both of great value and importance, must not be permitted to work against each other in the period ahead.[45]

As late as 1989 it was possible for Professor Michael Howard to write of Versailles 'Certainly the states established by the settlement have remained viable ever since'[46] but today almost the opposite would be true. Twenty-six million Russians are scattered about the wreck of the old USSR. Three million Hungarians live in seven states bordering on Hungary. On 31 December 1992 Czechoslovakia split into two states with a total population of 15 million, leaving 300,000 Slovaks and 60,000 Czechs on the wrong side of the new frontier. No such velvet divorce in Yugoslavia; this tragedy may not be a new phenomenon in the Balkans but it is a striking reminder of Lansing's fear in 1918:

> The gift of clever phrasing may be a curse unless the phrases are put to the test of sound, practical application before being uttered.... Think of the feelings of the author when he counts the dead who died because he coined a phrase![47]

Yet there can be no doubt that, as the *New York Times* put it in 1991, Wilson's ideas have the floor:

> From the Baltics to the Adriatic, from the Ukraine to the Balkans, oppressed millions have given new life to his imperative – and often troublesome principle. Indeed if results are the measure, Wilson has proved a more successful revolutionary than Lenin.[48]

Put another way, the genie refuses to go back into the bottle.

NOTES

1 Speech reprinted by H.W.V. Temperley, *A History of the Peace Conference of Paris* (six vols), Oxford: Oxford University Press, 1920–1924, vol. 1, p.438.
2 Figures taken from Raymond Pearson, *National Minorities in Eastern Europe 1848–1945*, London: Macmillan, 1983, p.136.
3 Speech 11.2.18, in Temperley *op. cit.*, vol. I, p.399.
4 Quoted by Z.A.B. Zeman, *A Diplomatic History of the First World War*, London: Weidenfeld & Nicolson, 1971, p.193.
5 Temperley, *op. cit.*, vol. 1, p.433, pp.398–9 and p.407.
6 The establishment of the PID is covered in Alan Sharp, 'Some relevant historians – the Political Intelligence Department of the Foreign Office 1918–1920', *Australian Journal of Politics and History*, 1989, vol. 34, no. 3, pp.359–68, and two works by Erik Goldstein, 'The Foreign Office and Political Intelligence 1918–1920', *Review of International Studies*, 1988, vol. 14, pp.275–88 and *Winning the Peace: British diplomatic strategy, peace planning, and the Paris Peace Conference 1916–1920*, Oxford: Oxford University Press, 1991, pp.57–89. See also Kenneth Calder, *Britain and the Origins of the New Europe 1914–1918*, Cambridge: Cambridge University Press, 1976, *passim*. V.H. Rothwell, *British War Aims and Peace Diplomacy 1914–1918*, Oxford: Oxford University Press, 1971, *passim*. Hugh and Christopher Seton-Watson, *The Making of a New Europe: R.W. Seton-*

Watson and the last years of Austria-Hungary, London: Methuen, 1981, *passim*.

7   C.A. Macartney, *National States and National Minorities*, London: Russell & Russell, 1968 (reprint of RIIA 1934 original), p.184.

8   A. Cobban, *The National State and National Self-Determination*, London: Fontana, 1969, pp.49–50.

9   N.G. Levin, *Woodrow Wilson and World Politics*, New York: Oxford University Press, 1968, pp.13–49 and *passim*. See also Derek Heater, *National Self-Determination: Woodrow Wilson and his Legacy*, London: Macmillan, 1994, pp.32–6.

10   Cobban, *op. cit.*, p.63.

11   See Alan Sharp, 'Britain and the protection of minorities at the Paris Peace Conference, 1919', in A.C. Hepburn (ed.), *Minorities in History*, London: Arnold, 1978, pp.177–8. Temperley, *op. cit.*, vol. 1, pp.399 and 434.

12   Robert Lansing, *The Peace Negotiations: a personal narrative*, Boston: Houghton Mifflin, 1921, p.97.

13   Gilbert Murray, 'Self-determination of nationalities', *Journal of the British Institute of International Affairs*, 1922, vol. 1, p.8.

14   See Thomas G. Fraser, 'Germany and Indian revolution, 1914–1918', *Journal of Contemporary History*, 1977, 12, pp.255–72.

15   See Elizabeth Monroe, *Britain's Moment in the Middle East*, London: Methuen, 1965, pp.26–45. Michael Dockrill and Douglas Goold, *Peace without Promise: Britain and the Peace Conferences 1919–1923*, London: Batsford, 1981, pp.131–79. Alan Sharp, *The Versailles Settlement: peacemaking in Paris 1919*, London: Macmillan, 1991, pp.175–84. J. Nevakivi, *Britain, France and the Arab Middle East 1914–1920*, London 1969, pp.251–60. M. Kent (ed.), *The Great Powers and the End of the Ottoman Empire*, London: Allen & Unwin, 1984, *passim*.

16   Dockrill and Goold, *op. cit.*, p.141.

17   See also his Dublin speech 25.9.14. Rothwell, *op. cit.*, pp.18–19.

18   Fraser, *op. cit.*, p.255.

19   Zeman, *op. cit.*, pp.340–43.

20   Georges Clemenceau, *Grandeur and Misery of Victory*, London: Harrap, 1930, p.180.

21   D. Perman *The Shaping of the Czechoslovak State: Diplomatic History of the Boundaries of Czechoslovakia, 1914–1920*, Leiden: E.J. Brill, 1962, pp.13–16.

22   Murray, *op. cit.*, p.8.

23   See David Lloyd George, *War Memoirs* (two vols), London: Odhams, 1936, vol. II, pp.1477–90 and 1498–1503.

24   Speech to the TUC, 5.1.18, in ibid., p.1511. Speech to Congress, 8.1.18, in Temperley, *op. cit.*, vol. I, p.434.

25   S.H.Thompson, *Czechoslovakia in European History*, London: Frank Cass, 1965, p.326.

26   Perman, *op. cit.*, p.32.

27   Quoted in ibid., p.50. Temperley, *op. cit.*, vol. IV, p.105. Sharp, 1989, *op. cit.*, pp.363–64. Raymond Poincaré *Au Service de la France* (ten vols), Paris: Plon, 1933 onwards, vol. X, p.399.

28   Note 30.12.18, Lansing, *op. cit.*, pp. 97–8.

29 George Creel, *The War, the World and Wilson*, New York: Harper & Brothers, 1920, p.163.
30 Quoted in Perman, *op. cit.*, pp.105 and 169.
31 Sharp, 1991, *op. cit.*, pp.136–38. For further details see S.D. Spector, *Rumania at the Paris Peace Conference: a Study of the Diplomacy of Ioan I.C. Bratianu*, New York: Brookman Associates, 1962, and I.J. Lederer, *Yugoslavia at the Paris Peace Conference: a Study in Frontiermaking*, Yale: Yale University Press, 1963.
32 Sharp, 1991, *op. cit.*, pp.119–22.
33 Ibid., pp.105–16.
34 In their reply to the German observations on the draft treaty. Macartney, *op. cit.*, p.194.
35 Sharp, 1991, *op. cit.*, pp.138–42. See also R. Albrecht-Carrié *Italy at the Paris Peace Conference*, New York: University of Columbia Press, 1938. Heater suggests that Wilson may have been disingenuous in this statement and that perhaps he was seeking to trade the Tyrol for Fiume. Much would depend on when Wilson conceded the Tyrol – it may have been as early as 21 December 1918. Heater, *op. cit.*, p.76.
36 Temperley, *op. cit.*, vol. IV, p.429.
37 Letter 5.3.19. Agnes Headlam-Morley (ed.), *Sir James Headlam-Morley: a Memoir of the Paris Peace Conference 1919*, London: Methuen, 1972, p.44.
38 Temperley, *op. cit.*, vol. VI, pp.556–58. On Upper Silesia see F. Gregory Campbell, 'The struggle for Upper Silesia, 1919–1922', *Journal of Modern History*, 1970, vol. 42, no 3, pp.361–85.
39 Hardinge Minute, *c.*19.3.19 in FO608/51. Temperley, *op. cit.*, vol. VI, p.556.
40 Macartney, *op. cit.*, pp.4, 276 and *passim*. Sharp, 1978, *op. cit.*, *passim*. Carole Fink, 'The minorities question at the Paris Peace Conference', in *Germany and Versailles: Seventy Five Years After*, Cambridge: Cambridge University Press, forthcoming.
41 Pearson, *op. cit.*, p.136. Sharp, 1991, *op. cit.*, pp.155–8.
42 Piotr S. Wandycz, *The Price of Freedom: a History of East Central Europe from the Middle Ages to the present*, London: Routledge, 1992, pp.238–40.
43 The Foreign Office view was that 'Where the inhabitants of a country, irrespective of race, language or religion are guaranteed equal rights by a written constitution, or are in traditional and effective enjoyment of them, as is the case in the British Empire and in the United States, the claim of self-determination, or as it is called in the United States, the right of secession, can clearly be ruled out.' A.W.A. Leeper, *c.* 28.11.18 (P.I.D. 64/37 in FO371/4354).
44 Quoted by Heater, *op. cit.*, pp.207–8.
45 Quoted by Adam Roberts in the Foreword to Daniel Patrick Moynihan, *Pandaemonium: Ethnicity in International Politics*, Oxford: Oxford University Press, 1993, pp.xiii–xiv.
46 In 'The legacy of the First World War', in R. Boyce and E.M. Robertson (eds), *Paths to War: New Essays on the Origins of the Second World War*, London: Macmillan 1989, p.50.
47 On 20 and 30 December 1918. Quoted by Moynihan, *op. cit.*, pp.82–3.
48 Karl E. Meyer, *New York Times*, 14 August 1991, quoted in ibid., p.80.

Chapter 3

Yugoslavia
The search for a nation-state

Ann Lane

> The ideal of Yugoslav unity was conceived by literary men and visionaries; it was realised by men of action under conditions and with a quickness which would have been thought incredible even ten years ago.

These words, written by the Cambridge historian R.G.D. Laffan in 1921, form the opening sentence of his contribution to Harold Temperley's *History of the Peace Conference of Paris*, and are a reminder of the rapidity with which the Balkan Wars and the First World War transformed dreams into political realities. Recent developments in the Balkans have been an equally poignant reminder of the speed with which political certainties can become ethnic and social nightmares. In 1991 Yugoslavia, a proud successor state of the Habsburg and Ottoman empires, itself became submerged in a deleterious and devastating war of succession.

Events in Croatia and Bosnia have led political commentators to question why Yugoslavia collapsed. But perhaps it would be wiser to consider why it survived so long. After all, the Kingdom of the Serbs, Croats and Slovenes which emerged in 1918 seemed from the start to be wrought by internal contradictions. Its original name gave no recognition to the fact that it included Macedonians, some of whom regarded themselves as a separate nation, and the term Yugoslav could have been equally well applied to the neighbouring Bulgarians. When the First World War broke out in 1914, Serbia was still in the process of absorbing territories in the southern Balkans which it had recently acquired from the Turks, and which included peoples who did not regard themselves as Serbs and who were Muslim by religion. After four years of war and enemy occupation, Serbia virtually annexed its ally, Montenegro, a kingdom which pre-dated the emergence of modern Serbia, and became the dominant element in a union embracing peoples whose languages, religions and political institutions differed from those of the Serbs.

The 1991 civil war in Yugoslavia erupted as a direct result of the failure of that country's constituent parts to resolve their differences by purely political means. One by one the existing political institutions collapsed, without being replaced. This chapter will attempt, through an examination of the cohesive and disintegrative forces which shaped Yugoslavia's seventy-year history, to answer the question of how far his collapse was inevitable.[1]

The question of the political organisation of this region in the event of the collapse of the Ottoman empire had arisen as an integral part of the Eastern Question which had preoccupied European statesmen for much of the nineteenth century. In his seminal study of the South Slav question, published in 1911, R.W. Seton-Watson hardly mentioned Serb–Croat rivalry except as something fostered by foreign occupants.[2] The intention of the Serbs, Croats and Slovenes to unite had been proclaimed in the Corfu Declaration of July 1917, but this made no attempt to address the question of what constitutional form the new state might take. The seeds of subsequent problems can be seen in a cursory comparison of the various war aims which had to be reconciled.[3] The Serbs,[4] who had struggled for their independence from the Turks throughout much of the nineteenth century, a status which was formally recognised in the 1878 Treaty of Berlin, were concerned in 1914 that they emerge from the war having attained the liberation of the remaining, unredeemed South Slav lands, envisaging the incorporation of these after the war in a Greater Serbia. In practice, they wanted Bosnia-Hercegovina and an outlet on the Adriatic, as well as the Serb-inhabited lands under Habsburg rule known as the Vojvodina. Serbia did not need a Yugoslav state as such – it already controlled a compact national territory and by 1914 had influential foreign allies. But the military disasters of 1915 convinced the Serbian leaders that they could no longer ignore the ideas of Croat and Slovene nationalists. They now came to the view that Serbia's position might be re-established more successfully if they joined their forces with the Slovenes and Croats who had themselves united to campaign for their interests under the banner of the Yugoslav National Committee.

Croatia and Slovenia had enjoyed autonomy within the Habsburg empire as a consequence of arrangements arrived at with the Hungarians in 1868; many of these subjects were uninterested in complete autonomy. However, the émigré Yugoslav National Committee, led by Ante Trumbic and Frano Supilo, which represented their interests abroad during the First World War, aimed for an improvement on their existing status and desired in particular to create a state in which Croats and Slovenes could participate as equal partners. Their actions were dominated in part by the necessity of combating Italian ambitions for dominance of the Adriatic.

These somewhat conflicting war aims were counterpointed by equally contrary political and cultural traditions which had to be accommodated in the new state.[5] The first of these concerned the problem of political organisation. The differing historical experience of the Serbs on the one hand and the Croats and Slovenes on the other had resulted in these entities evolving politically in quite separate ways. Serbia had a unitary, centralist outlook following the French model which they had first experienced during their brief liberation from Ottoman domination during the early nineteenth century; Croatia was conditioned more by the ethnic and constitutional complexity reflected in the traditions of Austria-Hungary and therefore inclined much more towards the federal model. Other differences would also have to be reconciled, most notably perhaps those of religion. The schism between Rome and Byzantium was a particular manifestation of the historical fault line which runs through this region and was something each side could call into play should it choose to dwell on symbolic and historical differences.

Although the idea of a Yugoslav state had been in evolution since the early nineteenth century, these antecedents furnished little that was of practical value in resolving the constitutional problems posed by the contradictions inherent in the post-1919 Yugoslav state. Indeed, it is in any case questionable as to how far the intellectual and romantic notion of yugoslavism was shared by other sectors of the indigenous populations. Yugoslavism, or pan-slavism, flourished during the nineteenth century as part of the wider growth of somewhat nebulous nationalist philosophies and in response to the decline of the old order imposed by the Ottoman and Habsburg empires. To the extent that nationalism might be seen as a quest for security, the decay of empire provoked in the subject peoples the desire for a new security which might be based on smaller, national groupings.

Nationalism found fertile ground among the Balkan intelligentsia precisely because this philosophy was immediately relevant to local conditions. As this took hold, Balkan intellectuals became increasingly concerned with national languages, history and folklore. These philosophies provided not only a *raison d'être* for political activists who sought self-determination, but also served the interests of those who propounded such ideas by countering the divisive parochialism which was endemic in this region. It should be remembered, however, that nationalism was not a philosophy that found wide acceptance in the general population.

Internationally, the idea of a Yugoslav state received little overt support during the war.[6] This was partly due to Italian ambitions for the acquisition of lands along the Adriatic coast, and to the commitments of Britain and France to Italy under the Treaty of London. The climate changed only in 1918 when President Wilson became a supporter of the idea of a Yugoslav state largely because he had been become convinced by the arguments of those who advised that a settlement of the nationalities question with Austria-Hungary was unobtainable. But despite the emphasis placed at the Peace Conference on the principle of self-determination in shaping the post-war settlement, the peace treaties with Austria and Hungary were based more on historical and strategic claims. Thus, the successor state which emerged in the area we knew until recently as Yugoslavia encompassed eight recognised minorities and still had six of its seven borders in dispute.[7]

Yugoslavia had been unified, then, as a consequence of the collapse of the two great empires. Its creation was a response on the one hand to the aspirations of Croat and Slovene separatists who sought independence and security in a South Slav union; and on the other to the ambitions of the Serbs to achieve a dominant position in the western Balkans. In a world in which war had encouraged and nurtured expansive nationalism, Yugoslavia could provide disparate peoples with security through a union based on the tenuous notion of a shared racial identity. In this process, however, the question of political organisation had remained unanswered.

At odds, then, with most of its neighbours for whose governments revisions of the peace treaty became almost a *raison d'être*, the new kingdom was also internally divided at the most basic

level. The Hungarian Foreign Minister was prophetically pessi-
mistic about the Kingdom of Serbs, Croats and Slovenes. Having
spent many years in Serbia and Croatia his perception was that
these two races could never pull together: despite the fact they
spoke the same language, they were essentially different in all
their characteristics.[8]

As it emerged during the early 1920s, the Yugoslav state was to
all intents and purposes Greater Serbia: a fact which was given
oblique recognition in the way that British diplomats continued to
refer to the new kingdom as Serbia.[9] Indeed, Serbia's membership
of the victorious wartime alliance and international acceptance of
its claims to reparations tended to reinforce Serb dominance
within the union. This was also apparent in the Vidovan constitution of 1921, an instrument which satisfied most Serbs since it was
in effect an update of that under which pre-war Serbia had been
governed and, as such, it represented the triumph of the centralised Serbian experience over the Austro-Hungarian model of
federated feudalism. Moreover, the Serbs felt justified in their
predominance. They regarded themselves as the liberators of the
South Slavs from foreign oppressors, and argued that having
suffered most in war they deserved precedence in peace. Autonomous self-rule within each of the newly united provinces was
precluded by Serb rejection of a federal system. Instead they
sought to impose a patchwork majority consisting of Serb parties
and tactical allies onto parties that represented most of the non-
Serb groups.

The cost of this arrangement was that the majority of the
population never accepted the constitution, and there soon
emerged a Serb–Croat struggle which paralysed political life for
the next twenty years. Croats, who in pre-war Hungary had had
their own assembly and local leaders, had no intention of
abandoning their autonomous status. Lacking in general acceptance, then, the central government found its authority increasingly under challenge. Its response was to become steadily more
autocratic. Legal opposition was made difficult as criticism came
to be treated increasingly as treason. The successive political crises
which resulted during the 1920s culminated in the closure of the
parliament, the abolition of political parties and assumption of
personal dictatorship by the king, a situation which was enshrined
in the constitution of 1931.

These national political battles were exacerbated by the impact of the Great Depression on the region which severely undermined the predominantly agricultural and raw materials base of the economy: by 1932–1933 the prices of grain were one-third to one-half of those of 1929. The peasants, already indebted, were unable to meet taxes or payments on this debt. They were also affected by the widening of the gap between the values of agriculture and industrial goods.

Yugoslavia seemed indeed to be based on very shaky foundations. Its survival was due to a combination of factors, not the least important of which were first the fact that initially the Serbs were able to find allies among the non-Croat population of the state, and second the simple truth that for most of these peoples there was no obvious alternative to Yugoslavia. The Slovenes, for instance, historically belonged to the German states system. Their border with Croatia was, and is, one of the oldest in Europe, having been both the southern frontier of the First Reich and Austria's frontier with Hungary. Their language, though Slavonic, was markedly different from Serbo-Croat, something which worked to their advantage since it allowed them to maintain their cultural identity and assert their political autonomy. But in pre-1914 Austria, Slovene linguistic nationalism had had to compete not only with the German speakers to the north but also with the Italians to the south and west, and, in the aftermath of the war, Slovenia's inclusion in Yugoslavia was and remained its surest protection against the ambitions of an expansionist Italy. As it was, the peace treaties left over half a million Slovenes, and all of what might have been regarded as their Istrian coastline, in Italy. Likewise, it was a united Yugoslavia that demanded and secured the 1920 plebiscite in the Klagenfurt area of Austrian Carinthia; although in this instance the majority of the mixed German/Slovene population voted to remain part of Austria.

A third advantage perceived by the subjects of the Yugoslav state was the land reform which was undertaken during the 1920s in the former Ottoman and Habsburg lands where large estates had been maintained under Muslim, German or Hungarian ownership. This policy was successful in satisfying the demands of the First World War peasant soldiers for whom ownership of the land was a long-cherished ideal, and it had the by-product of reducing the attraction to them of Communist propaganda. In the long term, however, any increase in productivity was difficult since the land was having to provide a living for too many people.

In the early 1920s external pressures may also have made continued union with the Serbs attractive for the majority of Croats. The Italians had hoped that the largely Croat-speaking Dalmatia would become theirs after the war, and their residual claims and the seizure and virtual annexation of Fiume/Rijeka, Croatia's principal port, by a band of Italian freebooters, demonstrated the dangers to which too small and independent a nation might be exposed. There was also the possibility that a Habsburg restoration in Hungary, attempted twice (in 1920 and 1921), might add weight to Hungarian revisionist claims and threaten Croatia's unity. Eventually, however, both Hungarian and Italian revisionists were to exploit Croat dissatisfaction with Serb dominance in their effort to bring about the peripheral disintegration of Yugoslavia. Moreover, the success of Italian policies in Albania and the triumph there of the Italian-backed Ahmet Zogou Bey (the future King Zog) were both a challenge to Yugoslav influence and a potential threat to Serbian rule in Kosovo and Macedonia. The readiness of the Italian Fascist dictator, Benito Mussolini, to associate himself with the Bulgarians whose claims on Macedonia had precipitated the Second Balkan War, and with the Internal Macedonian Revolution Organisation (IMRO) which looked towards Bulgaria for protection and support, likewise encouraged the centrifugal forces in Yugoslavia.

Indeed, Serbia itself provided a unifying force. Alone among the nationalities which comprised Yugoslavia in having a highly developed sense of nationhood, it was perforce able in the interwar period to provide the symbols of Yugoslav unity through the monarchy and the army. The problem in the interwar period in essence was that the component parts of Yugoslavia were not prepared to evolve into consocialisation. The necessary co-operation did not feature among the aims of the various political leaders. Neither the Austro-Hungarian nor the Ottoman and post-Ottoman models was suitable for adaptation to the pluralistic political culture with which the new state had to deal. Domination through assimilation seemed to be the central government's objective and coercion its only recourse.

During the Second World War the Germans successfully exploited the fissures within the Yugoslav state to hold the region down, a position which only ceased to be viable when the Red Army arrived on Yugoslavia's eastern frontier in October 1944. Following the German invasion of 6 April 1941, Croatia was set up as a nominally independent entity under the Fascist government of Ante Pavelic who had received Italian sponsorship before the war. The Serbs, meanwhile, fell under direct German control through the quisling government of Milan Nedic. It was not the occupiers, however, but other Yugoslavs, especially the Croats and Bosnian Muslims or Albanians, who were commonly perceived by the Serbs as the most dangerous enemy. The perception was fuelled by the activities of the Pavelic regime in neighbouring Croatia where an attempt was made to expel the Serbs *en masse*. When the Germans put a stop to this, the Ustase sent huge numbers of Serbs to concentration camps. Many thousands were killed.[10] While these divisions assisted the Axis powers in their domination of the region, such policies inevitably generated among the Serbs a virulent anti-Croatian sentiment. After the war, these sentiments were given no room for expression – furthermore, the imposition of Communist rule was to some extent founded on the mythologising of the Communist-led wartime resistance which was notable for being predominantly non-Serb.

Indeed, Yugoslav wartime resistance was itself a manifestation of the divisions within the Yugoslav peoples, particularly of that between the Serbs and the other populations. Two resistance movements emerged: the Cetniks led by the Serbian General Draza Mihailovic who nominally at least was under direction of the Royal Yugoslav Government-in-Exile, and the Communist-led Partisans of the self-styled Marshal Tito. These had totally different long-term aims and were similarly opposite in tactical analysis. While Mihailovic believed his (and Serbia's) best chance was to lie low for the duration of the war in the expectation that the Western Allies would liberate the region, as had happened in 1918, Tito favoured active resistance and carried with him a large sector of the non-Serbian population, most of whom were principally concerned to ensure that post-war Yugoslavia would not be dominated by the Serbs as in the pre-war years.[11] Tito owed his victory in the civil war in part to the fortuitous arrival of the Red Army which liberated Belgrade in November 1944, but also to his understanding of the national concerns and to skilful exploitation of these for his own ends.[12]

By contrast with the inter-war period, the post-war period up to the mid-1980s might be described as one of stability and increased prosperity. It is in this that we find an explanation of current puzzlement at Yugoslavia's implosion. Closer examination reveals, however, that Yugoslavia's recent disintegration should not be so surprising.

Tito's success in maintaining the state, even after Yugoslavia's expulsion from the Soviet camp in June 1948, was founded on provision of what the greatest majority of Yugoslav peoples broadly wanted: protection from traditional enemies: the Slovenes from the Italians and Germans; the Croats from Italy but even more importantly from Serbia; the Macedonians from the Greeks, Serbs, and Bulgars. The central thrust of the 1945 Constitution was that Serbia be kept relatively weak. To this end Serbia was denied Bosnia which had been a key element in its national expansion programme since the middle of the nineteenth century and which the Axis powers had included in Croatia. Serbia was also obliged to abandon Macedonia, 'Old Serbia' in pre-war Yugoslavia, and thus forsake its version of *Drang nach Salonika*. The regions of Vojvodina and Kosovo were given semi-autonomous status within Serbia to achieve the reduction of Serbia while simultaneously appeasing its sensibilities. Meanwhile, the Serbs resumed their interwar prominence in both the army and the civil service, a position which only began to be eroded in the mid-1960s. None the less, Serbia entered the post-war world with less than the undisputed dominance it had enjoyed pre-war and the seeds of the present backlash lie there.

The central government gained its legitimacy through monolithic Communist dictatorship, personified in Tito, bolstered by marxist-leninism and a national mythology which elaborated heavily on the romanticism of wartime resistance. Opposition, as in the pre-war state, was ruthlessly stamped out. Examples were made of those who would challenge the new regime – the erstwhile King Peter's Minister of War, Draza Mihailovic, as a Serb patriot and Stepinac, the Archbishop of Zagreb, who personified for many the Catholic church in Croatia. This process was later repeated with Soviet sympathisers following the Tito–Cominform split in 1948 and still later with doubters from within the ranks, most notably the Communist Party ideologue, Milovan Djilas.

Tito's position within Yugoslavia was significantly reinforced by the expulsion of Yugoslavia from the Cominform in 1948. Since the cause of this schism in the Communist bloc was essentially Stalin's quarrel with Tito's leadership (and was aimed therefore at his removal) it forced a redefinition of Yugoslav communism as the Yugoslav leadership sought to justify itself in marxist-leninist terms. The result was socialist self-management, the Yugoslav variant of communism in which the control of economic units was to be devolved from the centre.[13] At the same time, Tito was able to identify the Soviet Union as the strongest and most likely predator on Yugoslav territory which provided a powerful unifying force and following from this, Yugoslavia now appeared as an attractive investment for Western governments which quickly moved to offer aid in order to stabilise the country as an independent entity. From a Western point of view it was an inexpensive means to the end of improving the defence of Italy and strengthening the Western alliance's strategic position in the southern Mediterranean.

By the 1960s with the revival of the 'old' nationalism and the weakening of wartime bonds of comradeship between the partisans and the old guard, the federal party structure, once a formality, began to emerge as the most important centrifugal force. The political battle remained that between the centralists and decentralists. But while protection from external threat and the constitutional balancing act, reinforced when necessary by coercion, are part of the explanation for Tito's success, the regime was also mediating a contest between economic strength and political weakness.[14] During the early 1950s, collectivisation programmes and the Five Year Plan were abandoned in favour of a more decentralised approach but the attempt made in 1965 at implementing major economic reforms was instructive in demonstrating the degree to which the demons of Yugoslavia's national problems could restrict the regime's ability to manoeuvre. These reforms, which were heavily backed by foreign money and in particular by the International Monetary Fund, were intended to set Yugoslavia on the road to market socialism. Imports were to be liberalised to provide competition for domestic enterprises while the dinar was devalued to stimulate exports. Many fixed prices were freed and the tourist industry opened up. The immediate consequences, however, proved destabilising: unemployment and emigration quickly combined with growing suspicion on the part of party apparatchiks of increasingly independent industry managers to frighten the central government into a speedy withdrawal. It now sought stabilisation through the implementation in 1968 of so-called consensus economics. This resulted in the fragmentation of industry into thousands of self-managing units, each with its own bureaucracy. Although this satisfied the party a high price was paid economically since these units were almost exclusively preoccupied with distributing rather than creating wealth. In practice this resulted in a steady rise in inflation as the state responded to the strains inherent in its inefficient economy by printing increasing amounts of money.

At the same time, aid from the West enabled individual Yugoslav republics to pursue, within the framework of official Yugoslav economic development policies their own unstated parallel policies.[15] For example, Slovenia insisted upon building a large port at Koper on the Adriatic which would operate in addition to the substantial and well-established port of Fiume/Rijeka which just happened to be in Croatian territory. Similarly the building of a third Adriatic port, this time at Bar in Montenegro, linked to Belgrade by a railway, was a project which was criticised as commercially dubious, not least because of the high construction costs of building such a route through extremely difficult mountainous terrain. It can be made sense of, however, in the context of land-locked Serbia's search since the nineteenth century for an outlet to the sea.

The economic weaknesses of the Tito era were compounded after his death. Very little of the foreign currency loaned to Yugoslavia as backing for the government's 'Long Term Stabilisation Programme' launched in July 1983, was used to build infrastructure and was absorbed instead in consumer spending. The combined problems of low productivity, antiquated capital plant, the black market and debt had driven up inflation which by the end of the 1980s had risen to 2,500 per cent.[16] These weaknesses were exacerbated by the uneven economic development of the north and south as Slovenia and Croatia prospered through industry and tourism, leaving the southern states, especially Serbia and Macedonia, which remained predominantly rural, economically disadvantaged. By the end of the 1980s, the Yugoslav economy was already in a state of civil war; the Serbs, believing that their economy had been discriminated against by the two dominant players in the Yugoslav economy, had declared a boycott on Slovenian goods.

Tito's policies, both external and domestic, were in large measure self-serving and tailored to meet short-term objectives: non-alignment in the essentially bipolar environment of Cold War Europe brought Yugoslavia the benefits of Western aid without the commitments consequent upon membership of a formal military alliance; at home, marxist-leninism, tailored to Yugoslav needs, supplied a supranational ideology which could be invoked to legitimise the state and set above more parochial symbols of national identity. In the process the post-war regime not only prevented the airing of grievances which had evolved as a consequence of the fratricidal strife which had raged in Yugoslavia during the Second World War, but its constitutional balancing act and economic policies were instrumental in fostering new ones.[17] Serbia, already reduced by the 1945 Constitution, lost further ground during the attempts at decentralisation during the 1960s, symbolised by the purging of the Serbian chief of policy and deputy to Tito, Aleksander Rankovic, in 1966. Serbia was effectively partitioned by the 1974 Constitution under which the provinces of Vojvodina and Kosovo were granted full autonomy, a development which allowed them direct participation in the decision-making process at the federal level, without recourse to Serbia, as had previously been the case. These grievances were nursed and particular resentment harboured towards the allegedly anti-Serb policy pursued in Kosovo by Albanian 'separatists' and 'irredentists' which were blamed for the steady exodus of Serbs. Action was taken by Slobodan Milosevic who found in this the starting point for the reassertion of Serb authority in Kosovo.[18]

This Serbian counter-offensive, which had begun in the mid-1980s[19] and reached its climax with efforts to destabilise Croatia, Bosnia and Hercegovina by inciting the local Serbs in these two republics against their democratically elected non-Communist governments, served only to strengthen the already strong feelings among many non-Serbs, particularly in Slovenia and Croatia, against Yugoslavia.[20]

The Slovenes, once the strongest supporters of the Yugoslav idea, had begun to call the union into question as early as the 1960s. By the 1980s these concerns had developed into complete disenchantment. The trigger which initially activated their inclination to separate was the Jugoslovenstvo project, initiated by the central government in 1958 with the unitarist objective of the eventual merger of the separate national cultures into a single Yugoslav culture. The Slovenes had been successful in preserving their identity and were not going to acquiesce in what they believed to be a revival of serbianisation. The question surfaced again in the early 1980s, this time in the shape of a plan for an all-

Yugoslav 'core' educational curriculum for subjects such as history and literature. It was largely due to Slovene opposition that this plan was dropped.

However, by 1990, Slovenia recognised that opportunity now existed to break away from the federation. Yugoslavia was no longer perceived by the Slovenes as indispensable for national survival – Slovenia had excellent relations with Italy and Austria and had enjoyed multilateral co-operation within the framework of Alpe-Jaeva (Alpen-Adria) regional co-operation which also included Croatia, four northern regions of Italy and five Austrian Lander, Bavaria and three western regions of Hungary.

Croatia, meanwhile, which in 1918 had welcomed union with Serbia to escape Hungarian and Italian claims, was also disenchanted. As a consequence of the union Croatia had lost the autonomous status it had enjoyed within Hungary between 1868 and 1918 as one of the historical nations of the Habsburg empire. Croatian separatism posed more problems than did that of Slovenia since Croatia was not geographically and linguistically separate from Serbia and as such its independence could be less clearly defined. Conversely, the threat of the possible revival of serbianisation seemed even more real – the linguistic closeness, once the ideological basis for the Yugoslav state, was now proving fatally divisive. Pro-independence sentiment in Croatia had been on the increase since the central government's repression in 1971–1972 of the Croatian national movement led by the reform Communists, known as the Croatian Spring. At the first multi-party elections, held in April/May 1990 Croatia's independent sentiment found renewed expression, which resulted in victory for the Croatia Democratic Union of Franjo Tudjman. The subsequent move towards independence was complicated, however, by the presence of the Croatian Serbs, already alienated from the Croat cause, who were strongly against independence: it was this conflict which emerged in the traditional stronghold of Serbian nationalism at Knin in southern Croatia, and this of course was the crisis which sparked off the war in 1991.

The immediate causes of the break-up have been traced by contemporary commentators to a variety of factors, most notably to economic weakness, the cessation of the security threat consequent on the collapse of the Soviet Union and the delegitimisation of communism as an ideology which followed upon this; it has also been ascribed to the political bankruptcy of the existing regime which responded to criticism during the 1980s by branding its opponents as nationalists, thereby giving them a common identity, and to the decision of the government in Belgrade to appeal to the Serb diaspora as a means of maintaining power. As various of Yugoslavia's component parts gave increasing expression to their disenchantment, so their determination also increased to emphasise whatsoever differences, however small, they could find between themselves and their immediate neighbours.

Any examination of the history of this troubled region prompts the conclusion that the idea of Yugoslavia was fantastic from the outset. After all, the nineteenth-century German nationalists could look back on a common German political structure – the Holy Roman Empire and the Germanic Confederation both embraced more Germans than Bismarck's creation. Italian nationalists could also look back on an Italian states system which had helped give to Italy a sense of political identity. There was nothing in recent South Slav history resembling these entities or systems – the Illyrian Provinces of the Napoleonic empire hardly contained fewer Serbs than Germans and Italians. Yet Croat visionaries of the 1860s dreamed of creating a Yugoslav state extending from the Alps to the Black Sea and the Adriatic and including Bulgars as well as Serbs, Slovenes and so on. The only element that unified these diverse peoples was the fact that nineteenth-century philologists defined their various languages and dialects as South Slav.

Perhaps the Yugoslav idea succeeded because it served to legitimise the aims of those seeking a greater Serbia and because, with the possible exception of the Croats, the other peoples of Yugoslavia had not in 1918 developed a strong sense of national consciousness. It is arguable that the Yugoslav idea ultimately failed because it created precisely the conditions in which national consciousness could develop among the indigenous people. Indeed, nationalisms might be said to have emerged and flourished in reaction to Serb domination.

Nevertheless, it may also be the case that there was no obvious alternative to Yugoslavia in 1918, or even in 1945. As Lord Palmerston had once remarked about the Austrian empire: 'If it had not existed it would have had to have been invented.' The Croats did not want reunion with Hungary and the Slovenes did not want absorption into Italy. Yet neither was a viable entity in its own right. But in 1990 this was no longer true. The main external threat to their independence had disappeared with the collapse of the Soviet Union, and two of the principal actors in the Yugoslav state had a viable economic basis independent of the Yugoslav union. For these, the European Union and the 'Europe of Regions' now provided the hope of a possible prosperous future.

The First World War brought to a close Ottoman and Habsburg domination of the Balkans. But in so doing it exposed the problem of how to effect stable political order in the absence of a consensus among the populations in question as to which might legitimately govern. The Kingdom of the Serbs, Croats and Slovenes was from the outset a polyglot state which was granted international acceptance partly in response to the expressed will of the native populations, but also because there was no other solution to hand. Without a consensus as to the internal organisation of this new state, the history of this region has been shaped by the working out of a series of internecine rivalries. Writing in 1948, the late A.J.P. Taylor, in his monograph on the Habsburg monarchy,[21] observed that it remained to be seen whether communism could provide a common loyalty which would transcend these rivalries. We now know that despite Tito's thirty-five year tenure of power in Yugoslavia, self-management socialism also failed to bring lasting stability and as a result of contemporary political and economic failures, changes in the structure of European politics combined with a legacy of ethnic complications and cultural diversity, nationalism has once again become a powerful vehicle for change in the Balkans.

NOTES

1   There are a number of general histories of Yugoslavia. The two standard works are B. Jelavich, *History of the Balkans: twentieth century*, vol. 2, Cambridge: Cambridge University Press, 1983, and I. Banac, *The National Question in Yugoslavia: origins, history, politics*, Ithaca: Cornell University Press, 1984. For a short overview see P. Lendvai, 'Yugoslavia without Yugoslavs: the roots of the crisis', *International Affairs*, 1991, vol. 67, no. 2, pp.251–61; C. Cviic, *Remaking the Balkans*, London: Frances Pinter for RIIA, 1991, and F. Singleton, *A Short History of the Yugoslav Peoples*, Cambridge: Cambridge University Press, 1985.

2   R.W. Seton-Watson, *The South Slav Question and the Habsburg Monarchy*, London: Constable, 1911. This point is developed by J. Horvat, *Politicka Povijest Hrvatske*, Zagreb: Globus, 1993.

3 W. Vucinich, 'The formation of Yugoslavia' and G. Stokes, 'The role of the Yugoslav National Committee in the formation of Yugoslavia', in D. Djordjevic and S. Fischer-Galatic (eds), *The Creation of Yugoslavia, 1914–18*, Oxford: Clo Books, 1980.

4 A. Dragnich, *Serbia, Nikola Pasic and Yugoslavia*, New Jersey: Rutgers University Press, 1974; M. Petrovich, *A History of Modern Serbia 1804–1918*, two vols, New York: 1986; T. Durham, 'Greater Serbia or Yugoslavia: Nicola Pasic and the Yugoslav Committee', *South Slav Journal*, 1992, vol. 13, nos 3/4 (autumn/winter).

5 D. Djordjevic, 'The idea of Yugoslav unity in the nineteenth century', in Djordevic and Fischer-Galatic (eds), *op. cit.*. See also R. West, *Black Lamb, Grey Falcon: a journey through Yugoslavia*, London: Cannongate Classics, 1942.

6 Stokes, *op. cit.*

7 I.J. Lederer, 'Yugoslavia at the Paris Peace Conference: a study in frontier making', M. Dockrill and B. Goold (eds), *Peace Without Promise: Britain and the Peace Conferences 1919–23*, London: Batsford, 1981; A. Sharp, *The Versailles Settlement: peacemaking in Paris, 1919*, London: Macmillan, 1991, pp.132–42; Vucinich, *op. cit.*

8 See, for example, PRO FO 370/209 L6205/152/402 Minute by Headlam Morley, 19 December 1925; see also W.N. Medlicott and D. Dakin (eds), *Documents on British Foreign Policy*, 1st series, vol. XXII; *Central Europe and the Balkans 1921, Albania 1921–22*, London: HMSO, 1980, *passim*.

9 For a general overview of the history of Yugoslavia in this period see S. Pavlowitch, *The Improbable Survivor: Yugoslavia and its problems 1918–1988*, London: C. Hurst & Co. 1988.

10 Jozo Tomasevich, 'Yugoslavia during the Second World War', in W. Vucinich, *Contemporary Yugoslavia: twenty years of socialist experiment*, Berkeley: University of California Press, 1969, p.78.

11 Ljubo Sirc, *Between Hitler and Tito: Nazi occupation and communist oppression*, London: André Deutsch, 1989; N. Anic, *The National Liberation War in Yugoslavia, 1914–45, vol. I*, Belgrade: Tanjug, 1985.

12 A. Djilas, *The Contested Country: Yugoslav unity and Communist revolution, 1919–1953*, Cambridge, MA: Harvard University Press, 1991.

13 J. Gow, 'Serbian nationalism and the Hissssing SSSSnake in the international order: Whose sovereignty? Which nation?', *Slavic and East European Review*, 1994, vol. 73, no. 3 (July).

14 Lendvai, *op. cit.*

15 O. Wilson Jr, 'The Belgrade–Bar railway: an essay in economic and political geography', in G.W. Hoffman (ed.), *Eastern Europe: essays in geographic problems*, London: Methuen, 1971, pp.365–94, cited in Cviic, *op cit.*, pp.56–7.

16 Cviic, *op. cit.*

17 S. Ramet, *Nationalism and Federalism in Yugoslavia 1962–1992*, 2nd edn, Bloomington: Indiana University Press, 1992.

18 A. Pavkovic, 'The Serb national idea: a revival', *Slavonic and East European Review*, 1994, vol. 72, no. 3 (July).

19   The immediate origins lie in the publication of the Memorandum of the Serbian Academy of Arts and Sciences which ascribed the cause of the profound economic and social crisis engulfing Yugoslav society to the nationally biased policies of the leaders of the Yugoslav Communist Party, which in their view favoured Slovenian and Croatian national interests over those of the Serbs in both constitutional and ethnic matters. The Memorandum was published as *Nacrt memoranduma Srpske acadmije nauka u Beogradu*, Canada: Srpska narodne odbrana, 1987.

20   On the present crisis see George Schöpflin, 'The rise and fall of Yugoslavia', in J. McGarry and B. O'Leary (eds), *The Politics of Ethnic Conflict Regulation*, London: Routledge, 1993; B. Margas, *The Destruction of Yugoslavia: tracing the break-up, 1980–82*, London: Verso, 1993; J. Gow, *Yugoslav Endgames: civil strife and inter-state conflict*, London: London Defence Studies, Brassey's, 1991; J. Gow, 'Deconstructing Yugoslavia', *Survival*, 1991, vol. xxxiii, no. 4 (July/August); L.J. Cohen, *The Disintegration of Yugoslavia*, Boulder: Westview Press, 1993; J. Seroka, 'Yugoslavia and its successor states', in S. White, J. Batt and P.J. Lewis (eds), *Developments in East European Politics*, Basingstoke: Macmillan, 1993; and M. Glenny, *The Fall of Yugoslavia: the Third Balkan War*, London: Penguin, 1992. For a discussion of the ethnic aspects see H. Poulton, *The Balkans: minorities and states in conflict*, London: Minority Rights Publications, 1993.

21   A.J.P. Taylor, *The Habsburg Monarchy 1809–1918: a history of the Austrian Empire and Austria-Hungary*, London: Penguin/Peregrine, 1964, pp.281–2.

Chapter 4

From Czechs and Slovaks to Czechoslovakia, and from Czechoslovakia to Czechs and Slovaks

W.V. Wallace

Comparatively speaking, the modern history of the Czechs and Slovaks has been less violent than that of their central European neighbours. So when communism disintegrated in 1989, it was hardly surprising that their break with the past earned the title of the Velvet Revolution. The citizens of Prague and Bratislava first trickled, then poured into the streets and discovered that their oppressors of four decades had more or less gone, leaving them free to shape their new future in peace.[1] They are still engaged in that process as they try to make policy through the ballot box and take on more than the rudiments of a market. But they have also chosen to go their separate national ways. The Czechoslovak state that had existed with but one interruption from the end of the First World War divided into the Czech and Slovak Republics on New Year's Day 1993. And even the divorce earned the title 'velvet'.

But if their history was so non-violent, why did they suddenly separate? They already had a federal state; was it so necessary to seek independence? Was it the opportunistic influence of a few ambitious politicians? Or was there a suppressed, internal resentment going back to the experience of the united state, or indeed to the Peace Settlement at the end of the First World War? The answers to these questions are that in fact Czech and Slovak history was only comparatively peaceful; the so-called federation was relatively recent and barely effective; and some post-1989 politicians pursued individual agendas; but at the same time the original marriage, however well-meant, was practically and contractually flawed, in need of greater internal and external understanding than circumstances allowed, and likely to end in divorce as soon the external constraints that held it together were removed.

The First World War and its aftermath had a profound effect on the destiny of the Czechs and Slovaks. Both peoples had gone through a cultural renaissance and a political reawakening in the previous hundred years or so and, if recent trends were to be followed, they would in due course have won greater autonomy, even independence. But the war hastened the process. Within Austria, the Czechs of 1914 have been described as being a nation without a state and not entirely dissatisfied. It was fear of German hegemony thereafter, combined with the nationalist ideology which eventually permeated French and British foreign policy in the course of the American entry into the war, that drove the majority of Czechs to seek full independence and get it. Within Hungary the Slovaks of 1914 were struggling for survival against a government determined to remove all traces of non-Magyar identity. So as the war ran its course, an impending Allied victory appeared to offer them a chance of rescue through the national carve-up of Austria-Hungary. The Czechs in particular contributed to the defeat of the Habsburgs and got their reward in a hearing at the Versailles Peace Conference, the Slovaks somewhat less so.[2] But victory belonged to the Allies, and so did much of the decision-making on the exact shape of the settlement.

The man who made the initial running on the Czech side was Tomas Masaryk, professor of philosophy, independent-minded politician, defender of victimised nationalities throughout the Habsburg empire. It took him six months to give up his pre-war idea of ethnic federalism to go abroad and win support for Czech national independence. In spite of his international reputation and the support of a bevy of extremely able émigrés and influential Western sympathisers, it took him three more years of travelling and talking to win the approval of Britain and France and, crucially, of the United States. But by the end of the war his case was made.[3] If the Poles could recover the independence they had lost in the eighteenth century, why not the Czechs who had lost theirs a century before? If national self-determination were to characterise the Peace Settlement, the Czechs had at least as convincing a case as anyone else.

But Masaryk was nothing if not a realist and quickly saw that military usefulness was a more powerful argument than sentiment or principle. Heavy losses in the middle of the war made the Allies hungry for whatever troop reinforcements they could get; and Masaryk capitalised on this by raising a legion from among young Czech conscripts who had deserted or been captured on the Eastern Front. Agreement in 1917 that they should be transported through the Far East (the only safe route then open) to fight against Germany in the west was an important factor in securing Masaryk's objective. The fact that on their way out in 1918 they came into conflict with the Bolsheviks added unintentional weight to the Czech cause. Western politicians, concerned lest bolshevism spread into the heart of Europe, were delighted to have some doughty Slav fighters on their side.[4]

What this meant, of course, was that the Czechs came to the Peace Conference with a tripartite case: they had history, nationality and geopolitical usefulness on their side. In an immediate sense this put them in a strong position. The ethnically German population of the Czech Lands could argue that they too, though incomers, were part of the history of Bohemia and Moravia, and should have equal treatment; or they could argue the ethnic case that they should either have territory of their own or be joined with Austria or Germany; but there was no way in which they could offer to provide good security, either against the defeated Central Powers or against the seductive tenets of bolshevism.[5] And so it was the Czech case that won.

However, in the longer run this was bound to weaken the Czech position if no reasonable satisfaction were given to the Germans or if the balance of power in Europe were to change. Also, seeking a specific frontier that was militarily defensible and economically viable, although on most points it had Allied support, led to the same short-term advantages and longer-term worries. Whatever the detailed settlement, its permanence would clearly depend upon how the new government would treat the whole of its population and upon whether Britain, France and America would continue to support the new state against the possible revisionism of Germany, Austria or Hungary, or the not impossible expansion of Bolshevik Russia.

But what was established, of course, was not just a Czech, but a Czechoslovak state. The Czechs and the next-door Slovaks are kindred peoples. Their languages are similar, their ethnic origins closely intertwined. The Great Moravian Empire of the ninth century, centred near Bratislava, encompassed both. But they were largely divided by the Magyar invasion; and although from the tenth century onwards their paths occasionally crossed, their development was different. It was 1620 before the Czechs' last army was defeated and their independence lost to Austria; and in between times, as in the Husite period, they were often at the heart of European history. The Slovaks by contrast, half as numerous and living on poorer land, had difficulty in keeping their identity under the Magyars until, at the turn of the eighteenth century, at about the same time as the Czechs, they began to rediscover their roots and express an ambition to look after their own affairs.[6]

But the Slovaks started from a much less well-endowed and self-conscious base; and they faced much tougher opponents, particularly after 1867 when Hungary secured parity with Austria within the Dual Monarchy and asserted its right to 'magyarise' all its subject peoples. In the half century before that, links had developed between the two nascent national movements.[7] And in the subsequent half century of persecution, the Slovak movement tended to depend on the Czech. Many Slovaks studied in Prague and some came to acknowledge Masaryk as their political mentor. Being half Slovak, he had a natural affinity with them, and in the two decades before the war he advocated extensive Czech–Slovak co-operation.[8]

At the outbreak of war the Slovaks had no spokesman prominent enough or free to speak on their behalf, at home or abroad; and it was left to Masaryk to voice their aspirations. Without an undisputed Slovak authority to consult he had to speak off his own bat after consultation with informed personal friends. In an early memorandum to the French and British governments he advocated the inclusion of the Slovak districts of Hungary within his proposed independent state. But however understandably in the face of Slovak formlessness and Western ignorance, he wrote of 'independent Bohemia' since 'the Slovaks are Bohemians, in spite of their using their dialects as their literary language . . . and accept the programme of union with Bohemia'.[9] And as late as 1917 Edvard Benes, Masaryk's wartime right-hand man, expressed identical ideas in a publication significantly entitled *Bohemia's Case for Independence*.[10]

The state that was eventually established, however, was not Bohemia, but Czechoslovakia. This outcome was arguably via a series of accidents. In Paris Masaryk and Benes discovered a former Slovak, renowned for his pre-war travels on behalf of the French Ministry of Marine and his wartime dogfights in the French air force. Milan Stefanik became a member of the independence trio and inevitably argued the Slovak case. The conscripts who found themselves in a position of influence behind the Russian lines included Slovaks. Prominent among the recent immigrants to the United States that Masaryk used to convince President Wilson of the justice of his case were the large numbers of Slovaks organised, on a par with the Czechs, into a political pressure group, the National Slovak Society. What also came through strongly as peace preparations were made was the preference of the Allies for larger rather than smaller states in the interest of their own security. If the South Slavs had to form a single state, so had the Czechs and Slovaks. It is true that in the course of the discussions that made up the Peace Conference doubts began to creep back about the good sense of the union, but they were swept aside in 1919 by the Franco-British reaction to what was seen as a real threat from the Bolshevik regime established in Hungary by Bela Kun.[11] Interestingly enough it was an American Slovak who led the Czechoslovak delegation that signed the Treaty of Trianon with Hungary.[12] But before that, the last word had lain with the West.

By the standards of previous and subsequent peace settlements at the end of long and bitter wars (not excluding what has happened since the conclusion of the Cold War) the creation of the Czechoslovak state made a great deal of sense. There was one particular anomaly that seemed nonsensical but could be justified. This was the decision to press Ruthenia on the new state, an area 60 per cent Ukrainian and more Hungarian, Romanian or German than Czech or Slovak. But the Ruthenians were Greek Catholic, not Ukrainian Orthodox; they were too few to stand on their own; and their connection with Slovakia was geographically plausible. Unfortunately there were other factors at work determining the outcome: distant pressure from the Greek Catholic Union in the United States; Western disinclination to cede territory to the emerging Soviet Union; and the Czechoslovaks' appreciation of Ruthenia's strategic value in a politically complex area. The interwar Czechoslovak government did not oppress the Ruthenians; indeed, it neglected them, given that it had so many other claims on its time and funds. In 1945 the Soviet Union simply seized for Ukraine territory it insisted belonged there; and in changed international circumstances the Czechoslovak government did not demur.[13]

A quarter of the population of the new Czechoslovak state was

German. Its representatives wanted complete separation or, failing that, frontiers more helpful to them and their parent countries. Population transfers were unthinkable to both sides, the Czechoslovaks for idealistic reasons, the Germans in order to sustain their claims. Some Czechoslovak and German representatives made demands that were inaccurate or excessive or both. In the event Czechoslovakia's frontiers with Germany and Austria followed historical lines, adjusted here and there to make it more viable both militarily and economically. Its frontier with Hungary was a little more difficult since there had been no medieval Slovak kingdom and there was little contemporary ethnic research on which to base it. The matter was settled by force when the French army drove the Magyars back. But within the new frontiers the Hungarian minority stood at 5 per cent.

All this should have tempered the Czechs and Slovaks. Together they made up only two-thirds of the population; and their representatives at the peace conferences had talked of establishing something resembling cantons on the Swiss model. Of course, once the post-Versailles international community had accepted Czechoslovakia's existence it had no constitutional right to intervene directly in its politics, although Czechoslovakia had signed the Minorities Treaty. Masaryk and Benes, as president and foreign minister, were aware of the need to protect Czechoslovakia against revisionism, not least by cultivating friendly governments and avoiding ethnic confrontations; and the constitution enshrined basic minority rights. However, anti-German and anti-Magyar sentiments were strong among the public at large as well as among political leaders. Germans and Magyars had enjoyed long years of political, economic and cultural supremacy; now it was the turn of the Czechs and Slovaks. Promoting German and Magyar autonomy through cantons or by other means was simply not an option. For their part, many Germans and Magyars continued to appeal for help to their co-nationals across the frontier, an action that did nothing to ameliorate Czechoslovak hostility. Yet as the international situation settled and the domestic economy improved, the politics of Czechoslovakia took on a less national character, and following the 1926 election it proved possible for two of the German parties to join a coalition government formed along social lines. The two small Magyar parties remained aloof, banking on continuing Hungarian revisionism.[14]

From the standpoint of later years it is possible to argue that twentieth-century multinational states were doomed. The First World War struck one blow, the Second another, and perhaps the Cold War a third. But Czechoslovakia in the mid-1920s seemed to provide evidence to the contrary. It was the Depression that ruined everything. The Sudeten regions of Czechoslovakia depended on exports, particularly to Germany, and suffered worse and took longer to recover than elsewhere in the country; they were inevitably prey to irredentism and in 1935 voted overwhelmingly for a recent creation, the Sudeten German Party, organised with Nazi money by Konrad Henlein. The link between the Depression and Hitler's own rise to power is all too well known; and it was no problem for him to play the irredentist card in Czechoslovakia, with Henlein as his agent.[15] The Depression was also among the constituents of Anglo-French appeasement; Western economic recovery – and lives – should not be sacrificed in the interest of an insupportable, unjustifiable, multinational society. The Peace Settlement had got it wrong; Germans should not be expected to live in a Czechoslovak state.

Under relentless pressure President Benes went all the way in 1938 to offering Henlein complete autonomy. But the powers that had authorised an all-embracing state twenty years before pushed harder. And in September, the Munich Agreement, a peculiar name for a settlement forced on a country not party to the talks producing it, severed the 'Sudetenland' from Czechoslovakia altogether. It was a curious remedy for multinationalism since there were still Germans in Czechoslovakia and Czechs were transferred to Germany. The full lie was exposed six months later in March 1939 when Hitler sent in his forces to establish a protectorate in the Czech Lands and to allow Slovakia to slip to the side in a bogus independence.[16]

Undoubtedly the Czechoslovaks made mistakes in their treatment of the disaffected German population. A concession towards some form of autonomy before the Depression might have been sufficient, though it is worth noting that the Minorities Treaty laid clear obligations on central governments but not on the minorities themselves. However, once the Allied powers agreed to the Czechoslovak state in the form it took, they were in duty bound to support it; and even if they felt that they might like to change it in some way, they were still obliged not to participate in its destruction. If there was a problem, they had helped to create it; and far from resolving it, they compounded it.

At the end of the war the Czechoslovaks found their own solution. Britain and France had no ground to stand on in trying to stop them. Characteristically, Benes sought a different outcome. But after their experience of Henlein's subversion and Hitler's occupation the public would have none of it and drove the Germans out. It was a sad result, strangely close to current 'ethnic cleansing'. But it was done without unnecessary violence and remedied a situation not of the making of the Czechs and Slovaks alone.[17]

From the start the German question had an important bearing on the relationship between the Czechs and the Slovaks. The Czechs were so concerned to prevent the Germans from breaking away from their new state that they deliberately created a highly centralised form of government. This meant centralised in Prague with respect to the Czechs as well as to the Slovaks, but to the Slovaks it had much more meaning. It tended to reinforce the earlier prejudices of Masaryk and Benes that the two peoples were the same, or rather that the Slovaks were more or less Czechs. Another factor producing an apparently unfair relationship was the lack of an outstanding array of Slovak politicians. One or two Slovaks who had for some years aired pro-Czech views were included in the first government. Tragically, Stefanik, who might have done a great deal to develop equality of treatment, was killed in a plane crash on his way home from Russia in 1919. Andrej Hlinka, a middle-ranking figure in Slovak politics, found himself squeezed out of the centre for personal reasons (that were not particularly his responsibility) and began to exercise his talents in opposition to unity.[18]

Another awkward issue was the so-called Pittsburgh Agreement. This was concluded by Masaryk in May 1918 while in the United States drumming up support for independence. In joint talks with the National Slovak Society and the Czech National Association he envisaged that the new state would be some kind of federation in which Slovakia would have its own administration, assembly and law courts. Although he was careful to point out at the time that it would be for the Czechs and Slovaks at home after the war to draw up the actual constitution, his speculation was regarded by many Slovaks as a binding promise.[19] In the event, the National Assembly that gathered late in 1918 to debate and establish the constitution was composed of 256 members of whom only 40 were Slovaks; and the addition of another 14 in the spring of 1919 made little difference. Votes inevitably went the Czech centralist way.

These numbers were not wholly rigged. The Czech population outnumbered the Slovak by two to one; yet the ratio in the Assembly, even when improved, was four to one. The various experiments with local government did not help. A series of regions was established in 1920 in imitation of the French prefectures. They were meant to break old Czech provincial loyalties; but the effect on the Slovaks was to challenge what they quite reasonably considered as their national cohesion. Interestingly enough, this experiment was undermined by local resistence in the Czech Lands. So in 1927 provinces were allowed to reappear; and Slovakia, which had never enjoyed such a position, took its place alongside Bohemia and Moravia-Silesia with its own governor, administration and representative assembly. This had the appearance of a positive move that, incidentally, might go some way towards assuaging Slovak hurt. But the government immediately diminished it, in the Czech case as well as in the Slovak, by appointing the governors, the administrations and one-third of the assembly members. On centralist principles the provinces' powers were also restricted, a move that led to the unintended result that Slovaks were regularly brought together to discuss, of all things, their complaints.[20]

One feature of the constitution that did assist the Slovaks was proportional representation. It enabled them to get a fair return on the votes cast for their parties, and in particular guaranteed a political platform for the more outspoken among them. Yet another of the government's best intentions went badly astray. As a result of decades of 'magyarisation' within pre-war Hungary there was a severe shortage of Slovak experts in all walks of life, from administration and business through to education and medicine. So the government encouraged specialists from the Czech Lands, Slovaks trained in the Lands or Czechs, to move east for short periods to fill the gap. But particularly when Czechs decided to stay on, especially in the better-paid jobs, and became a barrier to newly trained Slovaks, there was deep-seated resentment.

Compared with the Czech Lands, Slovakia was not only short of expertise in 1918, it was generally underdeveloped. The issue was not simply one of a lesser endowment and a poorer quality of natural resources. Imperial Austria had exploited the agriculture of Bohemia and Moravia and provided the capital for industrial development. In the end, much of its richest farmland and 90 per cent of its industry were located in what became western Czechoslovakia. Imperial Hungary by contrast had been happy to take Slovak wine and copper and to attract Slovak migrant labour to Budapest; but it had established few plants in Bratislava or other Slovak towns. After 1918 the Czechs had to work very hard to re-orientate their economy to new markets beyond Austria and to interest Western investors. But the Slovaks inherited the more serious problem. Three-quarters of their population had to live off the land compared with only a half in the case of the Czechs. The post-war recession closed down two of their biggest industries, the Krompachy iron works and the Zvolen sheet-metal works, and left a quarter of their labour force out of work. Slovak peasants, though poor, enjoyed farming their own plots. There was a slight economic recovery in the late 1920s and some new industrial enterprises. But the restructuring process hit the out-of-date hardest, and this meant closing more Slovak than Czech plants. Even much-needed east–west railway construction seemed to take business westwards.

To be sure, the Czechoslovak government was in no way responsible for the size or the state of the economy it inherited in Slovakia. It was remarkably successful in the 1920s in making one large functioning economy out of the fragments of two markets that had collapsed. It was also careful to make its expanded social welfare provisions available throughout the country. But it can be argued that it might have weighted its reconstruction programme more generously in favour of the Slovaks since, whatever the reality, the appearance was different. Many Slovaks felt that they were getting the worst of the bargain; and there were politicians to feed their suspicions.

Post-war Hungary refused to give up its claim to Slovakia, twice involved itself in fruitless attempts to reinstate the Habsburgs and established a regency in their favour. But when these frontal assaults failed, it diverted its attention both to international propaganda and to politics in Slovakia. As things turned out, it was quite successful in wooing the owner of the *Daily Mail*, Lord Rothermere, to give the Czechs rather a bad press in Britain, but it made minimal headway with the Magyar minority in Slovakia since they were predominantly poor peasants no worse off than many of their Slovak neighbours. But for a time it looked as if they might have an ally in Hlinka. A Slovak through and through, he was not a separatist, but an autonomist. He appealed to the Peace Conference for autonomy for Slovakia and proceeded to build his party, the Slovak Populists, on the theme of the Pittsburgh Agreement. Rebuffed in Paris and Prague, he proved vulnerable for a time to the blandishments of some smooth Slovak turncoats and sharp Hungarian activists and was almost branded a traitor. The Hungarians were delighted. But he then made a little more headway at home when he doubled the number of his deputies from twelve to twenty-three between the 1920 and 1925 elections. As the leader of the largest Slovak party in the Chamber of Deputies, he was in due course invited to enter the government and agreed. Hungary lost out, and Slovakia seemed set to gain. Hlinka was unlikely to win autonomy right away, but at least he felt in a position to try to improve the lot of his electors.

In 1928 another issue was settled, apparently to his and his countrymen's satisfaction. Despite their Husite past and the sixteenth-century impact of Luther and Calvin, the Czechs of 1918 were basically Catholic. However, in addition to agnostics and atheists, there was also an influential sprinkling of Protestants; and the majority of the Catholics were somewhat independent-minded, influenced as they were by uncomfortable recollections of the close and long-standing Habsburg association with Rome. Slovakia had experienced protestantism, and several of its prominent historical and contemporary figures, were active Protestants. But circumstances had conspired to make most Slovaks firm Catholics, more devout and loyal than the Czechs. So when the Czechoslovak government came into dispute with the Vatican concerning the powers it should enjoy, there was some satisfaction among Czechs but a good deal of Slovak ill-feeling. Nevertheless, a special *modus vivendi* was negotiated that restricted papal powers within Czechoslovakia as a whole, but recognised that the state had obligations to the church. If this was not entirely to the satisfaction of many ordinary Slovaks, it had one aspect that pleased their clergy. They were liberated from the jurisdiction of the Archbishop of Esztergom in Hungary and were therefore able to devote themselves to the cause of separatism, or even of independence. Hlinka professed himself pleased, as did Father Jozef Tiso, who had entered the Czechoslovak government at the same time and was later to play a crucial role in pushing Slovakia towards independence.

Unfortunately, the government in Prague misinterpreted Hlinka's decision to join it as an abandonment of separatism. So he won no serious political concessions and was criticised by many Slovaks for betraying the cause. Even though he then withdrew from the coalition in time for the 1929 election, he lost four seats. By staying out he regained three of them in 1935. In the interval, of course, the Slovaks suffered much from the Depression. Given their overwhelmingly agricultural economy, they endured a longer period of low production and high unemployment than the Czechs, and they attributed this to their lack of autonomy and prejudice on the part of the government. Increased defence spending after 1935 came too late to make a noticeable impact. Slovak catholicism also gave a new twist to suspicion of the Prague government. Many of the clergy viewed Stalin and communism as more dangerous than Hitler and nazism and looked askance at ministers who tolerated the existence and activities of the Czechoslovak Communists and in 1935 joined the Franco-Soviet pact. To resentment at ethnic discrimination was added fear of Bolshevik subversion; and when the time came, Hitler utilised this mood against Czechoslovakia. Which was very soon.

Immediately after the *Anschluss* with Austria in 1938 the Slovak Populists sensed their opportunity. A delegation of American Slovaks brought the original of the Pittsburgh Agreement to Bratislava in May, and at a huge open-air meeting in June Hlinka demanded that the Slovaks be given their autonomy. Benes guaranteed them any concessions he might have to make to the Sudeten Germans, an attitude consistent with his previous policy of resisting Slovak autonomy for fear of raising unpalatable Sudeten demands. Hlinka died in August. Tiso, who succeeded him, was unwilling to accept this formula; and though Munich made no provision for a change in the Slovak–Czech relationship, he was able through the so-called Zilina Accord to wrest virtual autonomy from Benes's successor. The circumstances might not be the most desirable, but Tiso had achieved what Hlinka had been aiming at. A long struggle had come to an end; and other things remaining equal, Slovakia and the Czech Lands might have settled down to the business of negotiating a federation.

Hitler had a different target, the destruction of Czechoslovakia denied him at Munich. Over the winter of 1938 he encouraged the Slovak Populists to think in terms of complete separation, and in March 1939 he unapologetically bullied them into demanding it.

Tiso and his colleagues proved willing; and so Hitler had his pretext for marching on Prague. Within a matter of months Slovakia had moved from dependence to autonomy to independence. It was a triumph beyond belief.[21] But the fact and the method displeased many Czechs, and not a few Slovaks.

From the point of view of Benes, and of the many Czechs who worked with him in the wartime struggle to reassert Czechoslovak independence, the actions of the Slovaks in 1938–1939 were at best damaging, at worst destructive. There might have to be some kind of federation after the war; but disunity before it had undermined independence and all talk of a new Czech–Slovak relationship had to be set aside until well into the war. There were also Slovaks working with Benes, both in London and in Moscow, who thought the same. As in the First World War, Slovak conscripts deserted on the Russian front to join Czechoslovak fighting units. In due course a resistance movement built up within Slovakia that opposed Tiso for his dependence on Germany and the policies that this generated and that established connections with the Czechoslovak government in exile. Yet the resistance made no attempt to hide its wish for a different Czech–Slovak arrangement. Until the Tiso experience became unbearable, the feeling of being wholly separate from the Czechs and nourishing Slovak culture was something to be savoured. Communication with the Czechs was indirect; and this allowed Socialists and Communists also to develop a taste for a diluted link with their Czech colleagues. The Slovak uprising in 1944 was directed against the Tiso regime and its Nazi backers and it united many strands of political thinking; but more than anything else it was an expression of Slovak feelings that were only strengthened by its almost total defeat. Tiso might have shamed the Slovaks in 1938–39; but being Slovak from 1944 onwards was something to be proud of.[22]

By the end of the war most Slovaks therefore assumed that the pre-war centralised system of government would disappear. Obviously, total separation had been discredited. But the Slovak resistance record bore fair comparison with the Czech; and with the expulsion of the Sudeten Germans, one of the old arguments for an undivided union had finally been undermined. What reappeared, however, was the post-1918 case for unity in face of possible revisionism: maintaining the Czech-Slovak state's independence and providing security for the Second World War Allies.

Ruthenia might be hived off, but Slovakia should still be kept on a tight rein.

If this was an old argument, it was reinforced by a new voice. The Soviet Union might not have been able – or might not have wished – to rescue Czechoslovakia in the circumstances of appeasement in 1938; but by 1945 it had come to regard Czechoslovakia as an essential defence against Germany and a potentially hostile capitalist West. Because of its role in the defeat of Hitler and the liberation of eastern Europe it was also in a particularly strong position to influence Allied decisions and to help determine the pattern of events in Czechoslovakia. Specifically, the Red Army freed Prague while the Americans stopped at Plzen; and the Czechoslovak government that returned through Moscow was headed by Benes but included a sizeable faction of Communists, most of whom had spent the war years in the Soviet Union. It also excluded the Slovak Populists, proved advocates of Slovak separatism, and the Czechoslovak Agrarians, who were deemed to have collaborated with the Nazis and who had in their ranks those Czechs known to be most sympathetic to the Slovak point of view. The Slovak National Council that had organised and survived the Uprising and was initially recognised as part of post-war government machinery certainly entertained lively hopes of a better future, but it very soon found the odds stacked against it.[23]

Benes favoured a united, not a unitary state – 'equals with equals' – and never really changed his view. With the Communists it was different. A separate Slovak Communist Party was established in 1939, took part in the Uprising and remained active after 1945, all as part of Soviet military and political strategy. But objectives changed. Defence requirements apart, attacking Slovak autonomism became a useful post-war weapon in the hands of the wider Czechoslovak Communist Party in its struggle to move from a minority to a majority position in the government. The freedom of action of its Slovak partner was curtailed, and all sorts of obstacles were put in the way of the Slovak National Council and the Board of Commissioners that had been set up as its executive arm.[24] This was a policy that came easily enough to a Czechoslovak Party that was dominated by Czechs. It was also one that became an outright obsession with Stalin from 1947 onwards as he sought to stamp out the wartime nationalism that threatened the dominance of communism in the Soviet Union and the supremacy of the Soviet Union in the Communist world. Benes and his colleagues might look on the Slovaks with some favour. The new Slovak Democratic Party might bring together the best elements in society and have attainable aims. But once the various non-Communist parties lost their cohesion in February 1948 and let the Communists assume power by default, Slovak autonomy was off the political agenda.

In spite of scattered achievements along the way, the Communist period in Czechoslovak history now goes largely unsung. Czechs and Slovaks suffered more or less alike, politically in the early years and economically later. In a catching-up sense, Slovakia experienced more development than the Czech Lands. But the Slovaks were still outnumbered two to one by the Czechs. They had been out-manoeuvred by the Russians. They suspected Stalin of having deliberately slowed the Red Army's advance in 1944 to let their Uprising be defeated; they understood all too well his self-interested switch, in the years 1945 to 1948, from supporting their autonomy to torpedoing it; and in 1951 they had to face up to the fact that, in a show trial, Stalin murdered Vladimir Clementis, one of their wartime Communist heroes.[25]

Unlike the Germans, the Slovaks were still part of Communist Czechoslovakia and, short of a miracle, their aspirations were unlikely to disappear. In the late 1950s and early 1960s, the reverse happened. The economy faltered, absolutely as well as in comparison with the non-Communist West. Perhaps because the Slovaks had so often fared worse than the Czechs, or because they were by nature more courageous, they took the lead in criticising the essentially Czech government and implied that they could do better if they had more of their own way.[26] They were able to use the hollow remnants of their pre-1948 powers to start down the road that led first to autonomy and then to independence. In 1963 the Slovak Communist Party, otherwise under the thumb of its Czechoslovak superior, elected its own Secretary, Alexander Dubcek; and subsequently the Slovak Writers Union and other bodies took upon themselves the task of exploring publicly ways of reforming communism.[27] It was not least this, coupled with the uncertain Soviet behaviour of the 1960s, that led in 1968 to the Prague Spring and then in 1969 to the federalisation of the Czechoslovak state.

When at the end of 1967 the tide of resentment eventually turned on Antonin Novotny, the turgid General Secretary of the

Czechoslovak Communist Party, it was Dubcek who emerged as the person most likely to give communism a chance of winning back its authority by getting closer to what the public wanted. In the course of 1968 this brought him and his reforming colleagues into direct collision with the Soviet Union and led to the August invasion and the virtually complete reversal of their reform programme. But federalisation survived.

That it was taken seriously in the first place was due to the Slovaks' insistence; and they saw it as a historic moment when the Action Programme set out the reasons for seeking a new Czech––Slovak relationship.[28] But from the outset, the Czech view was different. A federation implied criticism of the existing pro-Czech arrangement and was justified only by the pressing need to win back support for the Communist Party. But it was a Slovak, not a Czech problem; so there was little call for change. In particular the Czechs were unwilling to yield the principle of Czech/Slovak voting equality as against Czechoslovak majority rule, or to localise very much in the way of decision-making. What resulted was a compromise that maintained inequality in senior appointments and excluded much of their economy from the Slovaks' control.

Nor were they able to draw much comfort from the fact that some of the new order persisted beyond 1968. The Soviet politburo was prepared to accept a federation in principle; but in the interest of its supremacy at home and throughout the Communist world, it was as opposed to nationalism as Stalin had been in 1948. So it ensured that the federation would be ineffective by insisting on the unity and supremacy of the single Czech-dominated Communist Party that proceeded once more to run the whole state as a single entity.[29]

In 1968–1969, therefore, the Slovaks' gains were mainly on paper. The final culprit might be the Soviet Union; and some of its aiders and abetters were Slovaks. After all the Slovaks had done before 1968 to create the opportunity for reform for everyone, they had some reason to feel betrayed by the Czechs, all the more so as some of their gains were then whittled away during the 1970s and 1980s.

It would not be true to say that in the 1980s there were greater pressures on the Slovaks to push for change than on the Czechs, or that one people sought it more actively than the other. Post-1968 consumerism eventually failed to satisfy either as the economy declined; and Gorbachev's reforms in the Soviet Union led both peoples to make bolder complaints. In some ways they were more united than ever and acted as Czechoslovaks in relishing top-level political resignations. When the moment came to parade on the streets, they called together for an end to communism.

Yet they threw up separate organisations: the Civic Forum in the Czech Lands and, in Slovakia, Public Against Violence. Despite that, they could still invite a Czech, Vaclav Havel, to be president and a Slovak, Marian Calfa, to be prime minister. Arguably as an acknowledgement of their comradeship in 1968, they made Dubcek chairman of the Federal Assembly. But within three years they had parted.

It will clearly be some time before there is an entirely satisfactory explanation.[30] Obviously, old attitudes and grievances played a part: Czech politicians refused to accept the Slovak proposition that there could be two republics and a united state; and Slovak politicians argued for extensive devolution of vital powers to republican governments. There were also new factors: although there was a massive popular turnout for the first free elections in June 1990, the results were unhappy in that nine parties gained seats, discussions among them were confusing and decisions therefore proved quite difficult. On the other hand, the Slovak National Party that called loudest for the break-up of Czechoslovakia gained only a modest number of seats. Yet, despite his intellectual skills, Havel as president lacked Masaryk's charisma and Benes's doggedness and found it increasingly difficult to induce political order.

The old economic conflict reappeared. The Czechs foresaw Slovakia draining off scarce investment funds. The Slovaks objected to rapid restructuring since they had some of the largest, least efficient enterprises, particularly in defence for which demand was rapidly declining; and they quickly ran up much higher unemployment figures. With more diversified industry and better-endowed agriculture the Czechs looked forward to getting quickly to the West German standard of living. The fact that Czechs and Slovaks were alike led astray by Western propaganda into believing that the economic millenium was at hand fuelled discontent and bred mutual suspicion.

It has also been suggested, with force, that some politicians, for reasons of personal or national ambition, actively sought separation. There is no doubt that the two current prime ministers,

Vaclav Klaus and Vladimir Meciar, both pursued tough policies following the more than respectable showing of their respective parties, the Civic Democrats and the Democratic Slovaks, in the June 1992 elections and proceeded to negotiate the separation.

But perhaps attention should be focused on some longer-term factors. Maybe it can be argued that the peacemakers, both domestic and international, got it wrong at the end of the First World War and repeated their misconception at the end of the Second. Alternatively, Czechs and Slovaks had been too long apart to come together, and the final separation was simply a tardy recognition of that fact. An influence not to be overlooked, too, was the collapse of the Soviet Union in 1991. Big Brother was no longer there to mount an invasion and stop a separation; and what was more significant, it had itself disintegrated on near ethnic lines.

Arguably all this can be restated. The Czechoslovak settlement was not ideal, but it suited the sharp international realities at the end of two world wars. The Czechs may have been somewhat insensitive, the Slovaks impatient; but together they survived and re-emerged. Now the international situation is totally different since neither Germany nor Russia offers threats of the old kind. In addition, unrequited nationalism, as in the former Yugoslavia, is a serious danger. So Slovakia was free, even encouraged to drift away, and to do so in the interest of the Czechs as much as anybody. In fact a new regional constellation has appeared, the European Union, and both the Czech Republic and Slovakia may shortly gain entrance. They have nothing to fear from the outside world and no need, therefore, to cling to each other. What they had to do was to part company, do their best economically on their own, then reunite as part of a European federation that in time will include eastern as well as western Europe. In contrast with previous turns of the wheel, this one has not so far called for a war, and will not do so.

Yet there is just an outside possibility that this happy analysis may be put to a severe test by the Magyars. Constituting 11 per cent of the population of the Slovak Republic with 11 per cent of the seats in the Slovak Parliament, they may conceivably be totally satisfied with their lot. But their location, too, is in part a legacy of the First World War and the Peace Settlement that followed it. So in the fluid circumstances of the 1990s they may find their present linguistic and cultural autonomy inadequate; and with a restive

Hungary next door, they also may find a divorce attractive. Which may be peaceful – or may not.

NOTES

1 T.G. Ash, *We the People: the Revolution of 89*, London: Granta Books, 1990, pp.78–130; N. Hawkes (ed.), *Tearing down the Curtain: the People's Revolution in Eastern Europe*, London: Hodder & Stoughton, 1990, pp.100–23.

2 W.V. Wallace, *Czechoslovakia*, Boulder: Westview Press, 1976, pp.53–61 and 91–122.

3 W.V. Wallace, 'Masaryk and Benes and the creation of Czechoslovakia', in H. Hanak (ed.), *T.G. Masaryk (1850–1937)*, vol. 3, London: Macmillan, 1990, pp.71–85.

4 G. Wightman, 'T.G. Masaryk and the Czechoslovak Legion in Russia', in Hanak (ed.), *op. cit.*, pp.57–70.

5 D. Perman, *The Shaping of the Czechoslovak State*, Leiden: E.J. Brill, 1962, pp.121–212.

6 P. Brock, *The Slovak National Awakening*, Toronto: University of Toronto Press, 1976, pp.3–19.

7 Ibid., pp.20–54.

8 T.D. Marzik, 'The Slovakophile relationship of T.G. Masaryk and Karel Kalal prior to 1814' in S.B. Winters (ed.), *T.G. Masaryk (1850–1937)*, vol. 1, London: Macmillan, 1990, pp.191–209.

9 T.G. Masaryk, *Independent Bohemia*, in R.W. Seton-Watson, *Masaryk, in England*, Cambridge: Cambridge University Press, 1943, pp.116–34.

10 E. Benes, *Bohemia's Case for Independence*, London: Allen & Unwin, 1917, pp.1–4.

11 Perman, *op. cit.*, pp.213–27.

12 C.S. Leff, *National Conflict in Czechoslovakia*, Princeton: Princeton University Press, 1988, p.20.

13 P.R. Magosci, *The Shaping of a National Identity: Subcarpathian Rus, 1848–1948*, Cambridge, MA: Harvard University Press, 1978, pp.76–102, 191–233 and 250–5.

14 Wallace, 1976, *op. cit.*, pp.125–80; E. Wiskemann, *Czechs and Germans*, London: Oxford University Press, 1938, pp.118–39; and J.W. Bruegel, 'The Germans in prewar Czechoslovakia', in V.S. Mamatey and R. Luza (eds), *A History of the Czechoslovak Republic 1918–1948*, Princeton, NJ: Princeton University Press, 1973, pp.167–87.

15 R.M. Smesler, *The Sudeten Problem 1933–1938*, Folkestone: Dawson, 1975, pp.243–55.

16 Wallace, 1976, *op. cit.*, pp.181–219; and W.V. Wallace, 'Britain and the origins of the Second World War', in B. Snajder (ed.), *The Last Days of a Restless Peace*, Prague: International Organisation of Journalists, 1989, pp.31–46.

17 R. Luza, *The Transfer of the Sudeten Germans: a study of Czech–German relations 1933–1962*, London: Routledge & Kegan Paul, 1964, pp.267–322.

18   E. Steiner, *The Slovak Dilemma*, Cambridge: Cambridge University Press, 1973, pp.17–26.
19   T.G. Masaryk, *The Making of a State*, London: Allen & Unwin, 1927, pp.208–9.
20   Much of this discussion of Czech–Slovak relations in the 1920s and 1930s is based on Wallace, 1976, *op. cit.*, pp.163–219 and Leff, *op. cit.*, pp.45–85.
21   J.K. Hoensch, 'The Slovak Republic 1939–1945', in Mamatey and Luza, *op. cit.*, pp.271–95.
22   A. Josko, 'The Slovak resistance movement', in Mamatey and Luza, *op. cit.*, pp.362–84.
23   Steiner, *op. cit.*, pp.77–92.
24   Leff, *op. cit.*, pp.86–98.
25   Much of this discussion of Czech–Slovak relations in the 1950s and 1960s is based on Wallace, 1976, *op. cit.*, pp.275–337, Steiner, *op. cit.*, pp.93–185, and Leff, *op. cit.*, pp.98–128 and 220–40.
26   V.V. Kusin, *Political Grouping in the Czechoslovak Reform Movement*, London: Macmillan, 1972, pp.143–50.
27   W. Shawcross, *Dubcek*, London: Weidenfeld & Nicolson, 1970, pp.81–144.
28   A. Dubcek, *The Action Programme of the Communist Party of Czechoslovakia*, published in Dubcek's *Blueprint for Freedom*, London: William Kimber, 1968, pp.123–212.
29   Leff, *op. cit.*, pp.243–73.
30   S.L. Wolchik, 'The politics of ethnicity in post-Communist Czechoslovakia', *East European Politics and Societies*, 1994, vol. 8, no. 1, pp.153–88; and various media reports.

Chapter 5

Trentino and Tyrol
From Austrian Crownland to European Region

Antony Alcock

On the eve of the First World War, the Austrian Crownland of Tyrol consisted of the present-day Austrian province of North Tyrol and the Italian Autonomous Provinces of South Tyrol and Trento. The first two were overwhelmingly populated by German speakers; Trento overwhelmingly by Italian speakers. The linguistic border was clearly marked, and coincided with the border between (South) Tyrol and Trento at the Salurn Pass.

For an Italian state set on unification with the motherland of those areas such as the Istrian peninsula and Trento which were substantially populated by Italians but under Austria, the Triple Alliance, which bound Italy to Austria and Germany, was an embarrassment, if not a contradiction. The fear of militant pan-germanism and the fear that Italy would not get what it wanted from a victorious Triple Alliance, and probably not from a victorious Triple Entente either, if it remained neutral, pushed Italy into war in 1915 on the side of the latter.[1] But what Italy really wanted was not only Trento and Trieste but also that part of Tyrol lying north of Salurn and south of the Brenner. The desire for the frontier at the Brenner rather than Salurn was based on two considerations. The immediate one was military: the Brenner frontier was a far better line of defence against the pan-German world than Salurn. The second was of much longer date: a belief that the land south of the mid-alpine line of the Brenner was geographically Italian. To the north, the rivers flowed to the Danube and the Black Sea. To the south, the rivers flowed to the Po and the Adriatic. The natural surroundings of this southern Tyrol – the olives, the citrus fruits, the climate – were Italian, in contrast to those of the valley of the Inn.[2]

The idea of the Brenner as the natural frontier of Italy had

already existed in the Middle Ages. It was given further prominence by Italian geographers in the 1890s. But the years before the
First World War saw the advocacy of a third reason for wanting
southern Tyrol, and this was based on the theory put forward by
Ettore Tolomei, an ethnographer from Trento and later a Fascist
senator, that the German population of the area was in the main
not descended from immigrant German families but from pre-
German elements that had been germanised over the centuries
and needed to be liberated and returned to their rightful culture.[3]

For their part, Austrian and German historians and geographers viewed Tyrol and Trento from Ala to Kufstein as a natural
geographic and political unit. The passes linking trans-alpine with
cis-alpine Tyrol made the whole region a country of transit
between the German and Italian worlds, organised to control
politically this relationship.[4]

In March and April 1915 Italy conducted intensive negotiations
with Austria and the Triple Entente. As a price for Italian
neutrality Austria was prepared to let go of Trento, but Italy
demanded the old frontiers of the Napoleonic Kingdom of Italy,
which ran in between Salurn and the Brenner. Austria refused.
One stumbling block was that the Habsburg dynasty considered
the German Tyrol its own personal fief, and the Emperor could
hardly consider amputation of one of his own territories.[5] In the
meantime, Italy was demanding from the Entente the Brenner as
the price for changing alliances. On 26 April Italy signed the Treaty
of London, in which the desire for the Brenner was satisfied. A
month later Italy and Austria were at war.

Although it appeared that the basis for the post-war settlement
would be President Wilson's principle of self-determination and
his Fourteen Points, Point IX of which referred to a 'Readjustment
of the frontiers of Italy along clearly recognisable lines of
nationality', Italy rejected the implication that this meant settling
for Salurn. The Allies were told that the 'readjustment' mentioned
in Point IX did not imply a mere rectification of frontiers but the
liberation of the provinces whose nationality was Italian and the
establishment of a frontier that offered the essential conditions of
military security. The Italians then went on to make a reservation
against Point IX, and later on, during the Versailles Peace Conference itself, Wilson declared that he realised Italy was not bound
by the Fourteen Points.[6]

At the conference, faced by the fact that obtaining Tyrol south of the Brenner meant obtaining an area with a population of 250,000, 86 per cent of whom were German, the Italians argued that geographically the southern Tyrol and Trento were one, and that since in that area Italians were in a clear majority, it was only correct that the whole should go to Italy.[7]

The Austrians bitterly contested the coupling of South Tyrol with Trento. They pointed out that the Brenner had never formed even an administrative frontier within Tyrol; far from separating the Tyrolese on both sides of the Brenner it was a link between them. The method of cultivating the soil, the system of agricultural holding, the formation of the villages, the architecture, arts and crafts, in sum all that constituted the national character of a people was identical in all German Tyrol and separated it from Trento.[8]

But a new Europe was coming into being which heralded the end of multinational empires and the zenith of the nationalism which had overthrown them. And another consideration was the need to strengthen those states surrounding the defeated powers so as to curb any movements of revanchism. Thus borders were drawn to provide military or economic advantage to such states as Czechoslovakia, Poland and Romania but they left large numbers of Germans and Hungarians in them as resentful bitter minorities, angered at the failure to have the principle of self-determination applied to their areas. Indeed, the irony of Versailles was that the newly created or enlarged states that came into being, far from being the monocultural political entities expected, came to be as multinational as the multinational empires that had been overthrown in the name of monoculturalism.

In so far as South Tyrol was concerned, since Italy did not receive all it expected for changing sides, particularly in regard to the Dalmatian coast, it was vital that the promise of the Brenner was respected, all the more so as Italy was expected to be a powerful watchdog against German or German-Austrian revanchism. In Tyrol there was profound shock at the decision to ignore Point IX and transfer the land south of the Brenner to Italy. On the one hand an area was being divided whose political unity dated from the thirteenth century. On the other hand, the decision on their destiny had been taken out of the hands of a people with a long history of democracy and of self-determination.[9]

Tyrolese attempts to keep their land's unity intact went so far as having political representatives of all parties in the Innsbruck Diet offer the Tyrol as a whole to Italy during the Versailles Conference.

The offer was made on the grounds that the Tyrolese were Tyrolese before they were Austrians and, bitter as the Austrian defeat was, bitterer still would be the dismemberment of the land of their fathers, the integrity of which it was their intention to keep. The offer was rejected by the Italians because they did not want to re-open the issue or be accused of intrigues by the Americans.[10]

With the failure both to remain with Austria and to maintain the unity of their land, the South Tyrolese now had to contemplate their future in the Kingdom of Italy. The main aim was to ensure that the political autonomy enjoyed by Tyrol in the Austrian empire was continued in an essentially centralist Italy.

In October 1919 all the political parties in South Tyrol united to form the so-called Deutscher Verband, and in March 1920 a delegation visited Rome and presented a complete political and economic programme. South Tyrol was to be an autonomous province. The exercise of autonomous legislative and adminis-trative powers was to be carried out by a parliament sitting in Bozen (now to be called Bolzano). The executive organ was to be a cabinet headed by a president. The state would be represented by a government commissioner. The legislative and administrative powers of the parliament should include, among other things, control of the local economy – agriculture, industry, tourism, exploitation of hydro power, and the local police. Basically all the powers in force in the former Crownland of Tyrol should be continued in South Tyrol. The cabinet should direct and control the autonomous provincial authorities and appoint their officials. All employees presently in public service were to keep their posts. Vacancies could be filled also by Austrian candidates, especially from North Tyrol, who declared themselves ready to become Italian citizens. Every person employed in public service who was not Tyrolese had to be able to speak and write German. With regard to finance, the province should be able to use the income from direct and indirect taxes, and Rome should be obliged to transfer the sums necessary to cover the province's financial requirements. The German language was to be equal to Italian in the province, to be used not only in relations with the autonomous administration, but also with state bodies in the province. The powers of the state should be restricted to foreign and defence policy, taxation, customs and trade policy, commu-nications (railways, posts and telegraphs) and justice.[11]

This programme was of great importance since it expressed an idea that was henceforward to be the cornerstone of South Tyrolese policy: autonomy wide enough to maintain as German the ethnic character of South Tyrol as compensation for the loss of the right to self-determination. But the country which, apart from the small French community of Val d'Aosta, had had no experience of dealing with minorities, had no difficulty in rejecting the South Tyrolese proposals. They were considered an attempt to create a state within a state, to create, indeed, a nature park for Germans, closed to Italians and to Italian political and economic influence. Furthermore the South Tyrolese made no secret of their refusal to accept as final their transfer to Italy. Calls for restoration of the right of self-determination were seen – as they were seen everywhere – as calls for separation and destruction of the integrity of existing states.[12]

But the dialogue between the South Tyrolese and the Italian government ended abruptly with the Fascist seizure of power in October 1922. Not only was the Fascist movement the most centralist of all Italian political parties, its policy towards all the ethnic minorities in Italy and their homelands was to make them Italian. And the man chosen to denationalise South Tyrol and the South Tyrolese was Ettore Tolomei.

Italian was to be the only official language in South Tyrol, and officials not knowing it sufficiently were dismissed. Schooling was to be entirely in Italian. All public inscriptions and place names were to be in Italian. Family names that derived from Italian or Latin had to revert to the original form; given names that 'offended Italian sentiment' were forbidden.

Until 1934 the economy of South Tyrol was predominantly rural, with alpine farms and the cultivation of fruits and wines in the hands of the Tyrolese while the Italians in the province were concentrated in the administration. But in order to take advantage of the hydro-electric facilities of the area it was decided to create an industrial zone outside Bozen/Bolzano. Land was expropriated in 1935, and a large number of Italians were sent from elsewhere in the kingdom to work there. The South Tyrolese did not participate in the industrialisation of the province. They had neither the skills nor the desire to participate, and in any case the Italians did not intend that they should participate: the Bozen Industrial Zone was to be a means of increasing the Italian population of the province. On the eve of the Second World War the population of South Tyrol had risen to 330,000, 25 per cent of which was Italian. However, if the South Tyrolese formed 75 per cent of the population 95 per cent of all public posts were filled by Italians.

These developments had two effects on community relations. First, the destruction of German schools and culture and the wholesale dismissal of South Tyrolese from public offices robbed the South Tyrolese of a whole generation of intellectual and administrative leaders. Second, the Italian population of the province, by its nature administrative and industrial, became centred almost exclusively in the larger urban centres, with their superior housing and educational facilities, while the South Tyrolese huddled on the land. The ethnic division between the South Tyrolese and the Italians was thus compounded by further divisions between town and country, and between industry and agriculture. Needless to say average Italian per capita income was higher than South Tyrolese income.

It was, therefore, no surprise that the South Tyrolese were determined that, should the occasion occur, the nation that had sought to rob them of their development, their names, and their homeland should never again have a say in their future.[13] That occasion seemed to have arrived at the end of the Second World War. Italy had entered the war belatedly and opportunistically in 1940 on the side of Nazi Germany but had suffered defeat at the hands of the British and Americans, whose landing in Sicily in September 1943 provoked the collapse of the Fascist regime. Northern Italy was taken over militarily by Germany and a rump Italian Fascist administration set up to govern it, while in Southern Italy the government which had replaced the Fascists changed sides and joined the Allies.

Thus it was all the more shocking for the South Tyrolese when, during the negotiations at the end of the war, the victorious British, American, French and Russian Allies rejected Austrian and North and South Tyrolese requests for South Tyrol to return to Austria. The main reason was the uncertainty over the general political situation – the deteriorating relations between America and the Soviet Union and the futures of Germany and Austria, both under Four-Power occupation.

For the Western powers, if the circumstances required a strong Italy, i.e. with South Tyrol, it would be absurd to transfer South Tyrol to a country whose future was in doubt, and alienate Italy. And, following the same argument used at Versailles, should there be a need to control a Germany that might want to reverse the decision of 1945 as it had tried to do with that of 1918 then clearly a strong Italy with South Tyrol was a better bet than an Austria strengthened by the return of South Tyrol.[14]

But there were other considerations. The fact that the Italian government had changed sides in 1943 meant Italy might deserve to be considered differently from the other Axis powers. And Italy had strong support – in the United States from the large Italian immigrant community, and in the Soviet Union because of the strength of the Communist Party and the prestige arising out of its record in the resistance. However, mindful of the treatment the South Tyrolese had suffered under Italian fascism, the victorious allies at the Peace Conference held in Paris in 1946 obliged Austria and Italy to come to a political settlement which involved granting South Tyrol autonomy.

The settlement, known as the De Gasperi–Gruber Agreement after the two foreign ministers who signed it on 5 September 1946, provided for the 'German-speaking inhabitants of the Bolzano Province and of the neighbouring bilingual townships of the Trento Province' to be assured a complete equality of rights with the Italian-speaking inhabitants 'within the framework of special provisions to safeguard the ethnical character and the cultural and economic development of the German-speaking element'. The populations of the above-mentioned zones would be 'granted the exercise of autonomous legislative and executive regional power'. The frame within which the said provisions of autonomy would apply 'would be drafted in consultation also with local representative German-speaking elements'.[15]

But the profound bitterness of this second failure of the South Tyrolese to obtain the right of self-determination led to repeated statements by North and South Tyrolese and much of the political and media establishment in Austria that the South Tyrolese would never give up the right of self-determination and that the De Gasperi–Gruber Agreement was only temporary. Italians noted, too, that the Agreement did not carry any renunciation of South Tyrol by Austria.[16]

The result was that the autonomy statute drafted by Rome in 1947 in fulfilment of the Agreement[17] was deliberately designed to ensure that the cultural, economic and social development of the South Tyrolese lay in Italian hands rather than in those of the South Tyrolese, consultation with whom was minimal, whose proposals on a draft autonomy submitted in 1947 were almost entirely ignored and whose agreement to its contents was not obtained without pressure. It was, therefore, restrictive and would be applied restrictively. There were seven main features of the autonomy as it affected South Tyrol and the South Tyrolese.

First, South Tyrol was joined with the Province of Trento in one region Trentino-Alto Adige. Whereas in South Tyrol the South Tyrolese formed two-thirds of the population, in the region they formed only one-third. Second, whereas both Trento and South Tyrol had provincial parliaments and both parliaments would combine to sit as the regional parliament, it was the region with its Italian majority that enjoyed legislative competence with regard to the important section of the economy, primary legislative competence with regard to agriculture and tourism, and secondary legislative competence with regard to industrial production. In contrast, with the exception of housing, and 'preservation of the countryside' the provinces had few primary legislative powers and secondary competence in regard to education.[18] Third, since Italy was a regional rather than a federal state, all laws passed by regional and provincial parliaments required approval by Rome before they could come into effect. More often than not there were long delays before approval came, if it came at all. Fourth, political power-sharing was institutionalised. The cabinets of the regional government and the provincial government of South Tyrol had to be composed of Italians and South Tyrolese in ethnic proportions. Thus, for example, of nine assessors or ministers in the Bozen/ Bolzano parliament, six had to be German-speakers and three Italian. The South Tyrolese were always represented by the Südtiroler Volkspartei (SVP), which regularly obtained over 80 per cent of the German ethnic vote, while the coalition partners were Italian parties of a similar ideology, Christian Democrats (DC) or Social Democrats. In the regional parliament it was vice-versa. Fifth, whereas it was stated in Article 14 of the Autonomy Statute that the region 'normally' exercised its executive functions by delegating them to the provinces, in practice the Italian-dominated region did not do this with regard to South Tyrol, and this stance was upheld by the Constitutional Court.[19] Sixth, Article 1(d) of the De Gasperi–Gruber Agreement had provided for 'equality of rights as regards the entering upon public offices with a view to reaching a more appropriate proportion of employment between the two ethnic groups'. The South Tyrol believed that this meant ethnic proportions in all public bodies – state and semi-state as well as regional and provincial operating in the province. But the Constitutional Court ruled that in the case of public bodies whose jurisdiction extended beyond the province, the principle of representation had to be applied 'in a matter compatible with the structure of the body itself'.[20] Seventh, financial power, particularly relating to economic development, rested with Rome. The region and provinces had little of their own.

The South Tyrolese were angered by the way the De Gasperi–Gruber Agreement was implemented, particularly by the coupling of Trento with South Tyrol. They argued, reasonably enough, that the autonomy was intended solely for them. The Italians of Trento did not need an autonomy because the state was behind them.

There were other causes of discontent. One was language. German was not considered an official language in South Tyrol. Under Article 1(b) of the De Gasperi–Gruber Agreement, it was 'parified' with Italian. But the Council of State ruled that if the negotiators of the Agreement had meant German to be an official language they would have stated it in the text. One side effect of this situation was that Italians working in the public administration did not need to learn German – and few did so, even though there was a financial bonus for those who did.[21]

The general dissatisfaction came to a head over the key issue of housing. With the so-called 'flight from the land' all over western Europe it was essential to bring the under-employed South Tyrolese down from their poor alpine farms into the towns so as to get jobs in commerce or the administration. This meant building houses, and housing was an area in which the province enjoyed primary legislative competence. But in order to maintain the Italian nature of South Tyrol it was essential for Rome to ensure the development of the Bozen Industrial Zone and if workers went there from elsewhere in Italy they too would need housing. Unfortunately for the South Tyrolese it was the Italian state which had the money for housing and therefore decided where the houses should be built and how they should be allocated. To the South Tyrolese the housing policy of the Italian state in South Tyrol aimed at flooding the province with Italians.[22]

The view that the Autonomy Statute was a disaster and no fulfilment of the De Gasperi–Gruber Agreement accounted for the fall, in May 1957, of the very moderate South Tyrolese leadership that had accepted it. The main aim of the new hardline leadership

that replaced it was to break the link with Trento and have South
Tyrol become a region in its own right, with the appropriate
legislative and executive powers. In the meantime, the first acts of
violence – placing bombs under electric pylons and on railway
lines – had already taken place, as South Tyrolese sought to draw
attention abroad to their situation.

In 1958 the SVP submitted a draft autonomy statute to the
Italian parliament, proposing that South Tyrol became a region in
its own right, with primary legislative and executive power in
regard to thirty-two matters, including all the important sectors of
the economy. Ethnic proportions were to be applied in all public
and semi-state bodies. The indigenous population should have
priority in appointment to public offices and private employment.
Candidates for public jobs should have priority if they knew both
German and Italian. A five-year residence qualification was
required for the right to vote. Finally, legislation by South Tyrol
would not require approval by Rome.

The draft was considered by Rome as going further than the
SVP proposals of 1947 and was considered to be more in line with
that presented by the Deutscher Verband in 1920. Unsurprisingly,
it was brushed aside – condemned as being a danger to the
integrity of the state by setting up a state within a state. There was
also the fear that the Industrial Zone, considered openly by the
South Tyrolese as uneconomic as well as environmentally and
ideologically unacceptable, would be run down and, together
with the requirement of ethnic proportions and bilingualism in
public employment, there would be a massive departure of
Italians and their families, putting in doubt Italy's future in South
Tyrol.[23]

In the meantime, in May 1955 Four-Power occupation had
ended in Austria and the country had become fully independent,
adopting a federal constitution. Among the nine Austrian provinces were North Tyrol and Vorarlberg. Under the State Treaty
the frontiers of Austria were laid down as those of 1 January 1938,
that is, without South Tyrol, and since these were guaranteed by
the Four Powers, it was clear that the chances of South Tyrol
returning to Austria were remote. The first Austrian intervention
on behalf of the South Tyrolese was brusquely rejected. Vienna
was told by Rome that South Tyrol was entirely an internal Italian
affair. This was unwise. Refusal to talk to Vienna and the SVP
created a political vacuum and in this vacuum terrorism rapidly

increased. The original group of terrorists, who had merely wanted to separate from Trento, had been arrested but their place was taken by others seeking instead separation of South Tyrol from Italy. Support in the form of arms, equipment, money and the media was to be found over the border in North Tyrol.

Italian obduracy led Austria to bring the South Tyrol question before the United Nations in 1960. If Austria did not obtain its main aim, that the United Nations should recommend that South Tyrol be raised to the status of a region, Resolution 1497 XV did oblige Italy to negotiate with Austria on all differences relating to the De Gasperi–Gruber Agreement, and thus ended any pretensions that the autonomy was solely an internal Italian affair.[24]

The following year terrorist attacks grew so severe that Rome decided to open a dialogue with the SVP as well. Tripartite talks between Vienna, Rome and Bozen continued until 1969 when agreement was reached on a package deal (known as the *Paket*) which provided for a far-reaching revision of the autonomy in which a large number of South Tyrolese demands were met.[25] The main features of the new autonomy[26] were four-fold.

First, if the Region Trentino-Alto Adige was not abolished, its name was changed to Trentino-South Tyrol, and most of its important powers (including those relating to agriculture and tourism) were taken away and transferred to the now so-called Autonomous Provinces of South Tyrol and Trento. Altogether the provinces would enjoy primary legislative competence and administrative powers in regard to twenty-nine matters, and secondary competence in regard to another eleven, including industrial production. Second, the principle of ethnic proportions would be applied to all state and semi-state bodies operating in the province with the exception of the Ministry of Defence and the various police forces, and had to be achieved by the year 2002. Third, all employees in the public service in the province, of whatever sort and whatever rank, would in future have to pass a compulsory examination to prove competence in both German and Italian.

Finally, the province would receive guaranteed sectoral grants from state programmes and be able to dispose of the money as it willed. However, on the negative side, provincial laws would still require the approval of Rome. In itself the *Paket* involved some 137 points and an operational calendar according to which, after Italy had carried out the last of the 137 points, Austria would give a Declaration that the dispute between the two countries over the fulfilment of the De Gasperi–Gruber Agreement was now closed. It was not until 1992 that the last point was fulfilled. The Agreement had thus taken no fewer than forty-six years to be fulfilled satisfactorily! South Tyrol was economically and socially transformed, and the beneficiaries were indeed the South Tyrolese.

The massive inflow of funds, investment and sectoral, into the province provided for an economic development which rapidly made South Tyrol the area with the highest living standards in Italy. The main thrust of this development was agri-tourism. Money for agriculture also came from the European Community's Agricultural Guidance and Guarantee Fund.

More and more South Tyrolese were getting jobs in an administration which expanded nearly six-fold as offices were set up to administer the sectors for which the province now had primary legislative competence. On the other hand, things were less comfortable for the Italians. Few owned land or were farmers to profit from the expansion in agriculture and tourism. Many posts in the public administration (particularly state offices) hitherto filled by Italians would have to go to South Tyrolese by the year 2002. Economic stagnation and inflation brought about by the oil crises of the 1970s had adversely affected the industrial sector, still overwhelmingly filled by Italians, and in any case the tourist-conscious government with its SVP majority placed great importance on the environment and had no intention of allowing industrial expansion.

Much of the way society was organised in South Tyrol depended on a Declaration as to ethnic identity. Each person at the time of the ten-yearly census had to declare whether he or she was German, Italian or Ladin (a small Rhaeto-Romansch group). There is some evidence that Italians were declaring themselves as German in order to benefit from the presumed economic advantages, and sending their children to German-language schools.[27] Indeed, it has since been claimed that in Bozen some 20 per cent of Italian children are attending German schools.[28] According to the 1991 census the population of South Tyrol was 440,500, of which 68 per cent were German, 4.35 Ladin and 27.65 Italian. The Italian population had thus dropped nearly 6.7 per cent from a peak of 34.3 per cent.[29]

The concern at the decline of the Italian population, which

suddenly felt itself a local minority rather than part of the national majority played into the hands of the neo-Fascist MSI (Movimento Sociale Italiano). By 1988 this party, which was hostile to the *Paket* and wished to abolish South Tyrol autonomy, had become the largest Italian party in both the South Tyrol parliament (polling 10.3 per cent), and the Bozen City Council (30 per cent). In the 1993 general elections, now operating under the title Allianza Nationale, it even won one of the four provincial seats in the Rome Chamber of Deputies provided for under the new first-past-the-post system introduced as part of the wide-ranging reforms of the Italian state.

In many ways the South Tyrol *Paket* of 1969 heralded the dawn of a new age for western Europe's ethnic, cultural and regional minorities.

The key factor in this development was the process of western European economic and political integration. Borders, with the exception of that between Northern Ireland and the Irish Republic, had all been accepted and ceased to be of significance. And, again except in Northern Ireland, minorities were decreasingly seen as threats to the integrity of states.

One of the most important features in the process of western Europe integration was the rise of regionalism. Promoted initially by the Council of Europe, it was based on rejection of the centralistic nation-state as well as the threatened anonymity, cultural uniformity and soullessness of industrial life. Its advocates sought a return to historical and cultural roots for two main reasons, which found their expression in the famous Bordeaux Declaration of 1978.

First, regions were seen as

> heirs to the history of Europe and the richness of its culture ... an irreplaceable and incomparable asset of European civilisation ... the symbol and the guarantors of that diversity which is the pride of the European heritage in the eyes of humanity and to which every European both bears witness and contributes. Every European's right to 'his region' is part of his right to be different. To challenge this right would be to challenge the identity of European man and ultimately of Europe itself.

Second, there was increasing demand for more popular participation in decision-making and rejection of decisions being made in distant capitals by unrepresentative 'faceless' bureaucrats. The aim was to change the situation under which regions were the objects of distant planners to one in which regions administered themselves and took basic political decisions through a regional legislature armed with legislative, administrative and financial powers. This would promote not only a more meaningful democracy but facilitate cultural pluralism.[30]

Regionalism developed in two ways. At national level, it took off or accelerated in a number of countries. Following the death of General Franco in 1977 and the restoration of democracy in Spain, Catalonia and the Basque Country received substantial autonomies, and the Spanish government has declared that any other region that wanted an autonomy could have it. In Belgium federalism, in the words of one observer, has been introduced, 'by stealth',[31] and the provinces and peoples of Flemish Flanders and French-speaking Wallonia been given wide-ranging economic and cultural powers. Even in centralist France cultural charters were granted to Brittany, the French Basques and Corsica, and the latter even received a *statut particulier*. At subnational level the regions of Europe, particularly those with legislative, executive and financial powers to carry out decisions, themselves became active in promoting cross-border and trans-frontier cooperation, and in this process Austria, although not (then) a member of the European Community took the lead.

Between 1970 and 1985 three important regional groupings (among others) or Arges were formed: in 1972 the Arge (Arbeitsgemeinschaft) Alp – Bavaria, Baden-Württemberg (West Germany), North Tyrol, Vorarlberg, Salzburg (Austria), South Tyrol, Trento, Lombardy (Italy), Graubünden, St Gallen, Ticino (Switzerland); in 1975 the Arge Adria – Upper Austria, Styria, Carinthia (Austria), Venice, Friuli-Venezia Giulia (Italy), Slovenia, Croatia (Yugoslavia) and Gyor-Soprón and Vas (Hungary), with headquarters in Klagenfurt (Carinthia). And in 1983 the Arge Pyrenées was set up between the French and Spanish regions of Aquitaine, Languedoc-Roussillon, Midi-Pyrenées, Aragon, Catalonia, the Basque Provinces, Navarre and Andorra.

The aim of these Arges was to develop common policies in regard to agriculture, transport and communications, tourism, cross-border national parks and the environment, particularly in mountain areas. These Arges have no independent bureaucracy. The annual conference of heads of regional government sets the policy priorities. On-going contact between the regions takes place at civil-service level.[32] Until 1989 the Arges represented Austria's commitment to Western integration and East–West co-operation. But within the new Europe post-1989 they have become potentially models of the new 'Europe of the Regions'.[33]

In May 1980 the Council of Europe adopted the Madrid Outline Convention on Transfrontier Co-operation between Territorial Communities or Authorities, in which the participating states agreed to promote cross-border co-operation, including the right of local and regional authorities to make agreements with their neighbouring foreign opposite numbers in the fields of competences as laid down by domestic laws.[34] Both Italy and Austria have ratified the Convention, which came into force in December 1981. In addition to all these activities the European Commission has been promoting cross-border co-operation through its INTEREG scheme, particularly in the fields of the environment, tourism, transport and education.

The years 1989–1992 brought about stunning changes to the European political landscape. South Tyrol was affected by three of them.

Most dramatically, there was the collapse of communism and the Soviet Empire and the end of the Cold War. One result was a reaction in eastern Europe to central political and economic direction, but as these were swept away ethnic antagonisms, so long held in check, re-emerged. During this time the South Tyrolese were active in advising newly independent east European governments and ethnic groups on protection of minorities through regional autonomy, based on their own seventy-year struggle.

Second, there was the onward march of the European Community to a European Union which was expressing itself eager to expand, initially by taking in states of the European Free Trade Area, and later states from eastern Europe. For the South Tyrolese there were two aspects of interest. One was the application of Austria to join the Union. The other was the establishment, with the 1992 Maastricht Treaty, of a Committee of the Regions. It was true that this Committee only had consultative powers in regard to a restricted list of activities but it was the first occasion that the EU treaties had recognised the existence of local and regional government and admitted that the regions of Europe had a place in the construction of Europe.[35] It was thus seen as a step in the right direction by all those advocating a Europe based on its regions rather than its states, that one day the regions should form a second chamber of the European Parliament on the model of the German Bundestag.

Finally, there were startling developments in Italy itself. Disgust at the widespread corruption, involving almost all the national political parties, that linked virtually all activity, business or administrative, to party connections and party deals, led to electoral reform which in turn caused the collapse of the old parties and their replacement by new groupings. Prominent among these was the Lombard (later Northern) League, with a programme of Europe federalism on the basis of the regions rather than the states, and transformation of Italy into a federal state based on three units, North, Centre and South, with the islands of Sicily and Sardinia grouped with the last.

Equally, in Trento, long were gone the days when the Trentini saw themselves as watchdogs over the South Tyrolese and had done much to ensure the 1948 Autonomy Statute was applied restrictively. In the 1970s the Partito Autonomista Trentino-Tirolese (PATT) had advocated more powers for the autonomous provinces and closer links with the South Tyrolese. With the collapse of the traditional parties the Northern League had made big inroads in the province. For the South Tyrolese these events seemed to provide a wonderful opportunity. The power structures of Versailles and Yalta had at last been broken, and at a time when the fulfilment of the *Paket* meant that the dispute over the De Gasperi–Gruber Agreement was also over.

What now? In SVP thinking, one thing was obvious: as events in eastern Europe had shown, there could be no lasting peace in Europe if solutions were not found to ethnic and minority problems. Equally, in many border areas it was clear that not all problems could or indeed should be solved by inter-state foreign policy. There was a need for a lower-level foreign policy, where problems could be discussed and solved by local politicians and civil servants.

But how to proceed at European level? No plans were in existence. There were far too many differences among Europe's regions in regard to their size, economic strength, powers and aims. Clearly a new course had to be decided, and hopefully, South Tyrol could give a lead.[36] Reunification of Tyrol had never been far from the minds of Tyrolese, North and South, and the South

Tyrolese had continually stressed that they had never renounced self-determination. On the other hand, the region as it was at present was no longer a threat; indeed it had been emasculated. The *Paket* was all very well as far as it went, but provided no absolute cast-iron guarantee of South Tyrolese rights. What was wanted was a real autonomy, with full financial sovereignty on the model of the Swiss cantons, an end to the need for approval by Rome of legislation, and transfer of almost all powers to the regions leaving Italy (and eventually all other nation-states) only with those relating to defence, foreign policy, justice and monetary policy. And European regions were already in existence. All these issues – Tyrolese unification, a true autonomy, self-determination, a positive future for the region – could be solved at one stroke with the creation of an Autonomous European Region Tirol (AERT), to include North and South Tyrol and Trento and, if its population so wished, Vorarlberg.

There were a number of other considerations. The first was population size. South Tyrol by itself with a population of 440,000 was far too small. But with North Tyrol (630,000) and Trento (450,000), the AERT would have a total population of 1.52 million. Admittedly this was still small compared to other existing and future Euro-regions, but a second consideration was its physical size linked to its economic functions. Using the same arguments as those advocated at Versailles in 1919, the proponents of the AERT pointed out that the region was an extensive and coherent transit area, linking two powerful economic zones, the Lombardy plains of northern Italy and the Danubian basin of southern Germany. It also provided an area of rest and recreation for those working in those zones, and indeed for Europe as a whole.

Third, it was essential to include Trento in the AERT. Trento had a common history, unbroken at least with South Tyrol, for very many centuries and with North Tyrol for not much less. The inclusion of Trento was necessary in order to reassure Italians who might have felt abandoned as a small minority of barely 10 per cent in a purely Tyrolese region. As it was, the AERT would be 61 per cent German, 37 per cent Italian and 2 per cent Ladin. And there was also the point that if the Trentini did not go in with the Tyrolese then their likely fate would be to be swallowed up by a large Veneto region in which they and their historical traditions and identity would be swamped. In any case the idea of the AERT was generally supported by Italian political parties and politicians in Trento, with the obvious exception of the National Alliance, and the Greens.[37]

Leading on from this, there was some concern at the continued advance of the MSI. Following the 1994 Italian general elections, under the name National Alliance, this party had been included in a coalition government led by Forza Italia and the Northern League, and the South Tyrolese and Trentini had their doubts about the stability of a government composed of one party openly euro-federalist, the second still perceived to be nationalist-centralist, and the third and dominant party apparently far less committed to a single European state than its predecessors, closer indeed to the British position on the process of European integration. There was the real fear that the National Alliance was the strong one in the coalition, and therefore there was a need to create a strong region in Trento and Tyrol as a bastion against anti-democratic forces.

Finally, within the framework of the Madrid Convention, Italy and Austria had already signed a cross-border agreement in January 1993 applying, in Italy to the regions, and provinces and municipalities of Trentino-South Tyrol, Venice, and Friuli Venezia-Giulia, and enabling the authorities concerned to sign agreements, within the framework of the powers they enjoyed in domestic law, in regard to fourteen matters, including transport and communications, energy, environmental protection, cross-border nature parks, health, culture and sport, tourism, cross-border commuters, handicrafts and vocational training, trade promotion, agricultural improvements, economic and technological research, with the possibility of extending the list.[38] This agreement was ratified by the Italian parliament in October 1994.

But how would the AERT come into being? For one thing, Austria would have to join the European Union. But much more important, the way forward lay not in changing political frontiers or state constitutions but by ensuring that the individual Austrian and Italian provinces possessed the same legislative and administrative powers and institutional and social organisation. At the time the powers relating to some sectors lay with the regions or provinces in one state but with the central government in others, while in some cases powers were divided between the state and the region.

Another consideration was that if the Austrian regions could make international agreements that were relatively unlimited with states or subdivisions of states bordering Austria in those sectors where they enjoyed the appropriate powers, Italian regions and autonomous provinces were only empowered to do so following approval from Rome and if the activity concerned had only an international – and thus no internal – significance.[39] There would therefore have to be constitutional changes in both Austria and Italy regarding sectors of regional competence and the level of powers to be enjoyed.

In the AERT itself German and Italian would be official languages in all institutions and offices (Ladin in the Ladin-speaking valleys of Trento and South Tyrol). Ethnic proportions in public employment would continue to apply in South Tyrol and be extended to all regional offices in the other provinces. And the AERT would have its own police force.[40]

This vision of an Autonomous European Region Tirol as a model for the future has not, of course, lacked its critics. Austrian and Italian sovereignty would continue to exist in their respective parts of the AERT. And how could one speak of a unified Tyrol if south of the Brenner Italian civil and criminal law, the police and military service continued to exist? Even if the AERT came into being, there was no sign that other countries would follow the example of Austria and Italy. And even if this model were accepted in the EU, was such a Eurotopia of 75 mini-states of 5–10 million inhabitants really desirable? In the meantime one important step in the autonomists' programme took place. On 12 June 1994 Austria voted by a two-thirds majority to join the EU, and the federal movement in the Union could expect correspondingly to be strengthened with Austrian accession on 1 January 1995.

NOTES

1   Imperiali to San Giuliano of 14 August 1914 and San Giuliano to Imperiali of 16 September 1914 in *Documenti Diplomatici Italiani*, fifth series, vol. 1, 1914–1918, quoted in A.E. Alcock, *The History of the South Tyrol Question*, London: Michael Joseph, 1970, p.18.

2   According to Giuseppi Mazzini, whose views were reproduced in *La Nazione Italiana*, 1890, vol. 1, no. 32 (October), Rome, quoted in Alcock, *op. cit.*, p.11.

3   *La Nazione Italiana, op. cit.*, vol. 1, nos 1, 6 and 27, 1890; *Archivio per Alto Adige*, nos 10 (1915) and 40 (1945), quoted in Alcock, *op. cit.* pp.13–14.

4   Alcock, *op. cit.*, p.12.
5   A. Salandra, *Italy and the Great War*, London: Arnold, 1932, p.55; Alcock, *op. cit.*, p.18 and fn. 68.
6   R.S. Baker, *Woodrow Wilson and World Settlement*, London: Heinemann, 1923, vol. 2, p.133; P. Mantoux, *Les Délibérations du Conseil des Quatre*, 24 Mars–28 Juin 1919, Paris: Centre National de la Recherche Scientifique, 1955, vol. 1, p.295. C. Seymour, 'Woodrow Wilson and self-determination in the Tyrol', in *The Virginia Quarterly Review*, 1962, vol. 38, no. 4, p.574. Alcock, *op. cit.*, p.20.
7   M. Toscano, *Storia Diplomatica della Questione dell' Alto Adige*, Bari: Laterza, 1967, pp.26–8; Alcock, *op. cit.*, p.21.
8   N. Almond and R.H. Lutz, *The Treaty of Saint-Germain*, Stanford: Stanford University Press, 1935, pp.350–3; Alcock, *op. cit.*, p.21.
9   For example, the 1342 Great Letter of Liberty by Count Meinhard II that no new taxes or legislation would be enacted without the consent of the Tyrolese Estates; the support of Tyrolese representatives in 1363 for the decision by which Tyrol passed by the marriage of the *Landesfürstin* Margaret to Rudolf IV into the possession of the Habsburgs; the right granted to the Tyrolese Estates in 1511 by the Emperor Maximilian I to obtain prior consent for any Tyrolese involvement in war and exemption from campaigning outside their land. M. Forcher, *Tirol*, Vienna: Panorama Verlag, 1974, pp. 13–40.
10 Toscano, *op.cit*, pp.36–43, quoted in Alcock, *op. cit.*, p.22, fn. 88.
11 *Meraner Zeitung*, 17 December 1919; G.A. Barghese, *L'Alto Adige Contro Italia*, Milan: Treves, 1921, pp.57–75, quoted in Alcock, *op. cit.*, pp.27–30.
12 Barghese, *op. cit.*, pp.34–7.
13 Alcock, *op. cit.*, pp.33–45.
14 A.E. Alcock, 'La Gran Bretagna e l'Accordo De Gasperi–Gruber sul Sudtirolo del 5 Settembre 1946', in *Premesse Storiche e Quadro Internazionale dell' Accordo De Gasperi–Gruber*, Trento: Istituto Trentino di Cultura, Informa, 1/1987, pp.9–11.
15 Text of the Agreement in Alcock, *op. cit.*, pp.473–4.
16 Ibid., pp.138–44.
17 Ibid., pp.475–92.
18 According to Articles 4, 5, 11 and 12 of the Autonomy Statute, under primary legislative competence regional and provincial legislation had to respect the Constitution, the legal principles of the state, international obligations and national interests as well as the fundamental rules governing the social and economic reforms of the Republic (Italy had been a republic since 1946 following a referendum on the monarchy). Under secondary legislative competence such legislation had also to respect principles established by state law.
19 Ibid., p.286.
20 Ibid., p.276.
21 Ibid., p.188–9.
22 Ibid., p.290.
23 Ibid., pp.294–303.

24 Ibid., pp.347–8.
25 Text of the *Paket* in A.E. Alcock, *Geschichte der Südtirolfrage – Südtirol seit dem Paket 1970–1980*, Vienna: Braumüller, 1982, pp.211–37.
26 D.P.R. of 31 August 1972, no. 670, in ibid., pp.238–74.
27 Ibid., p.57.
28 Information from Dr F. Pahl, Vice-President of the Autonomous Region Trentino – South Tyrol, November 1994.
29 Information from Dr F. Pahl, Vice-President of the Autonomous Region Trentino – South Tyrol, November 1994.
30 Council of Europe, *Bordeaux Declaration*, Bordeaux: Conference of Local and Regional Authorities of Europe, 30 January–1 February 1978.
31 John Fitzmaurice in *Dutch Crossing*, London: University College London, April 1989.
32 See *Arge Alp*, Munich: Bayerische Landeszentrale für Politische Bildungsarbeit, 1978; F. Esterbauer, *Regionalismus*, Munich: Bayerische Landeszentrale für Politische Bildungsarbeit, 1978, pp.137–47; D. Morrow, 'Regional policy as foreign policy: the Austrian experience', in *Regional Politics and Policy*, London: Cass, 1992, vol. 2, no. 3 (Autumn), pp.27–44.
33 Morrow, *op. cit.*, p.35.
34 Text of the Convention in Autonome Region Trentino–Südtirol, *Die Grenzüberschreitende Zusammenarbeit*, Trento: Vorschläge für Ihre Entwicklung, 1993, pp.95–101.
35 F. Brouwer, V. Lintner and M. Newman, *Economic Policy Making and the European Union*, London: Federal Trust, 1994, pp.103 and 107.
36 H. Frasnelli, *Südtirol – Tirol/Trentino – Österreich – Italian – Europa: Autonomie und Europaintegrationspolitik*, n.p.o.d., Bozen/Bolzano: 1994. Dr Frasnelli is Deputy Chairman of the SVP, a former MP, and Leader of the SVP group in the South Tyrol Parliament.
37 Speech of the President-Elect of the Region, Tarcisio Grandi (PPI), 18 March 1994, to the Legislature and Reply of Dr Franz Pahl (SVP), Vice-President of the Region, 19 April 1994.
38 Text in *Grenzüberschreitende Zusammenarbeit*, pp.157–62. Note that at time of writing this Agreement had not been ratified by either party.
39 Constitutional Court Judgments no. 179/1987 and no. 472/1992.
40 F. Pahl, *Einführende Bemerkungen zur Autonomen Europa– Region–Tirol; Eine Grenzregion für Europa*, Politischer Drei- Stufenplan für die Bildung der Autonomen Europa–Region–Tirol; n.p.o.d., Bozen/Bolzano: January–April 1994.

Chapter 6

Hungary
A state truncated, a nation dismembered

Raymond Pearson

By constituting the fourth-largest national minority in inter-war Europe, the largest national minority in post-war Communist Europe and the third-largest national minority in post-Communist Europe, the Hungarians have collectively proved to be the longest-running, most intractable European minority concern of the twentieth century. While some minority phenomena have suddenly appeared (like the Unexpected Diaspora of Russians precipitated by the collapse of the Soviet Union), others have gradually diminished (like the Dissolving Diasporas of Germans and Jews) and a few are only just being acknowledged (like the Forgotten Diaspora of Gypsies). The Enduring Diaspora of Hungarians, however, has persisted fundamentally unchanged and conspicuously unresolved from the First World War through to the present day.

In one sense, contemporary Hungary satisfies a cardinal, even classic nationalist requirement for a nation-state. The detailed recent official census of 1985 revealed that the state population of 10.65 million comprised few non-Hungarian national minorities and only a modest non-Hungarian aggregate: 320,000 Gypsies; 230,000 Germans; 130,000 South Slavs; 130,000 Slovaks; 80,000 Jews; and 25,000 Romanians together mustered 915,000 people, or just 8.6 per cent of the total population.[1] With one criterion of nation-statehood being ethnic homogeneity, the figure of 91.4 per cent for the proportion of the state population which is Hungarian might well lead a casual observer to conclude that the close demographic match brings Hungary near to the nationalist ideal of nation-statehood.

That same nationalist ideal, however, presupposes that the nation-state simultaneously excludes all non-nationals and includes all co-nationals. Hungary's predicament in the 1990s (as for most of the twentieth century) lies not in the first but the second criterion. Significant numbers of Hungarians populate all seven of Hungary's neighbouring states: between 1.65 million and 2.1 million in Romania; 567,000–650,000 in Slovakia; 345,000–450,000 in Serbia; 158,000–200,000 in Ukraine; 70,000 in Austria; 20,000–40,000 in Croatia; and 10,000–5,000 in Slovenia.[2] Though estimates differ spectacularly, the predictable expression of a combination of self-interest and wishful thinking which induces Hungary to 'maximise' and neighbouring states to 'minimise' the presence of Hungarian minorities, the existence of a trans-state Hungarian diaspora on a scale second only to that of the Russians since 1991 cannot be gainsaid. If the voluntary emigrants and involuntary émigrés resident in western Europe and America are excluded, some 9.7 million Hungarians reside within Hungary and between 2.8 million and 3.5 million in a 'Hungarian archipelago' of enclaves across the immediate geographical vicinity of Hungary.[3] According to even the modest figures furnished by Hungary's neighbours, Hungarians outside Hungary comprise 22.4 per cent of all Hungarians; according to (perhaps inflated) Hungarian statistics, Hungarians outside Hungary muster as much as 26.6 per cent of Hungarians.

Far from constituting a Hungarian nation-state, the Hungary of the 1990s embodies a glaring geopolitical mismatch between statehood and nationhood, merely a Hungarian territorial heartland politically detached from, but in tantalisingly close physical proximity to, about one-quarter of all people who identify themselves as Hungarians.

To understand how a twentieth-century Europe supposedly wedded to the principle of nation-statehood can contain such an anomaly, an appreciation of Hungary's pre-twentieth-century historical legacy is essential. The scattered nature of Hungarian settlement over the mid-Danube basin is the part-fortuitous, part-contrived product of a sequence of dramatic episodes in the history of Hungary. The Magyar tribes who comprised the original Hungarian proto-nation were not autochthonous European 'residents' but what might be disrespectfully termed 'illegal Asian immigrants'. Depending on self-interested national viewpoint, the Hungarians who occupied Pannonia from the late ninth century were either peaceful settlers who colonised a deserted terrain or barbaric interlopers who forcibly expelled the indigenous population to establish their own exclusive military-political ascendancy from the late tenth century.

The Kingdom of Hungary was maintained until the advance of the Ottoman Turks in the sixteenth century (and most dramatically the rout of the Hungarian army at Mohács in 1526) effected the dispossession and evacuation of much of the Hungarian population from Hungary. Over the seventeenth century, occupied Hungary comprised the most westerly province of the sprawling Ottoman empire. In the course of the early eighteenth century, the Austrian Habsburgs mounted a successful campaign to expel the Turks from Hungary but chose to compromise the Hungarian restoration by a divide-and-rule strategy of expedient plantation of non-Hungarians throughout the territory of Hungary. Forcible dispossession at the hands of the Turks and then partial repossession through Habsburg licence left Hungary politically dependent upon its Austrian benefactor and the Hungarians themselves more demographically dispersed than ever before.

Over the late eighteenth century, provoked by a combination of resistance to Habsburg ambitions for imperial centralisation (notably under Emperor Josef II) and resentment at Habsburg repression (to prevent the spread of French revolutionary ideas), the traditional aristocratic monopoly of the *natio Hungarica* began to broaden into a more multi-class Hungarian nationalism. Napoleon toyed with the idea of extending his strategy of favouring nations victimised under the *ancien régime* to Hungary, tempting the Hungarians with the prospect of preferment under the patronage of the new master of early nineteenth-century Europe. Appreciating the damage inflicted on the Austrian empire by the Napoleonic experience, Hungarians increasingly committed themselves to securing autonomy for Hungary within the Metternich-dominated empire after 1815. As the importance of political demographics became apparent, the Hungarians' ranking as close second to the Austrians in population size seemed to place Hungary at the head of the queue within the multi-ethnic empire for preferential political treatment.

Early in the so-called Year of Revolutions, Hungary exploited the discomfiture of a Habsburg establishment under pressure from the 'Springtime of Nations' to secure a 'lawful revolution', the surrender of substantive autonomy within the empire. However, once the Habsburgs recovered their nerve later in 1848, the concession to Hungary was rescinded on the grounds that under-takings extracted under duress have no legal force, provoking Hungary into defiance of imperial authority and, in early 1849, a declaration of Hungarian independence. To defeat and suppress the Hungarian rebellion, the new Emperor Franz Josef invited Tsar Nicholas I to help out a fellow autocrat by administering the *coup de grâce* to Hungary's military resistance, an episode which left the Hungarians with an abiding hatred of the Russians as the suppressors of their national aspirations.

The defeat of Hungary's ambitions in 1849 did not mean despair or disillusionment for Hungarian nationalism. Pride in Hungary's independent past was reinforced by her doughty, not to say heroic performance over 1848–1849: Hungarian nationalists took solace in the thought that it had taken the joint actions of the Austrian and Russian imperial armies to defeat them (and the ongoing frictions between Vienna and St Petersburg meant that the Russian army might well not be available to save the Habsburgs on a future occasion). Hungarian moral indignation at Vienna's reneging on its promise over 1848 was further heightened by the ferocity of Habsburg repression (notably the arbitrary redivision of Hungary into five non-historic adminis-trative provinces) and retribution (especially the 'martyrdom' of nine Hungarian generals by public hanging in late 1849). Over the 1850s and early 1860s, first the international isolation of the Austrian empire and then its humiliation over Habsburg Italy at the hands of France sapped imperial neo-absolutist morale and favoured the dogged Hungarian campaign for a restoration of the 'lawful revolution' of 1848.

Finally, Austrian defeat in the Seven Weeks' War with Prussia in 1866 provided the precipitant for the Ausgleich of 1867. By this 'compromise' or 'equalisation', the unitary Austrian empire was converted into the Dual Monarchy of Austria-Hungary. Accord-ing to the new constitution, all governmental functions other than the supreme military, diplomatic and dynastic competencies (which were reserved as imperial), were devolved under the separate jurisdictions of 'Cisleithania' (Austria) and 'Transleitha-nia' (Hungary). By the Ausgleich, the Habsburg establishment gambled that prudent compromise would render the Hungarian question manageable and stabilise an empire which threatened to become ungovernable. The Hungarians secured, in effect, a restoration of the autonomy granted in early 1848, a junior partnership which fell short of independent sovereignty but provided access to the accelerating economic modernisation as well as the military protection of the Habsburg super-state.

Nations other than the Austrians and Hungarians regarded the Ausgleich as a cynical deal struck between the two state-nations of the 'Dual Monarchy' (together comprising some 43 per cent of the total state population) for the joint suppression of the remainder of the multi-national populace. Within Hungary, early promises to respect the rights of the non-Magyar 58.8 per cent of the population (in 1880), notably by a Nationalities Law in 1868, were soon abandoned in favour of a sustained programme of magyarisation. In a spirit of 'we have re-made Hungary, now we must re-make Hungarians', the Hungarian language was foisted on the non-Magyar majority through advancing state control of the school and university systems. Non-Magyar representation in the Hungarian Diet at Budapest was filtered at parliamentary elections to derisory and tokenistic levels. Demographically a mini-empire in which the Magyars could never even (quite) muster a majority, Hungary claimed the *Magyarsag* or 'Magyar-land' as a Hungarian nation-state.[4]

It is important to consider why the Hungarians should adopt magyarisation with such relish. Neither the spirit nor the policy of magyarisation was born in the 1880s: Hungarian contempt for the smaller nationalities unfortunate enough to find themselves within Hungarian jurisdiction had been legendary for centuries and had contributed to the isolation and subsequent defeat of the Hungarian national cause in 1849. Fundamentally, the historical career of the Hungarian people predisposed them psychologically towards what might be tritely called 'insecurity-based aggression'. A pervasive sense of racial and linguistic isolation combined with a conviction that their resentful Germanic, Slavonic and even Latin neighbours were waiting for an opportunity to turn back the clock of history and expel the Magyars from their unlawfully seized real-estate back to the Asia from which they had swept in the ninth century. Indeed, the whole history of the Hungarians could be seen as a sequence of traumatic oscillation between possession, dispossession and repossession, most recently over the 1848–1867 period. A collective, almost genetically imprinted sense of insecurity pre-determined a pathological siege mentality which supported the magyarisation to which the supremacist establishment of Hungary committed itself from the 1880s.

As the twentieth century dawned, magyarisation generated three linked but distinct repercussions, all fateful for the long-term future of Hungary. The first was, predictably enough, the irrevocable alienation of all nationalities within Hungary unprepared to accept enforced Hungarian assimilation. Many Jews, some Germans and a few Slovaks were prepared to countenance acculturation, if not assimilation, by accommodating themselves to a regime which may have been ethnocidal but was never genocidal towards non-Magyars; but magyarisation generally forced on the pace of developing national consciousness and later stimulated growing ambition for political separatism among the majority of non-Magyar nationalities.

The second repercussion was that the accelerating progression towards secessionist ambition within Hungary did not exclude the Magyars themselves. Heralded by exultant celebrations of the millenium of the Hungarian state in 1896, an anti-Habsburg movement demanding a Hungarian national army fomented a political crisis over 1905–1906. In the event, a combination of direct military rule and the threat of the imposition of universal suffrage upon Hungary quickly brought the Magyar political establishment to heel.[5] Even so, a Hungarian consensus for mere autonomy could no longer be assumed after 1906: although Hungarian official and public opinion still tacitly supported the Ausgleich, the trend was towards entertaining aspirations for independence which could not be contained within the prevailing Dual Monarchy. As 'Vienna' became more liberal and 'Western European' while 'Budapest' became more repressive and 'Eastern European', an eventual split of the polarising, increasingly schizophrenic Dual Monarchy into separate sovereign states of Austria and Hungary seemed inescapable.

The third effect of magyarisation was the international bad press visited upon Hungary. The mass emigration of non-Magyars fleeing magyarisation reached epic levels in the run-up to 1914, profoundly influencing attitudes towards Hungary in the emigrant destinations of the West. When compared with later manifestations of 'integral nationalism' in inter-war eastern Europe, magyarisation does not appear exceptionally reprehensible (and in its non-racial rationale and practice may even be deemed tame); but in a world still unaccustomed to the abrupt transition from emancipatory 'Risorgimento nationalism' to repressive 'integral nationalism' often occasioned by the acquisition of state power, magyarisation was perceived as a peculiarly Hungarian aberration bringing disgrace upon the wider nationalist cause.[6] Hungary's high-profile conduct in the heart of Europe attracted opprobrium as the worst advertisement for nationalism and, significantly for the immediate future, alienated Western government and society opinion.[7]

The First World War proved Hungary's nemesis, although whether deserved or undeserved remains a matter of impassioned debate. When Vienna took the decision to confront Serbia in August 1914, initiating a chain reaction which culminated in world war, Budapest proved most reluctant to follow. The Magyar establishment headed by István Tisza calculated that Hungary was in a no-win situation: if the Dual Monarchy lost the war, the geopolitics of conflict made it likely that Hungary rather than Austria would be the supreme casualty at the hands of Serbia's ally Russia; if the Dual Monarchy won the war, then its Slav jurisdiction would be expanded by conquest, undermining the Ausgleich partnership which even in peacetime had come under mounting Czech-led pressure to convert into a Trialist federation. But although no benefits could be anticipated from either victory or defeat in 1914, Hungary found itself politically bound by the terms of the Ausgleich to join the Habsburg war effort.

It may come as a surprise to anyone whose only acquaintance with the Habsburg army comes from Jaroslav Hasek's propagandist *The Good Soldier Schweik* to learn that the military performance of Austria-Hungary over the years 1914–1918 was very creditable – too impressive for the Dual Monarchy's long-term political good. Within Hungary, although some Slav minorities were tempted to desert to the Russians, the Magyars had every reason for opposing tsarist Russia, identified since 1849 as the great enemy of Hungarian liberty. Always fighting outside the frontiers of Hungary (on Serb, Russian, Romanian and Italian fronts), the Austro-Hungarian army expanded the jurisdiction of the Habsburg state by over one-half by the time of the Russian separate peace signed at Brest-Litovsk in March 1918. Ultimately, however, the price-tag attached to military success proved to be political collapse and territorial disintegration. The strains of conducting a multi-fronted war of unprecedented intensity over four years precipitated the supreme crisis of Austria-Hungary in mid-1918. As the Allies turned against permitting the retention of the Habsburg state after the war, the minority nationalities within

Austria-Hungary were encouraged to advance claims for the creation of new peacetime nation-states. With eventual military defeat in November 1918, Austria-Hungary paid the capital penalty and suffered dissolution through a deadly combination of nationalist takeover and Allied *diktat*.

In a desperate bid at damage limitation, Hungary attempted to dissociate itself from the Habsburg establishment which bore primary responsibility for both the detonation and conduct of the Great War. In October 1918, a 'Chrysanthemum Revolution' belatedly brought to power in Budapest a Hungarian National Council, headed by Count Mihály Károlyi and committed to a separate peace with the Allies on the basis of Woodrow Wilson's celebrated 'Fourteen Points'. Uncomfortably aware of the unenviable international reputation earned by pre-war magyarisation, Károlyi attempted to impress the Allies favourably by announcing a new Hungarian federation, an 'eastern Switzerland' which would (under a programme administered by the newly appointed minister of nationalities, the liberal Oszkár Jászi) respect the rights of all non-Magyars in the population. The following month, Károlyi salvaged what he could from the final shipwreck of Austria-Hungary by proclaiming an independent liberal republic of Hungary.

Despite the best efforts of the Károlyi government, Hungary was to suffer the Treaty of Trianon, the second most territorially punitive of the five component treaties of the Paris Peace Settlement. The geopolitical impact of Trianon, signed on 4 June 1920, has reverberated through eastern Europe ever since. The territorial assets of the Kingdom of Hungary were unceremoniously stripped for the benefit of Hungary's neighbours. To the north, Slovakia and Ruthenia, combining 3.57 million people and comprising 22.3 per cent of pre-war Hungary, were granted to the new state of Czecho-Slovakia. To the west, part of the Burgenland, involving 290,000 people or 1.4 per cent of pre-war Hungary, was taken by the new state of Austria. In the south, the Backa, Baranya and western Banat, together incorporating 1.52 million people and 7.4 per cent of pre-war Hungary, went to the new Kingdom of the Serbs, Croats and Slovenes. To the east, Transylvania, eastern Banat and southern Máramaros, involving 5.24 million people and a massive 36.2 per cent of pre-war Hungary, were appropriated by an expanded Romania. At Trianon, Hungary lost more territory to Romania alone than it was permitted to retain for itself: 36.2 per cent as against 32.7 per cent of pre-war Hungary. The damage incurred by Hungary at Trianon was apocalyptic: in territorial terms, the 109,208 square miles of the Kingdom of Hungary were reduced to the 35,756 square miles of 'Trianon Hungary', a 67.3 per cent loss of jurisdiction; in demographic terms, the population of Hungary plummeted from 20.9 million in 1910 to 7.62 million in 1920, a loss of 73.5 per cent.[8]

The undeniable scale and apparent vindictiveness of the Treaty of Trianon were the product of a combination of political pressures released by the First World War. As already hinted, the treatment of Hungary was the result of an uncoordinated accommodation between nationalist appetite and Great Power strategy. Already recognised by the Allies as legitimate successors to the defunct Dual Monarchy of Austria-Hungary, Hungary's ambitious neighbours pre-empted the proceedings of the Paris Peace Conference commencing in January 1919, jumping the gun to claim squatters' rights over Hungarian territory. Over the three months following the end of the First World War, the Serb, Romanian and Czech armies opportunistically advanced into the Kingdom of Hungary to annex territory unilaterally, confident of a welcome from local co-nationals irremediably alienated by pre-war magyarisation. Once territory had been occupied by Hungary's neighbours, the ability of the Allies to enforce withdrawal was problematic – even if the Allies (especially France) had wished to disappoint their Serb, Romanian and Czecho-Slovak protégés.

The victorious Powers were determined to favour those nations and states which had committed themselves (with or without military success) to the Allied side and to license substantial successor-states to prevent the balkanisation of eastern Europe. If Czechoslovakia, Romania and the Kingdom of the Serbs, Croats and Slovenes were to be economically and especially militarily viable, their territorial aggrandisement had to be at somebody's expense – and defeated and discredited Austria and Hungary were the inevitable victims. Profoundly suspicious of the last-minute Hungarian conversion to liberal federalism announced by the Károlyi government, the Allies were then shocked by the apparent desertion of Hungary to bolshevism. From March to August 1919, a crucial period in Allied deliberations over the fate of Hungary, a Hungarian Socialist Republic led by Béla Kun,

inspired by an unstable blend of Leninist fanaticism and traditional patriotism, embodied the West's greatest nightmare of
Communist penetration of central Europe. Nothing in Hungary's
past or current record won any friends at the Paris Peace
Conference, instead confirming and reinforcing Allied commitment to the punitive Treaty of Trianon.[9]

So calamitous was the Treaty of Trianon that the question of
whether Hungary could have been treated worse has rarely been
addressed. It was not entirely beyond the bounds of possibility
that Hungary might have been liquidated as a political entity and
partitioned among its neighbours, replicating the fate of nineteenth-century Poland. The fact that Hungary was territorially
truncated, not completely partitioned in 1920 bears witness to the
Allies' appreciation that further reduction would have undermined all credibility in the Paris Peace Settlement's avowed prime
principle of national self-determination. Romania was certainly
encouraged to press into the heart of Hungary to topple the Kun
regime, inflicting the ultimate humiliation of the foreign occupation of the capital Budapest in August 1919; but once Hungary had
been brought firmly to heel, Romania was compelled to withdraw
to the Allied-determined new frontier in November 1919. For all
its manifest damage to Hungary, the Treaty of Trianon still did not
represent the worst-case scenario.

Moreover, the Hungarians could take some comfort from the
sweetening of the pill of Trianon by the earlier Treaty of St Germain
signed between Austria and the Allies in September 1919: an
admittedly solitary gain among all the losses was international
recognition for the first time of Hungary's sovereignty, formal
promotion to independent statehood after half a century of
constitutional autonomy within the Dual Monarchy.

How newly sovereign Hungary employed its unsought – until
the collapse of the Dual Monarchy – but now untrammelled
independence in inter-war Europe was almost entirely determined by its unequivocally hostile reaction to the Trianon Treaty.
Hungarians' chronic insecurity about possession and dispossession was compounded by a burning sense of legitimate grievance
about the iniquities of Trianon. The much-trumpeted prime
principle of national self-determination had been applied neither
to the 'beneficiaries of Versailles', who were granted more territory
than they 'deserved', nor to the 'victims of Versailles', who were
expected to rest content with less territory than they 'deserved'.

What distinguished a beneficiary from a victim was not the proved justice of its national claim but whether it had served on the winning or losing side in the war. Trianon was accordingly perceived as a treaty with an overwhelmingly, almost exclusively punitive rationale: Hungary was punished for its pre-war magyarisation policy, for its loyalty to the Habsburgs in 1914, for its robust military performance over 1914–1918, for its eventual defeat in 1918 and even for its despairing protest against imminent crucifixion by its defiant 'defection to bolshevism' in 1919.

Comprising almost exactly one-third of the territory of pre-war 'Greater Hungary', the 'Trianon Hungary' of the inter-war period represented a 'Lesser Hungary' insufferable to Hungarian *amour propre*. Indeed, in geopolitical terms, it could be argued that Hungary had been reduced to little more than a 'Greater Buda-pest'. Paralleling Vienna's relationship with the rump state of Austria, Budapest was a city whose developmental rationale as the capital of 'Greater Hungary' had been destroyed by Trianon. Budapest was now a demographic monstrosity, the grotesquely bloated and unhealthily top-heavy capital of the mini-Hungarian state. To an overwhelming majority of Hungarians, the only response to the demographic stunting, economic maiming and political humbling imposed by Trianon was the recreation of 'Greater Hungary' through the recovery of what may be termed, by analogy with the irredentist jargon of post-Soviet Russia, the Hungarian 'near-abroad'.

The forcible reduction in the jurisdiction of Hungary imposed at Trianon did not even possess the merit of shifting Hungarians significantly closer to nation-statehood, though it gave that super-ficial impression. According to the first national census of 1920, some 880,000 of Trianon Hungary's total population of 7.6 million were non-Magyars. Officially, the non-Magyars, dominated by 552,000 Germans, constituted 11.6 per cent of the state population, although if the estimated 473,000 assimilated Jews who tradition-ally registered as 'Hungarian' are added, the non-Magyar total rises to 17.8 per cent. Either figure was indisputably a substantial reduction on the 1910 non-Magyar proportion of 51.9 per cent, bringing Trianon Hungary closer to ethnic homogeneity than any other contemporary state in eastern Europe.[10]

Unhappily, Trianon reduced Hungary's internal minority pro-blem at the price of creating an external minority problem. From 1920, the shrinkage of Hungary's borders left a total of 3.23 million

Magyars outside the state: 1.67 million in Romania, 1.07 million in Czecho-Slovakia, 460,000 in the Kingdom of the Serbs, Croats and Slovenes and 30,000 in Austria. Proportionately, 67.6 per cent of all Hungarians lived in Trianon Hungary, 16.7 per cent in Romania, 10.8 per cent in Czecho-Slovakia, 4.6 per cent in the Kingdom of the Serbs, Croats and Slovenes, and 0.3 per cent in Austria. If the 'far-diaspora' of Hungarians in the West is disregarded, the 'near-diaspora' of 32.4 per cent of all Hungarians represented the second-highest expatriate proportion (after Albanians) and the third-largest expatriate total in inter-war eastern Europe.[11]

To the traditional 'far-diaspora' and Trianon-created 'near-diaspora' was now added an 'inner-diaspora': mainly professional and middle-class Magyars who quit the new enclaves to decamp to Trianon Hungary combined with the forcibly dispossessed (like the 105,000 Magyars leaving Czecho-Slovakia over 1918–1921) to experience a process dubbed the 'first ethnic cleansing' in the Hungarian historiography of the 1990s.[12] Displaced and impoverished, an estimated 350,000 political or economic refugees (some 4.6 per cent of the state population) became an extra burden on the straitened resources of Trianon Hungary, comprising a volatile and militant inner-diaspora committed to the recovery of 'Greater Hungary'.

Throughout the 1920s, the authoritarian Hungarian government headed by Regent Miklaus Horthy flew the state flag at half mast in mourning for the 'lost Hungarians' and geared its official efforts to convincing the Western Great Powers of the necessity of territorial revisionism. Diplomatic efforts to remedy the 'terrible mutilation' of Trianon were channelled through the League of Nations, targeting Article XIX of the League's Charter, which admitted the possibility of border revision.[13] Sympathisers outside Hungary were mobilised to press the revisionist cause, notably the historian C.A. Macartney and press baron Lord Rothermere in his ongoing 'Justice for Hungary' campaign launched in the *Daily Mail* in June 1927.[14] None of these constitutional initiatives brought any tangible rewards. The Western Allies were either, like France, adamant in their commitment to the Paris Settlement or, like Great Britain, intimidated into complacency by the daunting prospect of wholesale revision. Meanwhile, the new establishment of 'beneficiaries of Versailles' closed ranks to protect its gains: from 1921, a Little Entente of Czecho-Slovakia, Romania and the Kingdom of the Serbs, Croats and Slovenes operated as a self-interested, specifically anti-Magyar alliance ring-fencing Hungarian revanchist ambitions.

Rather than deflating Hungarian hopes, frustration only consolidated Magyar rancour. 'Nem, Nem, Soha' (No, No, Never) became the slogan of an abiding multi-class Hungarian solidarity of resentment at the injustice of Trianon. With Magyar enclaves viewed as Hungarian fifth columns by host states increasingly indulging their 'integral nationalism', a vicious circle of harassment-protest-persecution-defiance raised the political temperature to fever pitch.[15] The metaphor of mutilation was universally adopted and observed among Hungarians: the bloody product of 'cruel incursions into the living flesh of the Hungarian race', Trianon Hungary constituted the dismembered torso of the Hungarian nation; the enclaves of the near-diaspora were the amputated limbs of the Hungarian body-politic; the agony of forcible separation from now-isolated enclaves of Magyars acted like a 'phantom limb syndrome' on the new inner-diaspora within butchered Hungary.[16]

With the advent of the 1930s came a realisation that, first, no revision could be expected by constitutional or diplomatic means, and second, that only Great Power patronage could free Magyars from the constraints of Trianon Hungary. The success of Turkey in overthrowing the punitive Treaty of Sèvres (signed almost contemporaneously with Trianon in August 1920) and forcing its replacement by the more equitable Treaty of Lausanne in July 1923 demonstrated that revisionism could be forced upon the victorious Allies – but not by a state as small and beleaguered as Trianon Hungary. The plight of its near-diaspora, the broader socio-economic repercussions of the Depression and (above all) the exhaustion of viable alternative options gradually, and probably inexorably, forced Hungary into the clutches of Nazi Germany.

The argument of the pro-Axis Hungarian revisionists was that only the politico-military authority of Germany could break the bars of Trianon, that Nazi Germany was set upon a territorial rampage from which Hungary would emerge as a victim unless early collaboration were undertaken, and that Hungary's interests would be best served by a joint Rome–Berlin orientation. From 1934, such Hungarian arguments dovetailed with German geopolitical strategy for the economic and military penetration of eastern Europe. As early as September 1935, the Gombos government found German proposals to return to Hungary the Burgenland (once Austria was absorbed) and Slovakia (once Czecho-Slovakia was liquidated) in return for close military co-operation just too tempting. Hungarian conduct was too transparently mercenary and Hitler's personal dislike of Hungarians too undisguised for a love-match between Germany and Hungary; but, by the late 1930s, the German-Hungarian alliance represented an arranged marriage too mutually convenient and rewarding to resist.

Under the strengthening patronage of Nazi Germany (and faltering patronage of Fascist Italy), Trianon Hungary opportunistically expanded over 1938–1941 into a client 'Neuordnung Hungary'. Identifying the Czecho-Slovak foreign minister Edvard Benes as 'the architect of Trianon' and organiser of the Little Entente, Hungary needed little prompting from Hitler and Mussolini to participate in the partition of Czecho-Slovakia after the Munich Crisis.[17] By the (First) Vienna Award, signed by German and Italian foreign ministers Ribbentrop and Ciano in November 1938, Hungary was granted southern Slovakia and Ruthenia, involving 1.04 million people including 592,000 Magyars. In March 1939, Hitler authorised 'First Vienna Hungary' to occupy Transcarpathian Ruthenia (creating a common Hungarian–Soviet border for the first time) and a further slice of eastern Slovakia (creating a Hungarian–Polish border also for the first time). As part of the dismemberment of Romania demanded by Stalin, Hungary was granted most of northern Transylvania, involving 2.53 million mainly Magyar people, by the Second Vienna Award of August 1940. Finally, as payment for joining the Wehrmacht in the subjugation of Yugoslavia, 'Second Vienna Hungary' was licensed to take the Backa and part of Vojvodina in April 1941.[18]

Each instalment of expansion into the Hungarian near-abroad was accompanied by a state-sponsored Magyar 're-seeding', in which uprooted Magyars of the inner-diaspora reclaimed their lost lands, necessarily through the 'ethnic cleansing' of non-Magyars, who had now increased to over 25 per cent of the total population. The 'Neuordnung Hungary' territorially complete by mid-1941 contained, at 14.6 million, almost double the population of 'Trianon Hungary' and covered 52.9 per cent of the area of the 'Kingdom of Hungary'. The remaining *Hungaria Irredenta* of southern Transylvania and northern Slovakia (or 'Upper Hungary') was tantalisingly denied Hungary by Hitler's calculating grand strategy. Even so, although much less than a full restoration of pre-First World War 'Greater Hungary', the 'Larger Hungary' of Second World War Europe, was a substantial improvement on inter-war 'Lesser Hungary'.

'Neuordnung Hungary' proved all too short-lived. During 1943, the fall of Mussolini left Hungary with no Axis protection against German dominance, leading to the humiliating 'Operation Margarethe', the Wehrmacht takeover of Hungary in March 1944. Over 1944–1945, the military defeat of the Wehrmacht brought the Nazi Neuordnung crashing down. Not surprisingly, all the territorial gains in the near-abroad briefly enjoyed by 'Larger Hungary' were forfeited: by the terms of the Hungarian-Allied armistice signed in Moscow in January 1945, Hungary was returned to her 1937 borders. Indeed by the border-finalising Paris Peace Treaty of February 1947, a small extra bridgehead of Hungarian territory near Bratislava was transferred to a reconstituted Czechoslovakia.

It could have been worse: 'Yalta Hungary' may have been the smallest Hungary of the twentieth century but the inter-war 'Versailles matrix' was broadly restored in 1945. Although the geopolitical jurisdictions of the eastern European states were altered (and most were soon transformed from sovereign entities into satellites within the new Soviet Bloc), all states recognised by 'Versailles Europe' were recognised again within 'Yalta Europe'. By comparison with its harsh fate after the First World War and despite again ending up on the losing side, Hungary got off more lightly after the Second World War than might have been expected.

Even so, demographic changes occasioned by the Second World War significantly, though not fundamentally, altered the composition and context of 'Yalta Hungary'. An estimated 400,000 Hungarians were killed in the Second World War, some 4 per cent of the total Magyar population. A complex 'second ethnic cleansing' occurred during 1944–1948: some 500,000 Hungarian Jews were despatched to Auschwitz; 240,000 Germans were expelled under the Potsdam Agreement, halving Hungary's German problem at a stroke; in an act of 'self-cleansing', some 30,000 Hungarians fled Soviet takeover to join the far-diaspora; and inter-state 'vacuum cleaning' saw the deportation to forced labour in the Soviet Union of some 50,000 Hungarians and, by a Prague—Budapest Accord of February 1946, the exchange of 70,000 Hungarians and Slovaks.[19]

The net results of the ebb-and-flow of ethnic cleansing were that, first, Hungary became even more Hungarian, rising from an inter-war 82.2 per cent to a post-war 91.4 per cent Magyar, a 9 per cent increase which brought Hungary closer to ethnic homogeneity; and second, the Hungarian near-diaspora dropped from 32.4 per cent to between 26.6 and 22.4 per cent of the Magyar total, a substantial but still not definitive move towards Hungarian nation-statehood. Although shifted appreciably in the direction of nation-statehood over 'Trianon Hungary' by the Second World War, 'Yalta Hungary' still had considerable demographic distance to travel.

Whatever the manifold iniquities of 'Soviet empire', its role in bringing geopolitical stabilisation to eastern Europe is indisputable. For over forty years, a Kremlin-imposed 'Ice Age' put the still-unresolved Hungarian question on hold. Although the inner-diaspora was numerically increased by the second ethnic cleansing, reinforcing its inter-war reputation as the prime recruiting ground for irredentist para-military movements, the looming presence or proximity of the Red Army cooled and calmed relations between Hungary and its neighbours.

Over the decade following 1945, a conjunction of punitive Soviet exploitation and inherited Hungarian resentment provoked the first major national rebellion against the Soviet empire in 1956, which in turn permitted a haemorrhage of 200,000 political emigrants to the Hungarian far-diaspora. Thereafter, the Soviet Union and Hungary came together in a mutually expedient arrangement to forestall another '1956': Hungary resigned itself to uncomplaining 'membership' of the Soviet Bloc (and the smallest army in the Warsaw Pact) while a Hungarian—Soviet Pact signed in Moscow in March 1957 guaranteed Hungary 'favoured status' within the 'Socialist Family of Nations'. Preferential Soviet treatment permitted Hungary to develop its own distinctive 'goulash communism', which soon delivered the highest standard of living in the Soviet Bloc and converted Hungary into the 'happiest barracks in eastern Europe'. While on occasion mischievously dropping hints about its possible transfer of Transylvania as a ploy to mollify the Hungary of Kádár and intimidate the Romania of Ceauçescu, the Kremlin made it plain that the post-war geopolitical matrix of Yalta Europe was beyond local national revision.[20]

Even so, it is important to stress that under the Soviet empire, just as nationalism in general was not so much 'frozen' as 'refrigerated', so the Hungarian problem was competently managed rather than definitively resolved. The fundamentals of the Hungarian problem did not materially improve, indeed some grew worse. For instance, under Soviet patronage, Budapest doubled in size to become the third largest city in the entire Soviet Bloc (behind only Moscow and Leningrad), exacerbating the post-Trianon predicament of Hungary being constricted into a 'Greater Budapest'.

Over the *annus mirabilis* of 1989, two celebrated episodes underlined the pivotal role of the Hungarian question. In May 1989 Hungary became the first state of eastern Europe to dismantle its section of the Iron Curtain, thereby opening a 'Gateway to the West' for what became by September 1989 an East German exodus. Rendered more disrespectful of established borders than any other east European state by Trianon (and the unsettling experience of six different-sized 'Hungaries' over the twentieth century), Hungary took the lead in destabilising the Soviet Bloc by exploiting its geopolitical position at the frontier of East and West. In December 1989, attempts by the Romanian *Securitate* to expel Pastor Laszlo Tokes, the leader of the Hungarian community in Timosoara/Temesvár, triggered a chain reaction which within ten days had toppled the Ceauçescu regime by a 'Christmas Revolution'. Hungary and the Hungarian diaspora had staked their claim to top the agenda for post-Communist Europe.

Since 1989, the various interest groups of Hungarian political life have naturally disported themselves in a public manner denied under the Soviet empire. The Hungarians of the far-diaspora have polarised: the moderates are reconciled to channelling their support into the politically offensive but pragmatically unchallengeable Yalta-defined state of Hungary (through financial investment as much as personal commitment); while the militants see the 1990s as an era of geopolitical flux offering an unrepeatable opportunity for escaping the legacy of Trianon (with American Hungarians in particular 'parachuting into' the communities of the near-diaspora to agitate for border revision).

The Hungarians of the near-diaspora embody a whole spectrum of attitudes, generally determined by the particular circumstances of the individual enclaves. The reasonably prosperous Magyars in Austria and Croatia are broadly content with the treatment of their host states while the enclaves in Ukraine and Slovenia have been reassured by minority protection conventions passed in, respectively, June and November 1992.

In the post-January 1993, newly independent and nationally ebullient state of Slovakia, mounting fears of a government-sponsored slovakisation programme have agitated the Magyar minority even as the long-running quarrel over the Gabcikova–Nagymaros dam on the Danube continues to poison Hungarian—Slovak relations.[21]

In Romania, Ceauçescu intensified a long-standing campaign against the Magyar minority from the mid-1980s, inducing some 20,000 to decamp to Hungary over 1988–1989 alone. The downfall of Ceauçescu did not, however, bring an end to ethnic strife: Romanian–Magyar disturbances rocked Tirgu Mures/Marosvá-sárhely in March 1990; more recently, the provocative actions of Gheorghe Funar, Mayor of Cluj/Kolozsvár and leader of the ultra-nationalist PRNU (Party of Romanian National Unity) have exacerbated prevailing tense relations; and the HDFR (Hungarian Democratic Federation of Romania) in August 1994 demanded that Hungary insist on 'special protected status' for the Magyar near-diaspora in Romania.

The most potentially dangerous situation of all has emerged, predictably enough, from the débâcle of the disintegration of Yugoslavia. Warning signs for the 400,000 Magyars in Vojvodina came with Slobodan Milosevic's withdrawal of Vojvodina's protective autonomous status in February 1989 and official declaration that Serbian was the only official language throughout Serbia in July 1991. Since then, the moderate DCVH (Democratic Community of Vojvodina Hungarians) has become alarmed at Serbian allegations of mass Hungarian desertion from the federal army and Hungarian support for Croatia, which have induced another 20,000 Magyars to flee north to Hungary.[22]

If no overall consensus has emerged among a vulnerable near-diaspora anxious to avoid bringing unnecessary persecution upon its own head, unanimity of militancy characterises the inner-diaspora. The long-established dispossessed of the 1920s and 1940s have been augmented by some 50,000 refugees fleeing from the 'third ethnic cleansing' in 1990s Romania and Serbia. The inner-diaspora is growing in size and authority, raising demands for positive government action in the form of both a 'counter-cleansing' operation of magyarisation directed against the non-

Magyar minorities remaining within Hungary and the interventionist patronage of harassed enclaves in the Magyar near-diaspora.

The post-Communist governments of Hungary have consequently come under considerable pressure to, at very least, make noises sympathetic to the near-diaspora. On appointment as premier of the HDF (Hungarian Democratic Forum) coalition in 1990, Jozsef Antall announced that he headed a government of Hungarians not just a government of Hungary, implicitly assuming responsibility for the near-diaspora. In July 1991, Antall provocatively announced that the break-up of Yugoslavia meant that Serbia had no legal jurisdiction over Vojvodina, alarming Milosevic into repressive actions against the Magyar enclave. At the Third World Congress of Hungarians in August 1992, the largest international gathering of Hungarians for over half a century, Antall repeated his assurance that the government of Hungary would protect the Magyar diaspora.[23]

Over 1993, groups deriving their support from the inner-diaspora vilified the government for betraying the Magyar cause. For instance, angered by the Hungarian–Ukrainian accord of June 1992 (by which Ukraine promised its Magyar minority fair treatment in return for Hungary renouncing all territorial claims to Ruthenia/Transcarpathia), the populist nationalist HDF member István Csurka denounced his own government for selling out the Ukrainian Magyars. Csurka established an irredentist 'Hungarian Justice' faction in May 1993 which had to be expelled from the HDF with enormous embarrassment and considerable political damage the following month.[24] The inner-diaspora also applauded the reburial in his homeland in September 1993 of the remains of exiled Admiral Horthy, under whose leadership the Neuordnung Hungary of 1938–1941 had regained one-third of Magyar territory lost at Trianon.

The post-Communist government and (since May 1994) the post-post-Communist socialist government have, to date, appreciated the persuasive arguments favouring expedient stability while paying lip-service to the traditional sentiments of the inner-diaspora. The clear majority of the citizens of Hungary are relatively complacent with regard to nationalism, retaining a nostalgic, sentimental attachment to the near-diaspora but a wary scepticism towards the irredentist slogans of an inner-diaspora whose financial maintenance is increasingly resented. For this constituency, security and especially prosperity in the post-Communist era are first priorities. Both are perceived as lying with the West and specifically the European Union. Hungary has already attracted a full one-half of Western investment in eastern Europe since 1989 and in April 1994 Hungary became the first state in eastern Europe to make formal application for EU membership. A smooth and painless passage through the probationary 'ante-chamber' from associate to full EU membership is conditional upon firm economic stewardship, strict observance of civil rights and unqualified respect for existing state borders. The official strategy of Hungarian governments in the 1990s, so far, has therefore been to recognise reluctantly the borders inherited from Trianon but to seek to reduce their significance by fostering good relations with Hungary's neighbours to effect a closer community of all Hungarians.

'Trianon' represents an enduring historical inheritance and poisoned political legacy for the Hungary of the 1990s. At worst, Trianon inflicted wounds on the Hungarian body-politic which are still weeping and unhealed, and into which inner-diaspora fanatics are always ready to rub political salt. At best, Trianon has left indelible scars upon Hungarian national politics, which still disfigure Hungary's relations with its neighbours. The inherited Magyar historical trauma of alternation between possession and dispossession culminated in the 'Trianon syndrome' which has bedevilled the *Weltanschauung* of the Hungarian 'community of suffering' since the First World War.

The few eastern European optimists who survive argue that the twentieth-century 'in-gathering' of Hungarians has significantly reduced both the proportion of non-Magyar minorities within Hungary and the Magyar minorities outside Hungary, effecting an ethnic consolidation of Hungary and diminution of the destabilising Magyar near-diaspora. Moreover, the 1994 EU initiative to establish a standing conference on eastern Europe to defuse potential conflict and facilitate accord on borders and minorities may have displeased Hungary's neighbours, who feel they cannot gain and may lose from the so-called 'Balladur Plan', but has greatly heartened Hungary itself, which can hardly lose and may well gain from Western intervention.

Eastern European pessimists (many of whom are Hungarian) counter that the twentieth century provides irrefutable evidence of the passing impact and ultimate limitations of ethnic cleansing:

the three waves of 1918–1921, 1944–1948 and 1988 onwards have achieved neither a homogeneously Magyar Hungary nor a Disappearing Diaspora of Magyars. The fundamentals of the 'Hungarian question' posed by the First World War and precipitated by Trianon have not been substantively altered even by the Second World War and the Soviet empire. Although Hungary is currently on its best behaviour so as not to prejudice being the first eastern European state to gain admittance to the EU, an emotional and nationalistic act of defiance (as in 1849, 1919 and 1956) by the unreconciled and embittered 'victims of Trianon' can never be entirely discounted. In the mid-1990s, as capitalism is perceived as failing to deliver the expected prosperity, with 1994 unemployment in Hungary rising to 12 per cent and inflation to 22 per cent, the Hungarian potential for destabilising its seven neighbour-states at the very heart of Europe remains enormous.

Cast by Trianon in the unauditioned role of trouble-maker of eastern Europe, Hungary must now come to terms with its twentieth-century tragedy. The fortuitous near-coincidence of the 75th anniversary of the Treaty of Trianon (the ultimate national humiliation for the Magyars) in 1995 and the 1,100th anniversary of the founding of the Hungarian state (the crowning national triumph for the Magyars) in 1996 is setting the supreme test for a Hungary seeking security, stability and above all, self-fulfilment in the new Europe of the twenty-first century.

NOTES

1 J.K. Hoensch, *A History of Modern Hungary 1867–1986*, London: Longman, 1988, p.279.
2 M. Shields, 'Hungary's diaspora backed', *Independent*, 20 August 1992, p.6.
3 A. Barber, 'Tension over ethnic Hungarians', *Independent*, 11 January 1993, p.6.
4 Hoensch, *op. cit.*, p.28.
5 P.F. Sugar, 'An underrated event: the Hungarian constitutional crisis of 1905–1906', *East European Quarterly*, 1981, vol. 15, no. 3, pp.281–306.
6 R.W. Seton-Watson, *Racial Problems in Hungary*, London: Macmillan, 1908.
7 I. Hunyadi, 'L'image de la Hongrie en Europe occidentale à l'issue de la première guerre mondiale', in P. Aycoberry (ed.), *Les Conséquences des Traités de Paix de 1919–1920 en Europe Centrale et Sud-Orientale*, Strasbourg: University of Strasbourg Press, 1987, pp.173–82.

8   P. Teleki, 'Ethnographical map of Hungary', in A. Apponyi *et al.*, *Justice for Hungary: review and criticism of the effects of the Treaty of Trianon*, London: Longmans, Green & Co., 1928.

9   P. Pastor, *Hungary between Wilson and Lenin: the Hungarian Revolution of 1918–1919 and the Big Three*, New York: Columbia University Press, 1976.

10 R. Pearson, *National Minorities in Eastern Europe 1848–1945*, London: Macmillan, 1983, pp.170–4.

11 Ibid.

12 Coexistence/Egyuttélés/Spoluzitie, *From Minority Status to Partnership: Hungarians in Czechoslovakia/Slovakia 1918–1992*, Bratislava/Pozsony/Pressburg: Political Movement Coexistence/Egyuttélés/Spoluzitie, 1993, p.3.

13 J. Wlassics, 'Legal amendment of the Treaty of Trianon through the League of Nations and arbitration' in Apponyi, *op. cit.*, p.296.

14 R. Donald, *The Tragedy of Trianon: Hungary's appeal to humanity*, London: Butterworth, 1928; C.A. Macartney, *Hungary and Her Successors: the Treaty of Trianon and its consequences*, London: Oxford University Press, 1937.

15 R. Gower, *The Hungarian Minorities in the Succession States*, London: Grant Richards, 1937.

16 E. Nagy, 'The road towards rectification' in Apponyi, *op. cit.*, p.366.

17 Hoensch, *op. cit.*, pp.117–18.

18 H. Seton-Watson, *Eastern Europe between the Wars 1918–1941*, London: Cambridge University Press, 1946, pp.334–41.

19 Hoensch, *op. cit.*, p.177; Coexistence, *op. cit.*, pp.4–5.

20 Hoensch, *op. cit.*, pp.276–7.

21 Barber, *op. cit.*, p.6.

22 A. Barber, 'Budapest accuses Serbia of intimidation', *Independent*, 11 December 1991, p.6.

23 Shields, *op. cit.*, p.6.

24 E. Varadi, 'Expulsion splits Hungarian ruling party', *Independent*, 7 June 1993, p.6; Rebecca Ann Haynes, 'Hungarian National Identity: definition and redefinition', in Paul Latawski (ed.), *Contemporary Nationalism in East Central Europe*, London: Macmillan, 1995, pp.96–100.

Chapter 7

Ukraine
Between Eurasia and the West

Andrew Wilson

In the period 1917–1920 a weak and divided Ukrainian national movement was unable to seize the chance created by the collapse of the Romanov and Habsburg empires and establish an independent Ukrainian nation-state. On 24 August 1991 the supreme soviet of the Ukrainian SSR declared national independence by 346 votes to one, a decision subsequently endorsed by a 90.3 per cent vote in the national referendum of 1 December 1991. Despite the enormous difference in outcome, however, the two periods had more in common than is immediately apparent. The near-unanimity of the two votes in 1991 masked severe underlying ethno-linguistic and regional cleavages in Ukraine, which were either first revealed by the events of 1917–1920 or are in considerable part their long-term consequence.

The continuing importance of these divides was ably demonstrated by the 1994 elections to the Ukrainian parliament and presidency.[1] In western Ukraine and in central Ukraine west of the River Dnieper, areas dominated for historical reasons by Ukrainian-speaking ethnic Ukrainians, voters tended to back more or less nationalist candidates who took a firm line on national independence and sought gradually to move Ukraine away from Russia and towards integration with the political, economic and military structures of western and central Europe. On the other hand, voters in the east and south, home to Ukraine's huge (11.4 million) ethnic Russian minority and an even larger number of Russian-speaking ethnic Ukrainians, supported anti-nationalist and/or leftist candidates who preferred to define Ukraine's future as part of a 'common Eurasian home' along with Russia and Belarus.[2]

The division was revealed most sharply in the summer

presidential election, when the relatively nationalist incumbent Leonid Kravchuk lost a close race by 52 per cent to 45 per cent to the former prime minister Leonid Kuchma, who ran on a platform attacking nationalist policies of 'self-isolation' and urging the re-establishment of a 'strategic partnership' between Ukraine and Russia. Kuchma won every oblast to the east of the River Dnieper and in the southern coastal region, while Kravchuk won every oblast further to the west except one (Kirovohrad). Three years after the 1991 referendum, when the nationalist and pro-European camp appeared to be in the ascendant, the pendulum now seemed to be swinging back in the opposite direction.

The historical roots of this awkward balance of forces between east and west Ukraine can indeed be illuminated by a study of the twentieth century's two great periods of war and revolution. However, Ukraine's current problems do not all flow from a single defining crisis, as arguably those of Hungary date from the 1920 Treaty of Trianon, or Ireland's from the 1916 Easter Rising and subsequent civil war and partition. Both world wars had a major impact on ethnic politics in Ukraine, as did the fact that the united Ukraine of today was created (as the Ukrainian Soviet Socialist Republic, a constituent part of the USSR) not in 1917–1920, but in the vastly different circumstances of 1939–1945.

Ukraine did not appear on the map in 1914.[3] Ukrainian lands were divided between the Russian and Austro-Hungarian empires.[4] Moreover, unlike other then stateless nations such as the Irish or Poles, the Ukrainians as yet had little sense of their common existence as a nation. In the Russian empire Ukrainians were overwhelmingly peasants with a parochial world-view that centred on immediate economic concerns. They had a strong sense of loyalty to their locality or village and to the Tsar, but little conception of any social collectivity in between. The limited historical consciousness they possessed tended to be based in 'the pre-state, libertarian anarchic tradition of the Sich Cossacks and the Haidamack movement' (the Haidamacks were rebel peasant bands in the seventeenth and eighteenth centuries), rather than in any sense of belonging to a broader historical and ethnic group.[5]

Nearly all Ukrainians in the Russian empire lived in villages (80 per cent), of which 97 per cent were peasants.[6] The vast majority (87 per cent) were illiterate.[7] In the nine guberniias with an ethnic Ukrainian majority, 80 per cent of the total population claimed

Ukrainian (then known as 'Little Russian') as their spoken mother-tongue in the 1897 census, compared with only 32.5 per cent of the urban population.[8] The key cities, such as Kiev, Odessa/Odesa and Yuzovka (now Donets'k) remained the preserve of Russian, Jewish and/or Polish culture.[9] The tiny Ukrainian intelligentsia had begun to form social and political organisations around the turn of the century, but their 'isolation from the broad mass of the peasantry, lack of a clear socio-economic programme . . . organisational amorphousness, and lack of preparedness (or lack of desire) for intensive political activity' limited their influence.[10] Two tsarist decrees in 1863 and 1876 which severely limited the public use of the Ukrainian language made it extremely difficult for the Ukrainian intelligentsia to agitate among the peasantry and build a broad-based national movement.

Moreover, the intelligentsia was the only significant social group committed to the national cause. The Orthodox clergy in Ukraine, half of whom was Russian anyway, was largely quiescent and often impoverished, and the old Ukrainian (that is Cossack) nobility had nearly all been assimilated into the Russian elite in the late eighteenth and early nineteenth centuries.[11] A Ukrainian working class or business elite had yet to emerge. Partly as a consequence, the majority of Ukrainian activists continued to espouse a 'culturally-oriented apolitical Ukrainophilism' and to favour a federal relationship with Russia rather than outright independence.[12] The number of Ukrainian activists advocating an independent state in union with their ethnic brethren across the border was tiny.

In the Austrian territories of eastern Galicia and northern Bukovyna on the other hand relative political freedom encouraged a much higher degree of mobilisation among the local Ukrainian population. The same political freedom forced the Ukrainians to compete with rival movements organised by their traditional adversaries, the Poles in Galicia and the Romanians in Bukovyna, but the Ukrainians periodically enjoyed the support of the Austrian authorities who saw them as a potential counterweight to the more troublesome Poles.[13] Moreover, in Galicia most Ukrainians belonged to the Uniate church, which provided both elite leadership and institutional support and helped to maintain a sense of identity distinct from that of Orthodox Russians and Catholic Poles (most Bukovynan Ukrainians on the other hand were Orthodox). In Galicia therefore the rudiments of a Ukrainian civil society were in place by 1914. Ukrainians regularly voted for their own political parties, with increasing effect after direct and universal suffrage was introduced in 1907. On the eve of war in February 1914 the Habsburg authorities recognised the Ukrainians' growing strength by conceding a new provincial statute to east Galicia that would have granted the Ukrainians a guaranteed share of places in the local Diet and administration (although the Poles would still have remained the dominant social and political force in the region). Only the outbreak of war prevented the implementation of the plan.

Ukrainians also lived in Transcarpathia under Hungarian rule, but the area remained something of a political backwater. In contrast to the relatively liberal Austrians the Hungarians sought actively to magyarise their national minorities, and voting rights were restricted by the system of estate curiae that persisted up to 1918. Moreover, the Ukrainians had to compete with the rival Rusyn movement that claimed that the local Slav population was not Ukrainian at all, but a separate ethnic group, the Rusyns.[14] Like the Galicians most of the Transcarpathian population was Uniate, but they belonged to a separate branch of the church.

Although most west Ukrainians were, therefore, relatively pro-Habsburg, they did not forget their brethren to the east. On the contrary, the sense of belonging to a people of some twenty-six million was of vital psychological significance in the Ukrainians' struggle with the Poles, Romanians and Jews, and the basis of their sense of separate history was the idea of the common descent of all Ukrainians from the early medieval kingdom of Kievan Rus'. By 1900 radical Galicians were entertaining the idea of an independent pan-Ukrainian state. However, the feeling was not necessarily universally reciprocated on the other side of the border.

To a minority of nationally conscious Ukrainians in the Russian empire the vitality of Ukrainian life in Galicia helped to refute the argument that 'Ukrainian' was a pseudo-culture, a legacy of peasant parochialism, and its 'language' a mere dialect of Russian (the physical movement of individuals and banned literature across the border was also important). On the other hand Russian Ukraine had been a part of the Romanov empire for centuries. The Left, or eastern, Bank of the Dnieper effectively came under the Tsars' control in 1654 and the Right Bank and Volhynia in 1793–95. Moreover, much of southern and eastern Ukraine had never been part of the medieval Kievan state. Parts had been under the control of Ukrainian (Zaporozhian) Cossacks in the seventeenth and eighteenth centuries, but others had been annexed by Russia direct from the Crimean Tatars and Ottoman Turks.

Linguistic and religious proximity to Russia and an open career path in the empire for Ukrainian elites led many Ukrainians to take the 'Gogol option' and assimilate to Russian language and culture, if not 'as a marker of cultural identity', then at least 'as the acceptance of a common currency' and as the best means of access to world culture.[15] Most Ukrainians therefore believed that a local 'Little Russian' *landespatriotismus* was perfectly compatible with loyalty to the empire.[16] Some form of federal relation with a democratised Russia was therefore the limit of most national activists' ambition before 1914, even during the 1905–1906 Revolution.

With the outbreak of war, Ukrainian territory became the target for military strategy and political intrigue from both sides. In a manifesto issued in August 1914, the Galician Ukrainians declared themselves in favour of a united Ukrainian state, to be carved out of the Russian empire and placed under Habsburg protection, and formed a Supreme (later General) Ukrainian Council to promote this aim. The initial Habsburg response was lukewarm. Although they gave limited backing to the Council's activities, the Austrians were essentially fighting a defensive war on the Eastern Front and many accepted the Polish argument that the Ukrainians were 'unreliable'. It was only in 1917–1918 that the Central Powers, Germany in particular, came to realise that Ukrainian irredentism could play a crucial role in undermining the Russian war-effort.

On the other side of the border the Russian authorities viewed the Galician problem in a completely different way. Ever since the Bosnian crisis in 1908, the Russians, urged on by the nationalist Union of the Russian People, had been fomenting unrest in the region in order to counter the rise of Habsburg influence in the Balkans. Russia's claim was based on theories of dynastic right and the ingathering of 'ancient Russian lands from the time of Kievan Rus', rather than Ukrainian irredentism. Not only was the idea of creating a pan-Ukrainian state anathema to Russia's leaders, but they tended to assume that the annexation and pacification of Galicia would bring the additional benefit of ending Ukrainian 'intrigue' and allow the whole of Ukraine or 'Little Russia' to settle down into its natural state as a loyal province of an expanded empire.

During the Russian occupation of Galicia in 1914–1915, therefore, the local governor Count Georgii Bobrinskii attempted to
'russify' the region. Ukrainian activists were imprisoned or exiled
and Bobrinskii leant for support instead on the local russophile
movement, which argued that 'Ukrainians' were simply one part
of the broader Russian nation. Ironically, Bobrinskii's policies
might have had greater success in Galicia only a generation or two
earlier. Until the 1880s the russophiles had been a genuine political
force throughout western Ukraine, but the growth of Ukrainian
national consciousness had left them a fading force (in the 1913
elections to the Galician Diet the russophiles elected only one
deputy compared to the Ukrainian parties' thirty-one).[17] As a
result, russophile co-operation with Bobrinskii tended to be
perceived as collaboration and ultimately only served to accel-
erate their loss of support.

By the time Russian troops were forced to withdraw from
Galicia in May 1915, it was clear that Russia's preferred model of
an extended Little Russia under continued Russian hegemony,
although supported by many in Russian Ukraine, had no real
grass-roots support on the other side of the border (significantly,
there was only muted protest against Bobrinskii's policies from
the Ukrainian intelligentsia in the Russian empire, most of whom
continued loyally to support the Russian war effort until summer
1917; the only exception was a small group of émigrés, who in 1915
formed the Union for the Liberation of Ukraine and joined the
General Ukrainian Council in Galicia). Moreover, Russia was to
lose the war. It was, therefore, the Austro-German vision of
Ukraine's future that was to be experimented with in 1918.

The February 1917 revolution was not of Ukraine's doing. The
Ukrainian national movement in Russia was as disorganised in
February 1917 as it had been in 1914, and its political horizons had
yet to advance significantly beyond the federal project (although
some historians have argued that support for the Ukrainian
movement had nevertheless been growing steadily before
1917).[18] At first, therefore, Ukrainians largely reacted to events.
Although they began to seize the initiative over the summer of
1917, by the time an independent Ukrainian state was declared the
following January, successive Ukrainian governments found it
increasingly difficult to assert their control amid the social
maelstrom unleashed by the revolution and the collapse of central
authority (as unavoidable in Ukraine as in the empire as a whole).

Crucially, the Galicians were unable to come to the assistance of the Ukrainian experiment in the east until the Habsburg empire also began to fall apart in autumn 1918, by which time the Ukrainian government in Kiev was already a fading force.

Moreover, although the Provisional Government in St Petersburg was forced to recognise Ukrainian autonomy in July 1917, it did so only in the five central Ukrainian guberniias of Volhynia, Podillia, Kiev, Chernihiv and Poltava. The various Ukrainian governments of the period never had much support in either eastern or southern Ukraine, where the population tended to support the Bolsheviks, Whites or anarchists, or largely kept themselves to themselves. In 1918 the Bolsheviks even set up a rival Donets'k-Kryvyi Rih Republic in east Ukraine.[19] Although the main ethnic Ukrainian parties polled well in the November 1917 elections to the all-Russian Provisional Assembly (an average of 68 per cent in eight mainly ethnic Ukrainian guberniias), their support was markedly lower in the east and south (the Ukrainian parties polled 81 per cent in Poltava, but only 47 per cent in Katerynoslav).[20]

Moreover, the Bolsheviks were far from being a purely external force. Although less powerful in Ukraine than elsewhere, they drew considerable support from ethnic Ukrainians as well as from Jews and Russians in the main urban centres.[21] The struggle between the Bolsheviks and the various Ukrainian governments in Kiev was as much a Ukrainian civil war as a war of Russian reconquest. In the words of one author, 'although it is generally assumed that a Russian Red Army came [from Russia] to conquer the Ukraine and defeat the [Ukrainian] forces in early 1919, nothing could be further from the truth'.[22]

The first Ukrainian government in Kiev, the Ukrainian People's Republic (UNR), only lasted from November 1917 to April 1918. Its high-water mark was the Treaty of Brest-Litovsk signed in February 1918, when it seemed for a time that an independent Ukraine might actually come into being as a protectorate of the Central Powers (principally Germany, as Austria-Hungary was now preoccupied with its own internal problems). The Bolsheviks signed the treaty with reluctance, although they would repudiate it as soon as the Central Powers collapsed.[23] Brest-Litovsk granted the UNR control over a greatly expanded territory encompassing eleven tsarist guberniias; the five already mentioned in central Ukraine, plus Kharkiv, Katerynoslav, Kherson and Taurida (excluding Crimea) to the east and south, Chetm/Kholm in what is now south-east Poland and southern Grodno (now south-west Belarus). Nevertheless, the UNR's authority in many areas was little more than nominal.[24]

Some historians have argued that the Germans saw Brest-Litovsk solely as a 'grain treaty' (*Brotfrieden*), that is as a means to the colonial exploitation of Ukraine as a puppet-state.[25] The Germans certainly had little patience with the left-leaning UNR, and connived in the April 1918 coup that replaced it with a 'Hetmanate', led by a conservative landowner, Pavlo Skoropads'kyi. The Hetmanate abandoned the UNR's policies of social experimentation and backed local landowners in their struggle to preserve their estates from peasant land-hunger.[26] This satisfied the Germans' desire to maintain agricultural exports, albeit at meagre levels, but further alienated the already disaffected peasantry.

Others have argued that the Germans had a long-term vision for Ukraine derived from the writings of Friedrich Naumann and others on the concept of *Mitteleuropa*, as a stable and prosperous buffer state that could serve 'as a means of weakening the Russian colossus in the long term'.[27] Certainly Germany foresaw a greater geopolitical role for Ukraine in 1918 than it did in 1939–1945, albeit only as one of several satellite states in the region. Perhaps if the German occupation had lasted longer than nine months, then German protection might have substituted for the Ukrainian nationalists' lack of real internal strength, but the Western Armistice in November 1918 led to German withdrawal and Skoropads'kyi's enforced departure (he had assumed that the Germans would hold out until 1919 at least and give him time to form a proper army).[28] Skoropads'kyi was replaced by the restored UNR, whose administration was now known as the Directory, but its leaders were never able to recover the position they had enjoyed in 1917 and early 1918. First and foremost the Directory lacked an effective military force of its own, its initially enthusiastic peasant supporters having drifted away once hopes of rapid land reform were dashed. In February 1919 the UNR was forced to abandon Kiev to the combined forces of the Red Army and the Bolsheviks' east Ukrainian supporters.

On the other hand, the fall of the Habsburg empire gave the west Ukrainians the opportunity to enter the fray. The Galicians set up their own West Ukrainian People's Republic (ZUNR) in

November 1918, which formally declared union with the UNR in Kiev in January 1919.[29] In its brief nine-month existence the ZUNR claimed sovereignty over all of Galicia east of the River San, Lemko Ukraine (the Przemyśl region of Poland and what is now the north-eastern corner of Slovakia around the city of Prešov), Transcarpathia and northern Bukovyna. However, the ZUNR was too busy defending itself against Polish armies (backed by France) to be of much assistance to the UNR, which, in turn, was now preoccupied with its own struggle against the Whites and the Bolsheviks.

The short and bitter war between the ZUNR and Poles was effectively over by July 1919, with the Poles also gaining the north-western territory of Volhynia. Polish control of the latter was agreed relatively quickly by first Poland and the UNR (the 1920 Warsaw Agreement) and then by the March 1921 Treaty of Riga between Poland and the Soviet Republics. The east Galician issue, however, dragged on until March 1923, when the Conference of Ambassadors of the Entente powers finally recognised Polish sovereignty over the region, although this was made subject to promises of Galician autonomy which were never kept (Poland signed the Minorities Treaty of June 1919 which in theory allowed any League of Nations member state to complain about Poland's treatment of the Ukrainians, and the Polish Sejm passed but never implemented a statute on self-government for eastern Galicia in September 1922).[30] On the other hand, the 1918–1919 Polish–Ukrainian war set the seal on the growth of Ukrainian nationalism in Galicia and the Ukrainians became distinctly reluctant citizens of the restored Polish state.

In Transcarpathia rival Hungarian, Czechoslovak, Ukrainian, Rusyn, Russian and Soviet councils were formed from November 1918 onwards, but a combination of internal factors and external circumstances settled the issue in favour of the new Czechoslovak state. The Ukrainian movement was weak and many Transcarpathians were prepared to view Czechoslovak rule with equanimity, if only for lack of a suitable alternative; the ZUNR committed troops for a few days in January 1919, but the arrival of Czechoslovak forces in April settled the issue. The region's incorporation into Czechoslovakia was recognised by the Treaty of St-Germain in September 1919, albeit once again with a promise to provide a degree of autonomy that remained largely unkept (gerrymandering and malapportionment also limited Transcarpathia's voice in Prague).[31] The Treaty of Trianon a year later confirmed the division of pre-war Hungary.

The Bukovynan Ukrainians on the other hand, like the Galicians, only succumbed to force of arms. A brief uprising in November 1918 sought to join the region to the UNR, but the latter was unable to commit any troops to resist the immediate Romanian invasion.[32] Romanian control was confirmed by the treaty of St-Germain in 1919 as a reward for its support for the Entente after 1916, just as Italy was rewarded for swapping sides with the gift of South Tyrol (Romania also gained Bessarabia which had a large Ukrainian population). After 1924 Romania abandoned Austria's tolerant pre-war policies and began a programme of forcible romanianisation, making life increasingly difficult for the local Ukrainian movement.

From the middle of 1919 therefore the Ukrainians in the east were left to struggle alone, although an alliance of convenience between Symon Petliura, the military commander of the Directory, and the Poles prolonged their struggle into 1920, and the Bolsheviks were still mopping up isolated pockets of resistance into the early 1920s.[33] Once the Western powers withdrew from the region and the Russian civil war as a whole turned in the Bolsheviks' favour, the UNR's defeat was inevitable. Moscow restored control over nearly all of 1914 tsarist Ukraine, losing only Volhynia to Poland. Crimea was made a separate autonomous republic in 1921.

Historians differ in their assessments of the events of 1917–1920 in Ukraine.[34] One school of thought claims that the upsurge in Ukrainian national consciousness in these years forced the Bolsheviks to concede the creation of the Ukrainian Soviet Socialist Republic and a federal USSR, and laid the basis for the Ukrainian revival of the 1920s and for the periodic outbreaks of 'national communism' thereafter.[35] Moreover, the federal settlement of 1922, although largely a fig-leaf for a highly centralised state throughout most of the Soviet period, left a ticking time-bomb that ultimately undermined the USSR in 1991 when the Union fell apart along federal fault-lines.

Others have argued that the great mass of the peasantry in Ukraine was fundamentally uninterested in the national question and simply wanted the land. Each individual village either made tactical alliances with whatever political and/or military force happened to come along, or tried to keep itself to itself.[36] A third set of explanations have stressed the *force majeure* of external circumstances in overwhelming the efforts of Ukrainian leaders and peasants alike.[37] Ukraine was trapped between the Great Powers and the Bolsheviks, and in the face of German withdrawal and Anglo-American indifference was no match for the better-organised Bolsheviks, who had inherited most of the resources of the former empire, including the crucial central urban-industrial and communications heartland.[38]

A compromise view is that the Ukrainians were 'marked by social and geographical divisions and a profound ambiguity in their national and class orientations'.[39] To a degree 'the ethnic and socio-economic grievances of the Ukrainian peasant proved mutually reinforcing and provided the foundation for a political movement which combined nationalism with a populist social programme'.[40] However, despite 'the momentary coincidence of peasant voters and Ukrainian populists' in the Constituent Assembly elections of 1917, the opportunity was missed as Ukrainian governments were unable to organise agrarian reform, and leaders and masses drifted apart.

The truth lies somewhere in between the second and last points of view. Galician Ukrainians were already overwhelmingly nationalist in 1914, but the international conjunction of forces in 1918–1919 prevented them from breaking away from a newly resurgent Poland (3.5 million Ukrainians were no match for over twenty million Poles). On the Russian side of the border a minority of Ukrainians were politicised by the events of 1917–1920, raising the first fleeting possibility in nearly three hundred years for the reunification of Ukrainian lands, but the majority remained staunchly apolitical and would only attain a national consciousness during the vastly different conditions of the Soviet period. Moreover, 1917–1920 confirmed the lop-sided nature of the Ukrainian movement, weak in the east and south and unable to displace powerful urban elites who remained loyal to the pre-1914 vision of fraternal unity between Russia and Ukraine.

Nevertheless, although an independent Ukrainian state failed to emerge in 1917–1920, the years of war and revolution had a profound impact on local geopolitics. First, some 4.4 million Ukrainians in Galicia and Volhynia were now under Polish rule, although the Polish–Ukrainian war of 1918–1919 had left the two bitter enemies.[41] Instead of a delicate tripartite balance under Habsburg protection, Galicia was now racked by direct Polish—

Ukrainian conflict. Despite the promises it had made in 1922 Poland began a programme of forcible polonisation, harassing Ukrainian organisations, closing Ukrainian schools and promoting mass Polish in-migration. However, the Polish 'pacification' campaign only increased the intensity of the Ukrainians' reactive nationalism,[42] and their long, often violent, campaign of protest served to undermine political stability and the prospects for parliamentary democracy in inter-war Poland. As a consequence, post-war Poland would be shifted to the west at Germany's expense.

Smaller and less troublesome Ukrainian minorities, just over 500,000 in each state, also disrupted internal politics in Czechoslovakia and to a lesser extent in Romania. In relatively liberal Czechoslovakia the local Ukrainian movement was able to catch up on some of the ground it had lost under Hungarian rule before 1918. In the wake of Hitler's dismemberment of Czechoslovakia a short-lived Carpatho-Ukrainian state would emerge in 1938–1939.[43] The Bukovynan Ukrainians on the other hand were now caught up in the Romanian nationalist project of *Romania Mare* (Greater Romania), with bitter consequences after 1940 (see below).

The most important consequence of 1917–1920, however, was that the reunification of Ukrainian lands was delayed for another generation, until 1939–1945. Without western Ukraine, the 'national communist' camp in the Ukrainian SSR was much weaker than it otherwise would have been. Although the struggle to 'ukrainianise' the Ukrainian SSR in the 1920s was largely defeated by external factors (namely the victory of Stalin and his faction in Moscow), in the absence of the Galicians the 'Ukrainian' element in the Communist Party of Ukraine (largely composed of rural and small-town elements, and leftovers from the left-wing Ukrainian parties who joined the Bolsheviks in 1919–1920) was in a minority, and was unable to prevail over the russophile faction based in the Donbas and the key urban centres.[44]

The Stalinist reaction in the 1930s destroyed most of the gains of the 1920s. The national Communists were repeatedly purged throughout the decade (as Lev Kopelev pointed out, in Ukraine 'the year 1937 began with the year 1933').[45] Moreover, collectivisation and the Great Famine of 1932–1933, during which an estimated five to six million died, broke the spirit of the Ukrainian peasantry and its capacity for social organisation.[46] The traditional 'national awakening' strategy of the Ukrainian intelligentsia was therefore undermined and in Soviet Ukraine political dissent now lay dormant until the 1960s, ceding the ground to the militant form of right-wing nationalism that in west Ukraine and émigré circles was beginning to displace the ideas of 1914.

The new generation of radical nationalists blamed the failure to form an independent and united Ukrainian state in 1917–1920 on the provincial 'Moscowcentrism' and feeble-mindedness of the Ukrainian intelligentsia, and its inability or unwillingness to match Bolshevik political and military resolution. In place of the liberal or socialist populism that had dominated the Ukrainian movement before 1917 they therefore proposed a voluntaristic form of Ukrainian fascism termed the 'nationalism of the deed' (*chynnyi natsionalizm*), the main vehicle for which was the Organisation of Ukrainian Nationalists (OUN), established at a congress in Vienna in 1929.[47] The OUN's original supporters were mainly war veterans and radical youth, but the simultaneous onset of the Great Depression and defeat of the Ukrainian national Communists in the USSR helped the ultra-nationalists to build a broader base of support among impoverished workers and peasants, increasingly disillusioned with the failure of moderate Ukrainian parties to obtain concessions from the Poles, Romanians and Czechs, and no longer attracted to the alternative national Communist model in the Ukrainian SSR.

The OUN gathered strength during its terrorist campaign against the Polish state in the 1930s, and eclipsed constitutional nationalism after the Soviet occupation of eastern Poland/western Ukraine in 1939–1941 destroyed most of traditional Ukrainian civil society and deprived 'moderate' politics of any practical future. Unlike the largely spontaneous attempt to establish Ukrainian independence in 1917–1920, the second effort that came in the wake of the German invasion of the USSR in 1941 was therefore largely organised and imported by an outside force, the OUN.[48] Moreover, from the beginning it was bound up more closely with foreign intervention, as ideological affinity, shared geopolitical interests and the need for organisational support had encouraged the OUN to make an alliance of convenience with Nazi Germany before 1941.[49]

In many respects the Second World War had just as important a legacy in Ukraine as the events of 1917–1920.[50] The human cost of the war was particularly traumatic for Ukraine, including industrial and urban devastation, the loss of 4.6 million dead (not including those who perished in the 1930s),[51] the removal of 2.3 million so-called *Ostarbeiter* to Germany, and the decimation of the pre-war Jewish, Polish and German communities.

The Second World War also had profound political effects. The first was the nationalist uprising in western Ukraine, which lasted from the mid-1940s until the mid-1950s. Units of the radical faction of the OUN entered Ukraine with the Wehrmacht in 1941 and in June issued a symbolic declaration of Ukrainian independence in the Galician capital of L'viv. However, the German occupation forces, whose support for the OUN in the 1930s had been largely tactical, proved much less tolerant of nationalist activity than in 1918 and promptly arrested the group's leaders. Although Alfred Rosenberg and others favoured a reprise of the policies of 1918 in order to help detach the non-Russian peoples from the USSR, Nazi racial theory had largely displaced visions of *Mitteleuropa* and Ukraine's role in the Nazi New Order was to be confined to the provision of labour, land and raw materials.[52] In a sense, therefore, the OUN got the worst of both worlds, tainted with accusations of collaboration with the Nazis in the early stages of the war, but deprived of its practical benefits (many west Ukrainians also served alongside German forces in the Nachtigall and Roland divisions, and later in the SS-*Galicia*;[53] others were accused of involvement in anti-semitic atrocities).[54]

Disillusion with Germany led west Ukrainians to take matters into their own hands.[55] In 1941–1942 informal guerrilla units emerged all over west Ukraine and in 1943 united to form the Ukrainian Insurgent Army (in Ukrainian UPA), which at its peak in late 1944 had an estimated 90,000 to 100,000 men under arms.[56] The UPA was primarily a military rather than a political organisation, but the OUN's influence on its leadership and tactics was considerable (hence in Ukraine the two are often bracketed together as the OUN–UPA). The UPA fought a long and bitter three-cornered campaign against Polish, German and Soviet troops until as late as the early 1950s, but despite the formation of a broad-based Ukrainian Supreme Liberation Council in 1944 and the OUN's adoption of a more moderate programme embracing democratic slogans and key aspects of Soviet welfarism,[57] the military uprising remained largely con-fined to western Ukraine. Unlike 1917–1920, conditions in east, south and central Ukraine allowed only the briefest of flowerings of Ukrainian nationalist activity before Soviet troops returned in 1943–1944. OUN activists spread far and wide, but there was no popular groundswell of support for the nationalist cause equivalent to that in 1917.

Whether fairly or not, the saga of the OUN–UPA has therefore further contributed to the psychological division between Ukrainian lands. Regardless of the actual historical complexities outlined above, in western Ukraine and among the central Ukrainian intelligentsia the OUN–UPA are lionised as national heroes,[58] while in the east and south they are denounced with equal vigour as pro-Nazi collaborators and the Red Army is still regarded as the true liberator of Ukraine.[59]

The final union of Ukrainian lands in the 1940s therefore came about on rather more difficult terms than for a time seemed possible in 1918–1919. Times had changed. The new united Ukraine emerged under Moscow's auspices, and the nationalist stronghold of Galicia was even more out of step with the rest of Ukraine than it had been in 1918–1919. On the other hand Stalin, like Bobrinskii in 1914–1915, was wrong to think that Galicia could be quietly incorporated into a docile Greater Ukraine. Although the relationship between western Ukraine and the rest of the Ukrainian SSR remained ambiguous and difficult, not only was the nationalist virus able to survive, but it could now spread more easily to the east.

The second main consequence of the war was the belated union of most ethnographic Ukrainian territory.[60] In fact Ukraine, as the Ukrainian SSR, was the biggest single territorial gainer from the Second World War. Most of the western territories whose Ukrainian population had attempted to join the UNR in 1918–1920 were now secured, and the territorial settlement was completed by the transfer of Crimea from the Russian SFSR to the Ukrainian SSR in 1954.

Poland lost both eastern Galicia and Volhynia to the Ukrainian SSR, although it retained some ethnically Ukrainian territory in what is now south-east Poland (the Chetm, Przemyśl and Lemko regions). Savage population exchanges resulted in the late 1940s. The Poles were nearly all expelled from the east, largely ending a history of settlement dating back to the thirteenth century, while Operation 'Vistula' in 1947 either forced Polish Ukrainians in the opposite direction or dispersed them to the western territories newly acquired from Germany.[61] After 1950 therefore Galicia and

Volhynia were even more ethnically Ukrainian than before. The traditional local conflict with the Poles was effectively over, as was the 'Jagellonian idea' of Polish hegemony in the east, and Russian–Ukrainian confrontation more starkly exposed. Moreover, the local Jewish community was almost wiped out in the war, and a one-off influx of Russian administrators in the late 1940s and early 1950s failed to develop into a long-run trend. Despite Stalin's attempts to extirpate Ukrainian nationalism by a brutal series of deportations and purges in 1944–1953,[62] and the exceptionally tight security grip on the region maintained by his successors,[63] Galicia emerged virtually unscathed as the leading centre of nationalist revival in the late 1980s. As in inter-war Poland, persecution only served to strengthen nationalist resolve.

Most of the rest of western Ukraine was also incorporated into the Ukrainian SSR as a result of the war, although separate paths of development since 1918 (and earlier) had left their mark; both Transcarpathia and to a lesser extent Bukovyna now lagged behind Galicia in their commitment to the national cause. The pursuit of *Romania Mare* led Romania to back the wrong side in the war (Romanian troops had occupied Ukraine as far as the River Buh in 1941–1943), but the attempt by Stalin to trim back Romanian territorial ambition was less successful than the similar treatment handed out to Poland. Many Romanians and Moldovans were expelled, but hundreds of thousands remained on what now became Soviet Ukrainian territory in northern Bukovyna and southern Bessarabia (the coastal lands between the Dniester and Danube rivers, an ethnic patchwork of Ukrainians, Romanians/ Moldovans, Bulgarians and Gagauz). Moreover, Stalinist gerrymandering turned northern Bukovyna into the artificial modern oblast of Chernivtsi by the addition of the traditionally Romanian counties of Hertsa and Khotyn to the east (southern Bukovyna remained a part of Romania). The Moldovan SSR was also a gerrymandered entity, and ethnic troubles would re-emerge in all three regions in the late 1980s.

Transcarpathia's brief period of quasi-statehood as the Carpatho-Ukrainian Republic in 1938–1939 was ended when Hungarian rule was restored with Hitler's blessing in March 1939. However, Hungary only had five years in which to renew the pre-1914 magyarisation campaign before the Red Army occupied the region in 1944–1945. Transcarpathia's transfer to the Ukrainian SSR was ratified by the 1945 Soviet–Czechoslovak Treaty (thereby ignoring the period of Hungarian reoccupation). All Transcar-pathians were now classed as Ukrainians and Rusyn organisa-tions were suppressed. Nevertheless, both a Rusyn and a Hungarian movement would re-emerge in the late 1980s (some-where between 100,000 and 200,000 Hungarians were left on the Ukrainian side of the border).

As argued above, the inclusion of western Ukraine in the Ukrainian polity had ambiguous effects. On the one hand, the nationalist faction in Ukrainian life was now much stronger than in the 1920s and Galicia continued to see itself in Messianic terms, dedicated to spreading the true national faith to the rest of Ukraine.[64] On the other hand, the psychological gulf between Galicia and the rest of Ukraine remained wide. Despite the efforts of post-war Ukrainian dissidents and modern-day nationalists to distance themselves from the legacy of the OUN, for many Ukrainians (as well as Russians in Ukraine) nationalism remains an alien creed. This is not to say that they are hostile to the idea of a Ukrainian nation-state, but that they would prefer it to have much closer relations with Russia than would the Galicians.

This profound duality in Ukrainian social and political life has only been partly overcome by the dramatic social upheavals of the twentieth century and the long-term effect of the creation of the Ukrainian SSR. At the turn of the century the social structure of Ukraine was a multi-ethnic mosaic. The towns, as previously noted, were dominated by Russians, Jews and Poles, and although the surrounding countryside was mostly occupied by Ukrainian peasants, Polish landowners and Jewish middlemen were a prominent social force west of the Dnieper. To the east Russian and Ukrainian settlement intermingled to the extent that there was no clear ethnographic boundary between the two groups. Islands of German, Russian and other minority settlement existed throughout Ukraine, particularly in the south on the Black Sea coast where Crimean Tatars, Greeks, Bulgarians and Gagauz lived alongside Ukrainians and Russians.

However, the years since the First World War have drastically simplified the social structure in Ukraine. Minority populations have dropped considerably, with Ukraine's traditional Polish, German and Jewish minorities disappearing almost completely (although some 260,000 of the Crimean Tatars deported by Stalin *en masse* in 1944 returned to the peninsula in the early 1990s).[65] Furthermore, the ingathering of Ukrainian lands in 1939–1945 and the gradual penetration of the cities by ethnic Ukrainians has made Ukraine more Ukrainian, both in percentage terms and through the gradual transfer of traditional Ukrainian culture from rural to urban areas. On the other hand, the Russian population in Ukraine has continued to grow, encouraged by post-war resettlement programmes, ethnic proximity and the continued predominance of Russian language and culture in the cities outside of western Ukraine. There were 3.2 million Russians in Ukraine in 1926, but by 1959 their number had grown to 7.1 million, rising to 11.4 million by 1989.[66] The multi-ethnic Ukraine of 1897 had become a bi-ethnic (Ukrainian and Russian) society by 1989.[67]

More accurately, however, Ukraine is a bilingual society, split as much by linguistic as by ethnic divides. The brief ukrainianisation campaign of the 1920s was first stopped in the early 1930s, and then reversed in the post-war period. Outside of western Ukraine, Ukrainian cultural institutions went into sharp decline. By the 1950s the Ukrainian-language school had largely disappeared from the cities of eastern and southern Ukraine, and by the 1980s it was disappearing from many urban areas in central Ukraine too. The apparent numerical predominance of Ukrainian schools (73.6 per cent in 1989) masked the fact the majority of these were rural schools with low enrolment. In terms of the total number of pupils, only 47.5 per cent studied at Ukrainian schools in 1989.[68] Ukrainian media, including radio, television, press and publishing has also declined in relative and even absolute importance.[69] As late as 1993 the percentage of Ukrainian-language books in circulation in Ukraine was still only 35.6 per cent.[70]

The ethnic Ukrainian population, peasant and parochial in 1917, has undoubtedly strongly increased its levels of social mobilisation in the twentieth century and begun to develop a wider sense of identity.[71] However, without the influence of west Ukraine until 1945 and with Ukrainian cultural institutions on the retreat after the 1930s, Ukrainian peasants were entering an urban environment that was less Ukrainian than it otherwise would have been. Undoubtedly, the events of 1917–1920 and the creation of the Ukrainian SSR encouraged many to identify with Ukraine as their homeland. Stalin's insistence that the Ukrainian SSR become a founder member of the UN and its satellite organisations also provided important symbolic and status gains for Ukrainian nationalists.[72] Evidence for this proposition is provided by the millions of Ukrainians left outside the Ukrainian SSR by the borders established in the 1920s,[73] increasing numbers of whom identified themselves (or were identified) as Russians in subsequent censuses.[74]

On the other hand many peasants entering the cities for the first time seemed to have leapt straight from a parochial to a Soviet consciousness, rather than developing a Ukrainian identity, or have combined elements of local, Ukrainian, Russian and Soviet identities. The 'Eurasian' idea first formulated in the 1920s[75] – that Ukraine and Russia are naturally part of the same cultural and geopolitical space – has therefore continued to attract adherents among ethnic (or 'passport') Ukrainians, as well as among ethnic Russians living in Ukraine.[76] This orientation is not just, as Ukrainian nationalists would claim, the artificial result of forcible 'russification'[77] under both the Romanovs and the Soviets, although the brief flowering of Ukrainian language and culture in the 1920s was undoubtedly only brought to an end by coercive means. Rather, it is the not entirely surprising by-product of the 'ethnographic mass' of 1914 becoming socially mobilised under conditions in which Ukrainian culture and historical memory were stigmatised, and access to both highly restricted.[78] Moreover, the 'Little Russian' intellectual and social tradition in Ukraine, which overlaps considerably with the Eurasian world-view, has deep historical roots going back to at least the eighteenth century.

As a result, the Soviet census of 1989 reported that 33 per cent of the total population in Ukraine considered Russian to be their 'mother tongue' (*ridna mova* in Ukrainian, *rodnoi yazyk* in Russian). This figure included some 4.5 million ethnic Ukrainians out of a total of 37.4 million (12.2 per cent of all Ukrainians).[79] However, this is most probably a considerable underestimate, as 'mother tongue' is a highly ambiguous term, not necessarily indicating language of preference (possible meanings might include language spoken at birth, language spoken by parents or ancestors, language of psychological identification and so on). More recent survey data indicates that in terms of language of preference, because of the millions of ethnic Ukrainians who remain linguistically and culturally 'russified', Ukraine is effectively a bilingual society, split almost equally down the middle.[80] Moreover, this division tends to coincide with the historical divide between western and central Ukraine (at least on the Right Bank of the

Dnieper) on the one hand, and eastern and southern Ukraine on the other. This historical and ethno-regional legacy has meant that nationalist policies do not easily command majority support. The victory of the left parties in the parliamentary elections in spring 1994 and Leonid Kuchma in the presidential election later the same year confirmed the lessons of previous elections in 1989–1990 that the balance of political gravity in Ukraine lies more to the east than the west.[81]

Although Ukraine won its independence in exceptionally favourable circumstances in 1991, significant question marks remain about its future as an independent state. In contrast to both 1914–1920 and 1939–1945 Ukraine's western border is now reasonably secure. Poland seems reconciled to the loss of its eastern territories, and many Poles see a strong Ukraine as a useful bulwark against Russia. Moreover, the division of the Czech and Slovak republics and good relations between Ukraine and Hungary thanks to mutual enmity towards Romania has helped to confine any threat to Transcarpathia to marginal nationalist groups and émigré Rusyn circles. On the other hand, although the Second World War scotched the Jagellonian idea of a 'Greater Poland' to the east, it did not put an end to dreams of *Romania Mare*, and relations with Romania remain bedevilled by the issues of northern Bukovyna and southern Bessarabia.[82]

Nevertheless, the main threat to Ukrainian identity and security comes from the east. Not only have many Russians still to be reconciled to the idea of Ukraine as an independent nation-state, but Ukraine itself is divided internally. While Ukrainian nationalists seek a 'return to Europe', a substantial minority of the Ukrainian population, including millions of russophone Ukrainians, sees Ukraine as naturally part of a common 'Eurasian space' in close alliance with Russia if not actually part of the same state.[83] The 1994 Ukrainian elections demonstrated that Ukraine has yet to shake off this particular legacy of the past, as clear in the mid-1990s as it was in 1917–1920.

NOTES

1 Dominique Arel and Andrew Wilson, 'The Ukrainian parliamentary elections', and 'Ukraine under Kuchma: back to "Eurasia"?', *RFE/RL Research Report*, 1994, vol. 3, nos 26 and 32 (1 July and 19 August).

2   I am grateful to Dominique Arel for his first formulation of this problem. I would also like to thank George O. Liber for his helpful comments on an earlier draft of this chapter. Some of the themes raised in this chapter are covered in more detail in my *Ukrainian Nationalism in the 1990s: a minority faith*, Cambridge: Cambridge University Press, 1996, especially chs 1 and 2.

3   On Ukraine in the early twentieth century, see Orest Subtelny, *Ukraine: a history* (second edn), Toronto: University of Toronto Press, 1994, chs 16 to 19; I. Nahaievs'kyi, *Istoriia ukraïns'koï derzhavy dvadtsiatoho stolittia*, Kiev: Ukraïns'kyi pys'mennyk, 1993; and Taras Hunchak, *Ukraïna persha polovyna XX stolittia*, Kiev: Lybid', 1993. ('Hunchak' is a transliteration from Ukrainian; 'Hunczak' is an anglicised version of the same name.)

4   Russia won control of central Ukraine east of the Dnieper in 1654, conquered most of the east and south in the second half of the eighteenth century, and acquired central Ukraine west of the Dnieper in the final partitions of Poland in 1793–95. West Ukraine (Galicia and Bukovyna) had been under Austrian rule since 1772–74, and Transcarpathia under the Hungarian crown since the eleventh century.

5   Rudolf A. Mark, 'Social questions and national revolution: the Ukrainian National Republic in 1919–1920', *Harvard Ukrainian Studies*, 1990, vol. xiv, nos 1/2 (June), pp.113–31, at p.116.

6   Bohdan Krawchenko, 'The social structure of Ukraine in 1917', in ibid., pp.97–112, at p.106.

7   L.I. Yevselevs'kyi and S.Ya. Faryna, *Prosvita v Naddniprians'kii Ukraïni*, Kiev: Prosvita, 1993, p.10.

8   George O. Liber, *Soviet nationality policy, urban growth, and identity change in the Ukrainian SSR 1923–1934*, Cambridge: Cambridge University Press, 1992, p.12. Krawchenko, *op. cit.*, p.100, gives a figure of 30 per cent.

9   See the following studies: Michael F. Hamm, *Kiev: a portrait, 1800–1917*, Princeton: Princeton University Press, 1993; Patricia Herlihy, *Odessa: a history 1794–1914*, Cambridge, MA: Harvard Ukrainian Research Institute, 1986; and Theodore H. Friedgut, *Iuzovka and Revolution – Volume 2 – Politics and Revolution in Russia's Donbass, 1869–1924*, Princeton: Princeton University Press, 1994.

10 Heorhii Kas'ianov, *Ukraïns'ka inteligentsiia na rubezhi XIX–XX stolit': sotsial'no-politychyi portret*, Kiev: Lybid', 1993, p.68.

11 Andreas Kappeler, 'The Ukrainians of the Russian Empire, 1860–1914', in A. Kappeler (ed.), *The Formation of National Elites*, New York: New York University Press, 1992, pp.105–32.

12 Kas'ianov, *op. cit.*, pp.49–69. See also S. I. Bilokin' et al., *Narysy istoriï Ukraïns'koï inteligentsiï (persha polovyna XX st.)*, three vols, Kiev: Academy of Sciences, 1994.

13 Andrei S. Markovits and Frank E. Sysyn (eds), *Nationbuilding and the Politics of Nationalism. Essays on Austrian Galicia*, Edmonton: Canadian Institute of Ukrainian Studies (hereafter CIUS), 1982; and John-Paul Himka, *Galician Villagers and the Ukrainian National Movement in the Nineteenth Century*, New York: St Martin's Press, 1988. Where there

is no risk of ambiguity the text will refer simply to 'Galicia' rather than to 'eastern Galicia'.

14 See Paul Robert Magocsi, *The Shaping of a National Identity: Subcarpathian Rus' 1848–1948*, London: Harvard University Press, 1978, for the Rusyn point of view. For the Ukrainian side, see Ivan L. Rudnytsky, 'Carpatho-Ukraine: a people in search of their history', in Ivan L. Rudnytsky, *Essays in Modern Ukrainian History*, Edmonton: CIUS, 1987, pp.353–73.

15 Myroslav Shkandrij, *Modernists, Marxists and the Nation. The Ukrainian literary discussion of the 1920s*, Edmonton and Toronto: CIUS, 1992, p.3.

16 'Little Russian' was the standard term for Ukrainians in the Russian empire at the time, accepted by Ukrainians as well as Russians until late in the nineteenth century. See Zenon E. Kohut, 'The development of a Little Russian identity and Ukrainian nationbuilding', *Harvard Ukrainian Studies*, 1986, vol. 10, pp.559–76.

17 Hunchak, *op. cit.*, p.60. In the 1860s and 1870s the russophile movement was if anything the stronger of the two, given the power and prestige of the Russian empire and its firm anti-Polish stance at a time when the Austrians temporarily seemed to be favouring the Poles. However, the social conservatism of the russophiles and their insistence on using 'high' literary Russian gradually alienated them from the broad mass of the Ukrainian peasantry, who tended to prefer the ukrainophiles' co-operative socialism and more comprehensible propaganda. Austrian repression of the russophiles also played a role, as did growing awareness of how Ukrainians were treated on the Russian side of the border.

18 Ivan L. Rudnytsky, 'Trends in modern Ukrainian political thought', and 'The intellectual origins of modern Ukraine', in Rudnytsky, 1987, *op. cit.*, pp.91–141. For a critique of the view that the catalysts for the creation of the UNR were largely foreign rather than domestic, see Roman Szporluk's review of Hunczak, 1977, in *The Annals of the Ukrainian Academy of Arts and Sciences in the United States*, 1978–1980, vol. 14.

19 Friedgut, 1994, *op. cit.*, chs 8 and 9. Cf. Rex A. Wade, 'Ukrainian nationalism and "Soviet power": Kharkiv 1917', in Bohdan Krawchenko (ed.), *Ukrainian Past, Ukrainian Present*, London: Macmillan, 1992, pp.70–83.

20 Steven L. Guthier, 'The popular basis of Ukrainian nationalism in 1917', *Slavic Review*, 1979, vol. 38, no. 1, pp.30–47, at pp.37–9. No figures were available for Taurida.

21 I.L. Hoshuliak, 'Pro prychyny porazky Tsentral'noï Rady', *Ukraïns'kyi istorychnyi zhurnal*, 1994, no. 1, pp.31–44, at pp.36–7.

22 Arthur E. Adams, 'The great Ukrainian jacquerie', in Taras Hunczak (ed.), *The Ukraine, 1917–1921: a study in revolution*, Cambridge, MA: Harvard Ukrainian Research Institute, 1977, pp.247–70, at pp.259–60.

23 S.M. Horak, *The First Peace Treaty of World War 1. Ukraine's treaty with the Central Powers of February 9, 1918*, Boulder: East European Mono-

graphs, 1988; and Paul Robert Magocsi (ed.), *Texts of the Ukraine 'Peace'*, Cleveland: John T. Zubal Inc., 1981.

24   Paul Robert Magocsi, *Ukraine: a historical atlas*, Toronto: University of Toronto Press, 1985, pp.20–1. Skoropads'kyi later attempted to claim all Ukrainian ethnographic territory, that is including marginal Cossack lands to the east and south (Starodub, parts of Kursk and Voronezh and the area around Tahanrih and Rostov-on-Don).

25   Oleh S. Fedyshyn, *Germany's Drive to the East and the Ukrainian Revolution, 1917–1918*, New Brunswick: Rutgers University Press, 1971.

26   Taras Hunczak, 'The Ukraine under Hetman Pavlo Skoropads'kyi', in Hunczak, 1977, *op. cit.*, pp.61–81.

27   Peter Borowsky, 'Germany's Ukrainian policy during World War I and the Revolution of 1918–19', in Hans-Joachim Torke and John-Paul Himka (eds), *German–Ukrainian Relations in Historical Perspective*, Edmonton: CIUS, 1994, pp.84–94, at p.92. See also Vadym Levandovs'kyi, 'Ukraine in geopolitical concepts in the first third of the 20th century', *Political Thought*, Kiev, 1994, no. 3, pp.174–184; and S.V. Kul'chyts'kyi, 'Ukraïns'ka derzhava chasiv Het'manshchyna', *Ukraïns'kyi istorychnyi zhurnal*, 1992, nos 7/8, pp.60–79 at p.79, who denies that Skoropads'kyi's regime was 'a puppet collaborationist government'.

28   Jaroslav Pelenski, 'Hetman Pavlo Skoropads'kyi and Germany (1917–18) as reflected in his memoirs', in Torke and Himka (eds), *op. cit.*, pp.69–83, at p.77.

29   O.Yu. Karpenko, 'Lystopadova 1918r. Natsional'no-demokratychna revolutsiia na zakhidnoukraïns'kykh zemliakh', *Ukraïns'kyi istorychnyi zhurnal*, 1993, no. 1, pp.16–28.

30   Bohdan Budurowycz, 'Poland and the Ukrainian problem', *Canadian Slavonic Papers*, 1983, vol. XXV, no. 4 (December), pp.473–500.

31   Magocsi, 1978, *op. cit.*, pp.76–102. Magocsi argues that internal factors and Czechoslovak military force were decisive, not the diplomatic manoeuvrings among the Rusyn diaspora that produced the so-called 'Philadelphia agreement'; ibid., p.389, n. 40.

32   I.M. Nowosiwsky, *Bukovinan Ukrainians: a historical background. Their struggle for self-determination in 1918*, New York: Shevchenko Scientific Society, 1970.

33   Bohdan Nahaylo, 'Ukrainian national resistance in Soviet Ukraine during the 1920s', *Journal of Ukrainian Studies*, 1990, vol. 15, no. 2 (Winter), pp.1–18.

34   Two useful historiographical surveys are: Mark von Hagen, 'The dilemmas of Ukrainian independence and statehood, 1917–1921', *Harriman Institute Forum*, 1994, vol. 7, no. 5 (January); and I.L. Hoshuliak, 'Pro prychyny porazky Tsentralnoï Rady', *Ukraïns'kyi istorychnyi zhurnal*, 1994, no. 1, pp.31–44.

35   James E. Mace, *Communism and the Dilemmas of National Liberation: national communism in the Soviet Ukraine, 1918–1933*, Cambridge, MA: Harvard University Press, 1983; and John S. Reshetar, Jr, 'The

Ukrainian Revolution in retrospect', *Canadian Slavonic Papers*, 1968, vol. 10, pp.116–32.

36   John Reshetar, *The Ukrainian Revolution, 1917–1920: a study in nationalism*, Princeton: Princeton University Press, 1952; Adams, 1977, *op. cit.*, pp.247–70; and Mark, 1990, *op. cit.*.

37   Geoff Ely, 'Remapping the nation: war, revolutionary upheaval and state formation in Eastern Europe, 1914–1923', in Peter J. Potichnyj and Howard Aster (eds), *Ukrainian–Jewish Relations in Historical Perspective*, Edmonton: CIUS, 1988, pp.205–46.

38   David Saunders, 'Britain and the Ukrainian question, 1919–1920', *The English Historical Review*, 1988, vol. 103, pp.40–68; and Constantine Warvariv, 'America and the Ukrainian national cause', in Hunczak, 1977, *op. cit.*, pp.352–81.

39   Ronald Grigor Sumy, *The Revenge of the Past: nationalism, revolution and the collapse of the Soviet Union*, Stanford: Stanford University Press, 1993, p.30.

40   Guthier, 1979, *op. cit.*, p.32.

41   Budurowycz, 1983, *op. cit.*; and John-Paul Himka, 'Western Ukraine in the interwar period', *Nationalities Papers*, 1994, vol. 22, no. 2 (Fall), pp.347–63.

42   M. Shvahuliak, *'Patsyfikatsiia': pol's'ka represyvna aktsiia u Halychyni 1930 r. i ukraïns'ka suspil'nist'*, L'viv: Kryp''akevych Institute, 1993.

43   Magocsi, 1978, *op. cit.*, pp.234–49.

44   V.A. Hrechenko, 'Do istoriï vnutripartiinoï borot'by v Ukraïni u 20-ti roky', *Ukraïns'kyi istorychnyi zhurnal*, 1993, no. 9, pp.114–21; Yurii I. Shapoval, *Ukraïna 20–50-kh rokiv: storinky nenapysanoï istoriï*, Kiev: Naukova dumka, 1993, chs 1 and 2. See also Mace, 1983, *op. cit.*; Liber, 1992, *op. cit.*; V.M. Danylenko, H.V. Kas'ianov, and S.V. Kul'chyts'kyi, *Stalinizm na Ukraïni: 20-30-ti roky*, Kiev: Lybid' in association with CIUS, 1991, §1.

45   Liber, 1992, *op. cit.*, p.159. On the purges, see Shapoval, 1993, *op. cit.*, pp.149–222; 'Stalinizm i Ukraïna', *Ukraïns'kyi istorychnyi zhurnal*, 1991 and 1992 *passim*; and *Liudyna i systema (shtrykhy do portretu totalitarnoï doby v Ukraïni*, Kiev: Academy of Sciences, 1994; Heorhii Kas'ianov, *Ukraïns'ka inteligentsiia 1920-Kh–1930-Kh rokiv: sotsial'nyi portret ta istorychna dolia*, Kiev: Globus, 1992; and V.M. Danylenko *et al.*, *op. cit.*, pp.306–21.

46   On the famine, see Robert Conquest, *The Harvest of Sorrow: Soviet collectivisation and the Terror Famine*, London: Hutchinson, 1986; S.V. Kul'chyts'kyi and Serhii Maksudov, 'Vtraty naselennia Ukraïny vid holodu 1933 r.', *Ukraïns'kyi istorychnyi zhurnal*, 1991, no. 2, pp.3–10; and S.V. Kul'chyts'kyi (ed.), *Kolektyvizatsiia i holod na Ukraïni. Zbirnyk dokumentiv i materialiv*, Kiev: Naukova dumka, 1992. Serhii Pirozhkov, 'Population loss in Ukraine in the 1930s and the 1940s', in Krawchenko (ed.), *op. cit.*, pp.84–96, at p.89, cites a total figure of 5.8 million 'direct and indirect' deaths from the famine and the purges in the 1930s.

47   Alexander J. Motyl, *The Turn to the Right. The ideological origins and development of Ukrainian nationalism 1919–1929*, Boulder: East European Monographs, 1980; Zinovii Knysh, *Stanovlennia OUN*, Kiev:

Oleny Telihy, 1994; and Oleh Bahan, *Natsionalizm i natsionalistychnyi rukh: istoriia ta ideï*, Drohobych: Vidrodzhennia, 1994.

48   The best work on wartime nationalism remains John A. Armstrong, *Ukrainian Nationalism*, Englewood, CO: Ukrainian Academic Press, second edn, 1990.

49   The OUN was not itself a Nazi party. Its ideology was eclectic and attuned to specific Ukrainian circumstances, and its origins owed more to Italian fascism than to nazism.

50   Yurii Boshyk (ed.), *Ukraine during World War Two: history and its aftermath*, Edmonton: CIUS, 1986; and David R. Marples, *Stalinism in Ukraine in the 1940s*, London: Macmillan, 1992.

51   Pirozhkov in Krawchenko (ed.), *op. cit.*, p.93. Taras Hunczak, 'Between two leviathans: Ukraine during the Second World War', in ibid., pp.97–106, at p.104, gives a round figure of ten million for war deaths.

52   Ihor Kamenetsky, 'German colonisation plans in Ukraine during World Wars I and II', and John A. Armstrong, 'Ukraine: colony or partner?', in Torke and Himka (eds), *op. cit.*, pp.95–109 and 187–99.

53   Peter J. Potichnyj, 'Ukrainians in World War II military formations: an overview', and Myroslav Yurkevich, 'Galician Ukrainians in German military formations and in the German administration', in Boshyk (ed.), 1986, *op. cit.*, pp.61–6 and 68–87, argue that the Ukrainian units were more or less autonomous. See also the revisionist history, Mykhailo Slaboshpyts'kyi and Valerii Stetsenko (eds), *Ukraïns'ka dyviziia 'Halychyna'*, Kiev and Toronto: Visti z Ukraïny, 1994.

54   B.F. Sabrin, *Alliance for Murder: The Nazi–Ukrainian nationalist partnership in genocide*, New York: Sarpedon/Shapolsky, 1991, is polemical. Aharon Weiss, 'Jewish–Ukrainian relations in Western Ukraine during the Holocaust', in Potichnyj (ed.), 1988, *op. cit.*, pp.409–20; and Taras Hunczak, 'Ukrainian–Jewish relations during the Soviet and Nazi occupations', in Boshyk (ed.), 1986, *op. cit.*, pp.39–57 presents the case for and against Ukrainian anti-semitism.

55   Peter J. Potichnyj, 'The Ukrainian Insurgent Army (UPA) and the German authorities', and Taras Hunczak, 'OUN–German relations, 1941–5', in Torke and Himka (eds), *op. cit.*, pp.163–77 and 178–86.

56   Ustina Markus, *Soviet Counterinsurgency: the guerrilla wars in the Western Republics*, Ph.D. thesis, LSE, University of London, 1992, p.61.

57   Armstrong, 1990, *op. cit.*, *passim*; Peter J. Potichnyj and Y. Shtendera, *Political Thought of the Ukrainian Underground 1943–51*, Edmonton: CIUS, 1986.

58   Stepan Mechnyk, *U vyri voiennoho lykholittia: OUN i UPA u borot'bi z hitlerivs'kymy okupantamy*, L'viv: Krai, 1992; and Bohdan Zalizniak (ed.), *Zdaleka pro blyz'ke*, L'viv: Memorial, 1992. For examples of material in the nationalist press, see Borys Tymoshenko, 'Bilyi tsvit chornyts', abo pravda pro natsionalistiv', in the Republican Party's *Samostiina Ukraïna*, 1991, no. 11 (August); and 'OUN–UPA v dokumentakh', in the Democratic Party's *Volia*, 1991, nos 13–14 (August).

59   Attacks on the OUN–UPA are equally common in anti-nationalist literature in eastern and southern Ukraine. See, for example, P.

Neprych, 'Oberezhno: fashyzm!', *Tovarysh* (the central paper of the Socialist Party of Ukraine), 1992, no. 4 (June); or Nikolai Spiridov, 'Grozit li nam fashizm?', *Nash Donbass*, 1993 (January).

60 Areas still regarded by many Ukrainian nationalists as part of Ukraine's natural 'ethnographic territory' include south-east Poland, the Prešov region in north-east Slovakia, the area around Brest in south-west Belarus, Starodub and parts of the Voronezh, Tahanrih and Kuban' regions in south-west Russia. See for example F.D. Zastavnyi, *Ukraïns'ki etnichni zemli*, L'viv: Svit, 1993; and Volodymyr Serhiichuk, *Ukraïntsi v imperiï*, Kiev: Biblioteka Ukraïntsia, 1992, no. 3.

61 Halyna Shcherba, 'Deportatsiï naselennia z pol's'ko-ukraïns'koho pohranychchia 40-x rokiv', in S. Holovko (ed.), *Ukraïna-Pol'shcha: istorychna spadshchyna i suspil'na svidomist'*, Kiev and Przemyśl: Lybid', 1993, pp.248–55.

62 Markus, *op. cit.*, chs 3 and 7.

63 Heorhii Kas'ianov, ' "Sprava yuristiv" ta inshi: zvorotnyi bik "vidlyhy" ', *Vyzvol'nyi shliakh*, 1993 (December), pp.1497–505.

64 Yaroslav Bilinsky, 'The incorporation of Western Ukraine and its impact on politics and society in Soviet Ukraine', in Roman Szporluk (ed.), *The Influence of Eastern Europe and the Soviet West on the USSR*, New York: Praeger, 1975, pp.180–228; and Roman Szporluk, 'The strange politics of Lviv: an essay in search of an explanation', in Zvi Gitelman (ed.), *The Politics of Nationality and the Erosion of the USSR*, London: Macmillan, 1992, pp.215–31.

65 Andrew Wilson, *The Crimean Tatars*, London: International Alert, 1994, p.37. The number of Poles on Ukrainian lands has fallen from 2.2 million in the 1920s to 219,000 in 1989; V.I. Naulko, *Razvitie mezhetnicheskikh sviazei na Ukraine*, Kiev: Naukova dumka, 1975, p.64. There were 2.68 million Jews living on what is now Ukrainian territory in 1897 (9.3 per cent of the total population), and 2.72 million in the late 1920s. A mere 490,000 (0.9 per cent) were left in 1989, and emigration to Israel in the early 1990s has further reduced the total; Volodymyr Kubijovyc and Vasyl' Markus, 'Jews', in Kubijovyc (ed.), *Encyclopaedia of Ukraine*, vol. II, Toronto: University of Toronto Press, 1988, pp.385–93. A total of 434,000 Germans lived in Soviet Ukraine (plus Crimea) in 1926, and 136,000 in western Ukraine. Only 38,000 were left in 1989; Volodymyr Kubijovyc, 'Germans', in Kubijovyc, *op. cit.*, pp.46–7.

66 B. Kravtsiv, V. Kubijovyc, M. Prokop and A. Zhukovsky, 'Russians in Ukraine', in Danylo Husar Struk (ed.), *Encyclopaedia of Ukraine*, vol. IV, Toronto: University of Toronto Press, 1993, pp.461–8, at p.465. See also Bohdan Krawchenko, 'Ethno-demographic trends in Ukraine in the 1970s', in Krawchenko (ed.), *Ukraine After Shelest*, Edmonton: CIUS, 1983, pp.101–19; Roman Szporluk, 'Russians in Ukraine and problems of Ukrainian identity in the USSR', in Peter J. Potichnyi (ed.), *Ukraine in the 1970s*, Oakville: Mosaic Press, 1975, pp.195–217; and Roman Szporluk, 'Urbanization in Ukraine since the Second World War', in Ivan L. Rudnytsky (ed.), *Rethinking Ukrainian History*, Edmonton: CIUS, 1981, pp.180–202.

67   The one universal tsarist census was held in 1897; the last Soviet census in 1989.

68   Dominique Arel, *Language and the Politics of Ethnicity: the case of Ukraine*, Ph.D. thesis, University of Illinois at Urbana-Champaign, 1993, ch. 4, esp. pp.160 and 169.

69   Roman Solchanyk, 'Language politics in the Ukraine', in Isabelle T. Kriendler (ed.), *Sociolinguistic Perspectives on Soviet National Languages*, Berlin: Mouton de Gruyter, 1985, pp.57–105; and Oleksa Myshanych, 'Ukraïns'ka literatura pid zaboronoiu; 1937–1990', *Literaturna Ukraïna*, 18 August 1994.

70   Les' Taniuk, 'Prezydentovi Ukraïny L. M. Kravchuku', *Literaturna Ukraïna*, 18 November 1993.

71   Bohdan Krawchenko, *Social Change and National Consciousness in Twentieth Century Ukraine*, Oxford: St Anthony's/Macmillan, 1985; 'The impact of industrialisation on the social structure of Ukraine', *Canadian Slavonic Papers*, 1980, vol. XXII, no. 3 (September), pp.338–57; and Wsevolod Isajiw, 'Urban migration and social change in contemporary Soviet Ukraine', *Canadian Slavonic Papers*, 1980, vol. XXII, no. 1 (March), pp.58–86.

72   Ivan L. Rudnytsky, 'Soviet Ukraine in historical perspective', in Rudnytsky, 1987, *op. cit.*, pp.463–75.

73   As Ukrainian and Russian settlement areas substantially overlapped, the border between the Russian and Ukrainian republics was adjusted several times in the 1920s. B.D. Boiechko, O.I. Hanzha and B.I. Zakharchuk, 'Kordoni Ukraïny: istoriia ta problemy formuvannia (1917–1940 rr.)', *Ukraïns'kyi istorychnyi zhurnal*, 1992, no. 1, pp.56–77.

74   Robert J. Kaiser, *The Geography of Nationalism in Russia and the USSR*, Princeton: Princeton University Press, 1994, p.142.

75   On the development of the 'Eurasian' idea, largely by Russian émigrés in the 1920s, see Nicholas V. Riasanovsky, *The Emergence of Eurasianism*, Berkeley: University of California Press, 1967; and Riasanovsky's article of the same name in *Californian Slavic Studies*, 1967, no. 4, pp.39–72.

76   See the exchange of views between Rudnytsky and Holobnichy in the *Journal of Ukrainian Graduate Studies*, 1977, no. 3, and 1978, no. 4. The verification of this proposition is more properly a task for sociologists, but the results of the 1994 elections strongly suggest that this is the case. See note 1 above.

77   The term 'russified' is itself contentious, as it implies a previous or more 'natural' Ukrainian orientation.

78   Kas'ianov, 1993, *op. cit.*, p.45. See also Kenneth Farmer, *Ukrainian Nationalism in the Post-Stalin Era: myths, symbols and ideology in Soviet nationality policy*, The Hague: Martinus Nijhoff, 1980.

79   Arel, 1993, *op. cit.*, p.122.

80   Valeri Khmelko and Andrew Wilson, 'The political orientations of different regions and ethno-linguistic groups in Ukraine since independence', due for publication in 1996.

81   On the 1990 elections, see Dominique Arel, 'The parliamentary blocs in the Ukrainian Supreme Soviet: who and what do they represent?',

Journal of Soviet Nationalities, 1990–1991, vol. 1, no. 4 (Winter), pp.108–54. On the December 1991 polls, see Peter J. Potichnyj, 'The referendum and presidential elections in Ukraine', *Canadian Slavonic Papers*, 1992, vol. 33, no. 2, pp.123–38.

82 Vladimir Socor, 'Annexation of Bessarabia and Northern Bukovina [sic] condemned by Romania', *Report on the USSR*, RL 256/91, 19 July 1991.

83 For a more in-depth analysis, see Wilson, 1996, *op. cit.*, ch. 7.

Chapter 8

The Baltic states

Ken Ward

> Concepts of nationality are the products of historical change not the reflections of historical continuity.[1]

The concept of ethnicity has been an important issue in the debate on the character of nationalism since it is fundamentally concerned with national identity and national feeling. The link between ethnicity and political status arose from the movement towards national self-determination in European societies and the development of nation-states in the late nineteenth and twentieth centuries. In the course of this process many came to believe that ethnicity was a biological attribute, immutable and exclusive to the group sharing the same genetic characteristics and providing the basis of a national identity. Such a deterministic approach, with its emphasis on biological factors, provided a simplistic explanation of ethnic difference and its very simplicity offered an attractive solution to what was and continues to be a much more complex problem.

This emphasis on ethnicity as a 'racial' attribute was used to explain the superiority and inclusivity of a group, while excluding those who might claim, or seem to exhibit, a different racial outlook. The most extreme case of this was the anti-semitic stance of National Socialism in Germany which was embodied in government legislation between 1933 and 1945. The National Socialist regime argued that the German state and German nation were co-terminous and anyone defined by the state as a Jew could be neither a member of the German nation nor a German citizen. The Holocaust was the culmination of this extreme definition of ethnicity.

Such an approach took no account of the complex ways in

which ethnicity might be determined from within a group, rather than defined from outside. The most important aspect of ethnic identity is the creation, in the words of Anthony D. Smith, of a 'cultural collectivity' based upon social memory, myth, language and forms of common cultural practice, particularly religion.[2] Populations become aware of those elements which they have in common, and not only value them but positively use them to strengthen the sense of community. This approach, with its emphasis on the role of history as the interpreter of change is particularly appropriate for a study of the Baltic peoples – Lithuanians, Latvians and Estonians – whose development as national communities has continuously been predicated upon a dialogue between the past and the present. This is not an unusual occurrence, as will be clear from a study of many other national groupings, but it has been particularly important for small populations seeking to sustain a separate identity while confronted by more powerful economic and political entities.

Smith suggests six attributes of an ethnic community: a collective proper name, a myth of common ancestry, shared historical memories, one or more elements of a common culture, an association with a specific homeland, and a sense of solidarity among important sectors of the population. No one community may have all of these attributes but the more it possesses the greater sense of ethnic solidarity it may have. The crucial element would appear to be the shared historical memory and the means by which this has been communicated over time. Here we see the importance of symbolism attached to myth; the way in which the past might be re-worked in order to present a form of continuity of experience irrespective of the political and economic changes which affected populations.

Clearly associated with this idea of continuity is a sense of place. The influence of geographical factors upon indigenous cultures is hard to measure but in the case of the Baltic peoples it has been important in the development of different ethnic identities. Situated on the flat, north European plain, bounded in the west by the Baltic Sea and dominated by river systems, swamps and forests, the different populations of this area have always been susceptible to incursion and invasion, but also able to use the environment to their own advantage. The area, now known as Lithuania, had almost impenetrable forests which both protected and set it apart from the other Baltic peoples to the north.

This latter, more exposed, population settled along the rivers which connected the heartland of Europe to the Baltic Sea, worked the land and traded with their neighbours.

However, geographical divisions did not correspond to linguistic differences. The tribes who inhabited the southern two-thirds of the area (now Lithuania and Latvia) had migrated from central Europe and were of Indo-European stock, while the northern peoples (now Estonia) had much in common with the Finno-Ugric linguistic group. This division would have increasing importance in the future but in this earlier period all the peoples shared aspects of pagan popular culture and myth based upon their relationship with the rural environment, varieties of which existed across Europe before the arrival of Christian missionaries. These emissaries attempted to produce a form of uniformity, but found it difficult to eradicate the 'folk culture' of the people.[3] In many areas this persisted into the nineteenth century, and, it might be claimed, even later. In the Baltic area Christianity, in its various forms, was associated with the powers which sought to control the region and conversion was a form of political subservience.[4]

For the obvious geographical reasons outlined earlier the two most northerly peoples were most affected, suffering invasions and conquest by the Danes and Russians before the more systematic exploitation by the Teutonic Knights in the thirteenth century. These early incursions led to a political and territorial organisation of provinces which marked out the northern territory as Estonia, with Livonia to the south. The Danes colonised Estonia and established Tallinn (Reval) in 1219 as a main port of the region. Meanwhile, various Germanic military and religious orders began to dominate Livonia, establishing a major fortress and trading centre at Riga in 1201, and utilising their position to colonise the hinterland and establish the Christian religion. The indigenous peoples were unable to withstand the force of the Teutonic invasion, not least because of their hostility towards each other, and the Livonians used the German forces as protectors against both Estonians and Lithuanians. The Russians also had an interest in the north-eastern areas of Estonia, and also helped the local populations by defeating the German knights in 1242 on the frozen Lake Preipus, under the leadership of Alexander Nevsky. A feat celebrated in Russian and Soviet propaganda in the twentieth century.[5]

A century later the Danes sold their rights in Tallinn and the whole of Estonia to the Teutonic Knights, who dominated this area and Livonia for another two hundred years, but who found themselves continually harassed by a combination of Lithuanians and Poles. In this period of conflict the Lithuanians had been helped by their geographical situation and enjoyed strong leadership, most notably under Mindaugas, who founded a dynasty, and Jogaila, who effected a union with the Poles by marriage in 1386, and at the same time forced his subjects to become Christian. Paganism continued to be an important element in peasant culture, and there is evidence of substantial intermingling of various forms of Christian and other religions in the sixteenth century, but, as it increasingly came under Polish influence, the leadership in Lithuania imposed Catholicism more strictly.

The conflict culminated in a German defeat at the battle of Gruenewald (or Tannenberg) in 1410. The separate character of the Lithuanian peoples was established by this victory, which is still celebrated by the Lithuanians at the end of the twentieth century and this distinctive quality was reinforced by the Reformation, which coincided with the demise of the Teutonic Order. The military order was unable to sustain its domination and as its authority collapsed both Sweden and Russia sought to fill the vacuum. Sweden succeeded in capturing most of Livonia and Estonia, which secured the predominant position of Lutheranism by the end of the sixteenth century. In 1561 Poland partitioned Livonia, establishing a Duchy of Courland in the south which continued in the Protestant faith. In the middle of the seventeenth century the eastern part of Livonia came under Lithuanian/Polish control and was predominantly Catholic in religious outlook.

The most substantial influence on the Baltic countries had been German.[6] The orders had colonised Estonia, Livonia and Courland and by the early eighteenth century formed a land-owning aristocracy with substantial privileges over an indigenous population, and a merchant class with a monopoly of trade guaranteed by their position in the main cities. In 1721, when Russia took control of the area, Peter the Great confirmed the dominant position of the Baltic Germans in Estonia and Livonia and this privileged status lasted well into the final quarter of the nineteenth century. The Russian influence was increased by the three partitions of Poland which led to Lithuania and the Duchy of Courland as well as a small Catholic area of Livonia, Letgale, being absorbed by the Russian Empire in 1795. The Lithuanian aristocracy had become increasingly influenced by Polish culture and language during the period of the union, and the Catholic church had been, and would continue to be, an important factor in the cultural mobilisation of the Lithuanian peasantry. The area lacked the efficient economic and administrative organisation of the provinces to the north, and now faced an uncertain future in the Orthodox Russian empire.

At the beginning of the nineteenth century the political and cultural leadership of the Russian Baltic provinces lay with ethnic groups which had been associated with the region as conquerors and colonisers. It served the Russian leadership well to rely on the Baltic Germans to administer the northern provinces, and to encourage division between Poles and Lithuanians in the south. At this stage it could be argued that the only group with a clear sense of 'collective community' were the Baltic Germans, but three main factors would affect their role and encourage the growth of nationalist movements in Estonia, Livonia and Courland in the latter part of the nineteenth century.

The first was the re-organisation of the agrarian economies which followed the emancipation of serfs in all three provinces between 1816 and 1819 and the subsequent growth of commercial agriculture, offering opportunities for peasant farmers to become independent producers. The second was the growth of industrialisation and urbanisation in the latter part of the century leading to substantial peasant migration into the German-dominated towns. The third factor was the 'russification' of the Baltic area, particularly after the accession of Tsar Alexander III in 1881, who was unwilling to agree to the privileges given to the German aristocracy in 1721 and actively sought to undermine their administrative and cultural position with the aim of creating a more Russian-oriented administration.

The economic changes, allied with the growth of educational possibilities for many peasant families, led to the establishment of a small professional elite among the older indigenous populations in the north Baltic provinces. The first stirrings of a modern cultural nationalism began in the 1850s as a newly emerging intelligentsia began to construct a distinctive linguistic character. It was a movement which had been encouraged by the Lutheran church and German scholars, who were themselves much exercised with the issues of a national language in the construction of German national community. The challenge to the predominantly

German academic culture was small and muted and with no political potential, but as the peasant population began to move into the towns with the growth of industrialisation in the late 1880s, and an indigenous urban bourgeoisie developed, there was scope for the wider dissemination of Latvian and Estonian ethnic outlooks. The demographic complexion of the towns changed substantially with the influx of Estonians, Latvians and Russians so that their German character became less pronounced, but the political power of the Baltic Germans appeared to be invincible.

It was the tsarist policy of 'Russification' which melded the cultural and political issues. The government in St Petersburg saw the diffusion of the Russian language was the key to centralised political control, and this had clear ramifications for the Baltic Germans and the nascent nationalists. Neither group was satisfied when Russian became the official language of administration and education, but for nationalists, faced primarily with the immediate control by the Germans, it offered a means to undermine their cultural power. There was little opportunity for political expression, but the 1905 revolutionary uprisings in Latvia demonstrated the amount of popular opposition to the dominant group. In all, 184 country houses were destroyed as the rural population took revenge on their German masters, and the working class movement in Riga, comprising both Latvians and Russians demonstrated its strength by a general strike in October. In the face of these disturbances the Baltic Germans and the government of Nicholas II found they had much in common in suppressing by force the challenge to their power. A more difficult problem was how to cope with the growing articulation of ethnic communities who were moving from linguistic discussions to political programmes.[7]

The growth of a national consciousness in Lithuania took place at the same time as in the other Baltic areas but followed a different course. The long-term relationship with Poland led to an undermining of Lithuanian culture and language even after the dissolution of the political association in 1795. It was left to the Lithuanian gentry, influenced by German and Russian philologists, to begin to explore the unique character of their language. After the Polish insurrection of 1863, in which the Lithuanians were involved, the Russian government found it advantageous to encourage this development in the hope of distancing the Lithuanians from their old allies.

The economic and social determinants of change which affected the northern provinces in the later part of the century hardly impinged on Lithuania. Emancipation of the serfs only took place in 1861, and while there was growth in the agricultural sector there was not the expansion of industrialisation and urbanisation experienced elsewhere. The Lithuanians also had no experience of Baltic German cultural, economic and political domination, thus, unlike the Estonians and Latvians, the tsarist 'Russification' policy in the 1880s impinged directly upon them.

The other main factor was the role of the Roman Catholic church. Many of the clergy were Polonised, and Polish was the language of the mass for devout Lithuanians. Nevertheless, in a society which was very much less literate than the provinces to the north the priest was very often the key source for education in the Lithuanian language, even in a period of 'Russification'. Books in the Latin script, in Polish or Lithuanian, had been banned by the Russian government, but the church was instrumental in sustaining a flow of literature which was available to the intelligentsia. This was a small group which did not grow as there was substantial emigration to the United States from the 1860s until the First World War. By 1900 it is estimated that there were 100,000 Lithuanians in Chicago, making it the largest Lithuanian city anywhere in the world.[8]

It is clear that on the eve of the First World War, itself partly a result of nationalist and ethnic pressures upon traditional regimes, the political, economic and cultural character of the Baltic area was in a state of transition. In Estonia, Livonia, Courland and Lithuania there were competing ethnic forces, with the dominating groups being Russian and German. As a result of the upheavals of 1905 restrictions on the use of the indigenous languages were removed, and the provinces were represented in the Duma, but there was no concession by the government, or in the assembly, to the calls for greater autonomy for the representatives from the region. In fact, there was active persecution of those who sought to promote the national cause at a political level.

The ethnic group which felt most threatened, and had most to lose, were the Baltic Germans, who after 1905 found themselves increasingly isolated from the surrounding populations who were 're-creating' their own distinctive 'national' culture, claiming a longer and more distinguished heritage than that of the Germans who had dominated them for over five hundred years.[9]

The Baltic peoples were one of the many European populations affected by the political, ethnic and territorial changes arising out of the First World War. The establishment, by 1920, of three independent states (Estonia, Latvia and Lithuania) was only possible because of the demise of the Russian and German Empires which had dominated the area before and during the conflict. Such a possibility was far from anyone's mind in the spring and autumn of 1915 when German forces took Lithuania and Courland, eventually reaching the outskirts of Riga before being halted by Russian troops. Annexation and colonisation of the Baltic area became one of the German war aims. It was an ambition which seemed achievable after February 1917 with the fall of the tsarist government in Russia and the subsequent political crises leading to the Bolshevik coup in October. By February 1918 German forces had occupied Livonia and Estonia and were in a position to threaten Petrograd. In March 1918, under the punitive Treaty of Brest-Litovsk, Lithuania and Courland were ceded to Germany, followed, in August, by Livonia and Estonia. This was a crucial step in the movement towards independence since the provinces were removed from Russian political control, and a clear relationship with the German Empire had to be defined. While the military was unconcerned with political niceties and wished to exploit the provinces and utilise them against the Bolsheviks there were civilian politicians in Germany who were against annexation, seeking instead to come to terms with the principle of self-determination.

Estonian and Latvian leaders, who had been given positions of power by the Russian Provisional Government after the March Revolution, moved from a position of desiring autonomy within a Russian federation to outright independence once the Bolsheviks took power in October. The German successes gave the national leaders a crucial breathing space[10] but the military defeat of the Germans in November 1918 immediately changed the situation. Soviet troops moved into Estonia in the wake of German retreat but were held up by forces under Johannes Laidoner, and joined with the White Russians under General Yudenich in a move towards Petrograd. Eventually an armistice was agreed and subsequently, under the Treaty of Tartu, Estonia was recognised as an independent state by the Bolshevik regime in February 1920.

Meanwhile, the Latvian government, which had declared its independence in November 1918, was faced with more than one military threat to its existence. The first came from the Red Army which found some support among the industrial workers in Riga leading to the occupation of the city and the surrounding area, and the retreat of the government of Karlis Ulmanis to Liepaja on the Baltic coast. The second came from a combination of German troops who had either stayed in the region, or had returned as a Freikorps unit. They were joined by a military force of indigenous Baltic Germans, the *Landeswehr*, with all the units coming under the command of General von Goltz in February 1919.

By April the Germans had deposed Ulmanis, and in May Riga was captured from the Bolshevik forces. This was the highpoint of German intervention as the Allies sought to exercise control in the light of the Peace Treaty, the German government sought a new relationship with the Baltic countries, and the Baltic peoples took matters into their own hands.[11] Between June and October 1919 Estonian and Latvian forces combined to eradicate the influence of German and White Russian elements in the area thus leaving the way clear for negotiations with the Soviets over Latvian independence. This was recognised in August 1920 by which Letgale was also incorporated into the new Latvian Republic.

The Lithuanians had concluded a peace treaty with the Soviets in the previous month which allowed the latter to continue the conflict with Poland, but the defeat of the Red Army at the Battle of Warsaw in August effectively ended Bolshevik expansion in the region. It did not end the antagonism between Lithuanians and Poles, particularly over the possession of Vilnius, a predominantly Polish and Jewish city, which was considered by many Lithuanians to be their historical capital. It was seized by the Poles in October 1920 and became a fundamental source of antagonism between the two states. Kaunas became the 'provisional' capital of Lithuania, and the government flexed its muscles by annexing, in January 1923, the German port of Memel. It had once been part of East Prussia, but after June 1919 had become a League of Nations protectorate. The disputes over Vilnius and Memel opened up questions of ethnicity. The imposition of Kaunus as the capital satisfied more narrow nationalists who were suspicious of the 'cosmopolitan' character of Vilnius, while still undermining the willingness of Lithuanians to co-operate with their co-religionists in Poland. The annexation of Memel, while justifiable on economic grounds, cut against any argument about the consolidation of the national state, and led to considerable antagonism between Lithuania and Germany, particularly after 1933.

By 1922 the three independent Baltic republics had been internationally recognised as sovereign states but the process of 'state-building' had only just begun. There were considerable economic problems since city/ports such as Tallinn and Riga, which had developed as industrial centres and major entrepots for the Russian hinterland now found their trade declining and their position undermined. In the challenging international economic environment in the 1920s and 1930s the Baltic governments concentrated on developing their agricultural sector which engaged over 75 per cent of the population in Lithuania, and over 50 per cent in Latvia and Estonia. As with all primary producing countries they prospered in the 1920s as prices rose and then experienced substantial hardship during the Depression as markets disappeared and prices fell disastrously. In Estonia and Latvia the economic crisis of the 1930s was an important factor in the undermining of parliamentary government, but from the start all three republics had been susceptible to political instability.

One reason for this lay in the democratic constitutions which gave substantial power to elected assemblies which were made up of a large number of political parties, elected by proportional representation. As in other European states in the period, coalition governments were susceptible to pressure, and frequently fell, although there was a measure of continuity in personnel from one administration to another. However, the constitutional development of the states must be seen within the context of ethnic minorities and the re-organisation of economic and political power based upon the ownership of land.[12]

The construction of the new states presented the dominant national groupings with opportunities and obligations. They had the opportunity to use their position in power to develop the idea of a state based upon a national outlook constructed around their own dominant culture. However, they were also aware of obligations towards the ethnic minorities who made up 12 per cent of the population of Estonia, 25 per cent in Latvia and 16 per cent in Lithuania. Russians formed the largest minorities in Estonia and Latvia, while Jews predominated among the Lithuanian minorities. 3.2 per cent of the Latvian and 1.7 per cent of the Estonian population were German. Proportional representation led to the growth of more than one party to represent minorities in the national parliaments and cultural autonomy of the different ethnic groups was encouraged, particularly in Estonia, where legislation to this effect was enacted in 1925. In all three Baltic states the key to this development lay in the construction of independent school systems which allowed the study of the minority's language and culture. This was particularly important for the Baltic Germans, who had claimed an intellectual and moral superiority in their period of domination, but now found themselves under attack, not only culturally, but also at an economic and political level.

The attempts to secure the German position in the Baltic area after the Armistice clearly antagonised the political leaderships in Estonia and Latvia. As soon as possible after independence they put in hand land reform legislation which effectively deprived the Baltic Germans of their primary source of power.[13]

In Estonia the Germans had owned 90 per cent of the large estates which made up nearly 60 per cent of the agricultural land. In Latvia they had owned well over 50 per cent of the land. The estates were expropriated and distributed as small holdings, some of which the Germans were allowed to occupy as peasant farmers. The leadership of the minority in Latvia shifted to those engaged in industry and the professions and who were able to work more easily with the new state leadership. The key figure was Paul Schiemann, a lawyer and journalist with strong ties to Germany, who argued that the Baltic German position could only be preserved by the construction of a democratic state in which the rights of the minorities would be preserved.[14] Clearly this outlook would coincide with that of the Weimar Republic which sought a rapprochement with the new states in order to strengthen its financial and economic relationships in the region. The more positive outlook of Schiemann was not one shared by many of the German minority. Having lost their economic and social status they sought to preserve the only vestige of 'superiority' they felt they had left, their culture. The German school system, partly subsidised by the Reich, was a key element with other forms of cultural activity, in emphasising ethnic differences and acted as a statement of defiance towards the regime.

The question of minority rights was clearly bound up with the development of a democratic system of government, and the willingness and ability of minority groups to participate and use the system to their advantage. Once the parliamentary forum was removed as the central political element in the state the focus of government became more intensely chauvinist. This became clear in Lithuania in December 1926 when an army coup led to the dictatorship of two Nationalist leaders, Voldemaras and Smetona, who had found little support for their policies in elections after independence but were able to consolidate their power by isolating the main ethnic minority, the Jews.[15]

There had been a long history of anti-semitism in Lithuania not only encouraged by the Catholic church[16] but also by liberals faced with a greater preponderance of Jews in the professions and urban centres, particularly Vilnius. The loss of the 'capital' to Poland certainly affected the Jewish position in Lithuania since it was the intellectual centre for Yiddish studies, but of even greater significance was the attempt by the state to counter the educational backwardness of ordinary Lithuanians and create a middle-class which would be able to challenge the position of the Jewish minority in urban life. After the coup in 1926 the political leadership was able to build upon the resentment against the Jews which had been the basis of the policy, as well as the subsequent inability of the newly urbanised population to satisfy their social and economic desires. Voldemaras moved decisively to the right, eventually leading a para-military quasi-Fascist movement, Iron Wolf. Smetona, the president of Lithuania took an apparently more moderate line, eventually relieving Voldemaras of his office of prime minister in 1929, and then showing his true colours by creating a one-party state in 1934 with himself at the head.

The cultural bases of this 'national state' were the myths and legends of the pre-Christian period mixed with aspects of catholicism, a heady combination which demonstrated the contradictions in constructing an ethnic national culture for the new Lithuanian state. It was impossible to eradicate the influence of the church, and yet the rural/pagan/peasant themes offered the regime a form of historical legitimisation.

By 1934 Estonia and Latvia had also become dictatorships. This was primarily a response to the political problems caused by the continuing economic depression. The conservative/nationalist peasant parties which dominated the governments in both countries asked for more executive powers, and the Estonian constitution was changed in 1933 to allow for presidential elections, with the right of the head of state to rule by decree. Before elections could be held Konstatin Päts, the prime minister, assumed power as dictator on the basis of the constitution.

Similarly in Latvia, Karlis Ulmanis, head of the Farmers' Party, assumed dictatorial powers in May 1934. They were not only responding to external threats, but also to the growing popularity of right-wing radical groups: the League of Freedom Fighters in Estonia, and the Thunder Cross movement in Latvia. Influenced by events in Italy and Germany, a new generation of nationalists had sought to challenge those leaders who had been instrumental in the construction of the national state after 1919. The removal of the democratic constitutions allowed Päts and Ulmanis to deal with these movements, but also drastically affected the rights of minorities. As in Lithuania the dictators legitimised their actions by calls for national solidarity, and an emphasis on the ethnic qualities of the Baltic peoples. The defence of the state was constructed on the cultural myths of the past.

The accession to power of Hitler in January 1933 had important implications for the Baltic Germans. In his speeches he had called for the creation of a community embracing ethnic Germans living outside the Reich, and although how this was to be achieved was not clear it influenced some of the younger generation among the minority, and subsidies from the Reich were increasingly channelled towards those who supported National Socialism. The enhanced nationalism of the Estonian and Latvian states was countered by a greater stridency among the German minority, faced with few channels through which they might negotiate with the state. and a greater unwillingness to do so. It was not, however, the support of the German minority for Hitler which undermined the viability of the Baltic states but the increasing power of Germany and the Soviet Union in the late 1930s.

While the Baltic German minorities in Latvia and Estonia held little threat for the dictatorships of Ulmanis and Päts the port of Memel (Klaipeda) which had been annexed in 1923 posed difficulties for Smetona in Lithuania. After the resolution of the Czech crisis in the autumn of 1938 the tactics of National Socialists in encouraging the German populations in former German territories to mobilise against the host state, which had proved very successful in the Sudeten area of Czechoslovakia, were applied to the city of Danzig (now Gdańsk), in Poland, and Memel. In the light of the unwillingness of the western powers, Britain and France, to support the Czech state at the Munich Conference in September 1938 over the Sudetenland there was little the Lithuanian government could do except return Memel to the German Reich when this was demanded in March 1939.[17] It was unclear whether this was a prelude to the annexation of Lithuania by Hitler, in the wake of the absorption of Bohemia in the same month.

From March to August 1939 the fate of the Baltic states was bound up with attempts to stave off the expected German attack on Poland over Danzig and the Polish Corridor. The unconditional guarantee given to Poland by Britain and France at the end of March depended on the co-operation of the Soviet Union, which, it soon became clear, would only be forthcoming if it had a free hand in the Baltic area in the event of an expected attack by Germany on Poland. The Baltic states were caught between the devil and the deep blue sea and on 23 August 1939 both overwhelmed them when Germany and the Soviet Union concluded a non-aggression pact. The way was clear for Germany to act in Poland, and in a secret protocol Latvia and Estonia were declared to be part of the Soviet sphere of influence. Once again the Baltic area was to be partitioned between the Great Powers who had dominated it in the nineteenth century, but the result was a much more efficient and determined solution to issues of ethnic diversity.[18]

In August 1940 the three Baltic states were officially incorporated into the Soviet Union. This followed unsuccessful attempts to encourage the construction of popular front movements in the states and the opportunity to consolidate the Soviet position by more intimidatory means following the German advance into France in May 1940.

While left-wing elements might have welcomed the Soviet presence, the result was wholesale deportations of government leaders and officials as well as substantial numbers of those deemed to be enemies of the Soviet state. By the middle of 1941 over 150,000 people had been deported to the Soviet Union, with the likelihood that many of these had been killed.

In the period after the Nazi–Soviet Pact many Baltic Germans had been re-settled in former Polish territories, and thus were unaffected by the deportations. However, the German presence was re-established following the German attack on the Soviet Union in the summer of 1941. It was not now the old 'Baltic Barons' who began to impose a new authority over the whole area but ideologically motivated groups working under the aegis of different National Socialist leaders. The Baltic states were joined to Belorussia in the 'Reichskommissariat Ostland' and were subject to immediate racial 'cleansing', since all the Baltic peoples were deemed to be inferior to the Germans. The most obvious target was the Jewish population in Lithuania and Latvia. If they survived the death squads they were placed in ghettoes, and then, from 1943, in concentration camps. The ethnic antagonisms which had permeated life in the Baltic area were channelled by the German occupying forces into encouraging indigenous populations to collaborate with them against the Jews. The result was the virtual destruction of the Lithuanian Jewish population which, in 1939, had numbered over 250,000. This was the most extreme and devastating demographic change caused by the war, but large numbers of the majority populations were also deported or emigrated voluntarily in the course of both the Soviet and German occupations. The advance of the Red Army in the autumn of 1945 further exacerbated the situation but the greatest ethnic changes would take place in Estonia and Latvia during the Soviet occupation after 1945.

There was no possibility of the three Baltic states regaining their independent status at the end of the war. Occupied by Soviet troops, recognised to be within the Soviet 'sphere of influence' by the Western Allies and lacking any indigenous political leadership, the states began to be incorporated within the economic, political and nationalities structure of the Soviet Union. They were set to conform to the main aspects of Soviet nationality policy which has been defined as 'mobilising ethnic populations to accomplish Soviet-style modernisation, while maintaining internal stability'.[19] The policy of encouraging ethnic diversity while keeping it rigidly controlled within the Soviet ideological and bureaucratic structures was well established and applied as far as possible to the Baltic states, but the opposition in both Estonia and Latvia posed particular problems for the Soviet authorities. Since there was only a very small Communist Party in Latvia a political leadership made up of russified Latvians was imposed on the country. Apart from a short period following the 'thaw' in Soviet politics between 1957 and 1959 the Russian 'latovichi' dominated the government of indigenous Latvians until the late 1980s.[20] This was also the case in Estonia where the political system was dominated by non-native Estonians and Russians. Ethnic interests were subordinated to a centralisation policy which alienated many intellectuals who formed the core of an opposition movement in the 1980s.[21]

If there was an attempt to politically neutralise ethnic issues in Estonia and Latvia the development of the economies of both countries substantially exacerbated them. Once the Baltic states had been incorporated into the USSR there was a conscious decision by the central leadership to modernise and expand the industrial output of the region. Much of this development was centrally controlled and required the augmentation of the work-force in Estonia and Latvia, leading to substantial immigration from the other areas, notably the federal republic of Russia. For instance, in Estonia, before the Second World War, over 90 per cent of the population was ethnically Estonian, while fifty years later this had dropped to 61.5 per cent. Of the remainder 30 per cent were Russians. The position was worse in Latvia with ethnic Latvians forming just over half the population by the end of the 1980s. It appeared to many in these states that this was a conscious attempt to dilute the native population and create a new 'russi-fication' in the Baltic states. This view was encouraged by the emphasis on Russian as the language required for preferment within the economic and political system.

While the language issue also affected Lithuania the country had been spared other aspects of demographic change. There was less Russian immigration, since the development of the economy was more restricted, and the loss of Jewish and Polish minorities left a more homogeneous population; in fact, second only to Armenia in the USSR[22]. This population continued to grow because of a high birth-rate, which also marked Lithuania out from the other Baltic states, with their low birth-rates and ageing populations. This not only represented the difference in religious outlook but also responses in Estonia and Latvia to the social and economic pressures arising from industrialisation and the pres-sure of immigration. While both states enjoyed the effects of economic growth they also experienced problems in housing, much of which was prioritised for the immigrant populations.

There is no doubt that there was substantial resentment over their declining position among the indigenous populations in Estonia and Latvia but little opportunity for overt political opposition. There were individual incidents of dissident beha-viour, but the majority of the native populations appeared to take comfort in the standard of living which they were able to enjoy through industrialisation, a standard substantially higher than other republics in the USSR. They also sought a form of solace in cultural activities which, while not overtly, or predominantly political, kept alive the sense of 'ethnic difference' in a period of 'Russification' and political conformity. While Estonia and Latvia lacked an institution which could act as a focus for even muted opposition Lithuania had such a forum in the Catholic church. Its role in the definition of Lithuanian nationality has already been discussed, and in the 1960s and 1970s increased Soviet antagonism towards organised religion was perceived as an attack on Lithuanian culture. Subsequently, following the signing of the Helsinki Accords in 1975, this focused on the question of human rights, and the legitimacy of Soviet rule in Lithuania.

There was one further factor which affected all three Baltic states; the ecological crisis arising out of the indiscriminate exploitation of natural resources and the expansion of heavy industries. Oil-shale extraction had laid waste large areas of northern Estonia and plans to increase phosphate mining not only threatened further tracts of countryside, but also would mean the incursion of more Russian workers.[23] The proposed development of a nuclear power plant at Ignalina in Lithuania, in the wake of the Chernobyl disaster in 1986, led to substantial protests, not least because it was perceived as yet another form of Russian hegemony.[24] The opposition against destruction of the environment articulated a key element in the definition of ethnicity in the Baltic area, the sanctity of the homeland which had been represented in song and legend for centuries. The destruction of the environment by outsiders was the most tangible focus of popular opposition and source of unity.

The development of movements seeking greater freedoms was tolerated by the Soviet government because of the fundamental changes in the political and economic structures of the USSR initiated by Gorbachev after 1985. Perestroika and glasnost were intended to be the means whereby a restructured system would preserve the authority of the Communist Party but increasingly they offered opportunities for oppositional elements in the Baltic states to test Communist regimes increasingly perplexed by the initiatives from Moscow. In Lithuania the activities of the newly formed Freedom League acted as an irritant to the authorities from 1987, commemorating aspects of Lithuanian history, notably the seventieth anniversary of independence in February 1988. In the same year, *Sajudis*, the Lithuanian Reconstruction Movement, was established, offering a clearer political focus for debate within the existing structures. Its founding congress, in October 1988, brought together Lithuanians from all parts of the world, was televised throughout the country, and set an agenda for 'sovereignty' or political autonomy, which could be interpreted by some as independence. Similar movements were established in Estonia and Latvia by groups of intellectuals and reformers, including some Communist party members. The support for these Popular Front movements was tested in the spring of 1989 with elections to the Congress of People's Deputies, a body established by Gorbachev in an attempt to give his government a veneer of democracy. However, the success of reform movement candidates in the polls did nothing to stem the call for independence from some quarters in all three Baltic states.

This was given further impetus by the success of the 'Baltic Way' demonstration of August 23 1989, the fiftieth anniversary of the Molotov–Ribbentrop Pact which had effectively sealed the fate of the independent republics. A human chain of over two million people stretched from Tallinn (Reval) to Vilnius demonstrating their solidarity in condemning the illegality of the Soviet occupation. Over the next six months the demands for independence grew as the Communist parties, aware of the popular mood and the lack of support from Moscow, shifted towards a more nationalist stance. Events in other areas of eastern Europe, not least the fall of the Berlin Wall, encouraged the movements, and the declaration of independence by Lithuania on 11 March 1990 was not unexpected given the speed with which *Sajudis* and other movements had established themselves after free elections. However, the economic embargo imposed on Lithuania by the USSR in April re-emphasised the essential character of the relationship, and the declarations of independence by the Estonian Supreme Soviet on 30 March, and the Latvian Supreme Soviet on 4 May were more circumspect in their approach to dismantling their connections with Moscow.

During the second half of 1990 it appeared that Lithuania had become a test-case for the future of the Soviet federation, and the fate of independence movements in other republics. A meeting between the Lithuanian President Landsbergis and the Soviet Prime Minister Ryzhkov in October 1990 was inconclusive, and Landsbergis sought to gain US support for the independence movement on a visit to Washington in December 1990. The fears he expressed of intervention appeared justified on January 13 1991 when Soviet troops surrounded the television station in Vilnius[25]hoping to precipitate a Communist coup which would lead to intervention by the Moscow government. It totally failed in its objective since ministers and members of parliament continued to occupy the station and demonstrated their willingness to face imminent death. Within a week Latvia had experienced a similar coup attempt, and dealt with it in a similar fashion.

Part of the Gorbachev campaign was to encourage ethnic hostility between Lithuanians and the Polish and Russian minorities. They had most to lose by the secession from the USSR, but many Russians had become assimilated through mixed marriages, and recognised the fundamental changes occurring not only in Lithuania, but also in the Soviet Union itself. This was most apparent in August 1991 with the attempted coup in Moscow against Gorbachev which, while it failed, led to the end of a centralised Soviet government and political separation of the republics.

As should be clear from the preceding narrative, ethnic differences in the Baltic states would never be resolved by political independence. There were many who feared that secession from the larger federal union would instigate extreme ethnic conflict, but the homogeneous character of Lithuania, the willingness of large Russian populations to accept the independence of Latvia and Estonia, and the assurances of the nationalist movements secured a peaceful transition. New forms of political organisation would be required for new circumstances, and the experience of independence between the wars could not be a model for the future.

Nationalist movements in the 1980s took advantage of glasnost and perestroika, but the basis of their appeal to majority populations continued to be the essential aspects of ethnicity laid out by Smith – the importance of language, culture, and territory and religion. When the opportunity arose they became the basis of opposition – re-formulated by the freedom movements and gaining popular appeal. While emphasising historical continuity, they were effectively utilising historical change.

NOTES

1   James J. Sheehan, 'What is German history?', *Journal of Modern History*, 1981, vol. 53 (March), pp.1–23.

2   Anthony D. Smith, *National Identity*, Harmondsworth: Penguin, 1991, pp.20–4.
3   Peter Burke, *Popular Culture in Early Modern Europe*, London: Temple Smith, 1978, ch. 2.
4   Anatol Lieven, *The Baltic Revolution*, New Haven: Yale University Press, 1993, pp.38–48.
5   Richard Taylor, *Film Propaganda*, London: Croom Helm, 1979, pp.116–30.
6   John Hiden and Patrick Salmon, *The Baltic Nations and Europe*, Harlow, Essex: Longman, 1994, pp.14–18.
7   Lieven, *op. cit.*, pp.50–2.
8   Richard Krickus, 'Lithuania: nationalism in the modern era', in Ian Bremner and Ray Taras (eds), *Nations & Politics in the Soviet Successor States*, Cambridge: Cambridge University Press, 1993, p.163.
9   J.W. Hiden, 'The Baltic Germans and German policy towards Latvia after 1918', *Historical Journal*, 1970, vol. XIII, no. 2, pp.295–6.
10 Lieven, *op. cit.*, p.57.
11 John Hiden, *The Baltic States and Weimar* Ostpolitik, Cambridge: Cambridge University Press, 1987, ch. 1.
12 Royal Institute of International Affairs, *The Baltic States: a survey of the political and economic structure and the foreign relations of Estonia, Latvia and Lithuania*, London: RIIA, 1938; Georg von Rauch, *The Baltic States. Estonia, Latvia, Lithuania: the years of independence, 1917–1940*, London: C. Hurst, 1974.
13 Hiden, 1987, *op. cit.*, p.36.
14 For his views see Dr Paul Schiemann, 'Die neue nationalistiche Welle', *Nation und Staat*, 1932 (September), pp.1–13.
15 Krickus, *op. cit.*, pp.164–5.
16 Lieven, *op. cit.*, p.144.
17 Hiden and Salmon, *op. cit.*, pp.97–8.
18 Albert N. Tarulis, *Soviet Policy toward the Baltic States*: University of Notre Dame, 1959, ch. 8; Nils Muiznecks, 'Latvia: origins, evolution and triumph', in Bremner and Taras, *op. cit.*, pp.183–85.
19 Victor Zaslavsky, 'Success and collapse: traditional Soviet nationalist policy', in Bremner and Taras, *op. cit.*, pp.33–5.
20 Muiznecks, *op. cit.*, p.185.
21 Cynthia Kaplan, 'Estonia: a plural society', in Bremner and Taras, *op. cit.*, pp.206–7.
22 Krickus, *op. cit.*, p.166.
23 Lieven, *op. cit.*, p.220.
24 Krickus, *op. cit.*, p.170.
25 Ibid., pp.174–5.

Chapter 9

The Middle East
Partition and reformation

T.G. Fraser

It might at first sight seem that the inclusion of the Middle East in a book entitled *Europe and Ethnicity* would require some special pleading. But in the period 1914–1923 its future shape was at the disposal of the victorious Allied and Associated Powers. Moreover, the area concerned, that of the Ottoman empire, was very much part of the European 'system' during and just after the First World War. Modern Europeans conveniently forget how much of the continent's history after the fall of Constantinople in 1453 was shaped by the Turks and the vigorous Islamic religion and culture they brought with them. Much of the history of central and eastern Europe emerged out of the period after the siege of Vienna in 1683 when the Habsburg armies commanded by their great general, Prince Eugene, began to prise the Turks out of their conquests and restored these areas to Christendom. For much of the nineteenth century Turkey was widely viewed as the 'sick man of Europe', but however great the pressure the Turks came under in the Balkans, their hold over their extensive Middle Eastern territories remained firm, not least because Muslims saw the Ottomans as the one remaining buttress of the Faith, but also because the region provided the empire with its food supplies. Hence, in 1914 the Ottoman empire stood with those of the Habsburgs and Romanovs as the three great examples of multinational states which seemingly mocked the strident claim of nationalism to be the ideology of the age. But by 1918 the Turkish empire was in ruins, apparently at the whim of the victorious Allied Powers, its many peoples to be disposed of as the victors thought fit, and it is out of the decisions taken that the ethnic shape of the Middle East emerged. It remained to be seen whether the Allied statesmen would be able to dispose of the Middle East more wisely or successfully than the Ottomans had done over the previous four centuries.

An initial judgement might be that they did not do very well, for if we take as a definition of the Middle East the territories of the former Ottoman empire, then the recent history of the polities they created has been one of repeated ethnic conflict. The most obvious of these has been the Arab–Israeli conflict which has generated five wars, in 1948, 1956, 1967, 1973 and 1982. Lebanon experienced some of the bitterest internecine conflict of modern times in the civil war which broke out in 1975 and lasted for fifteen years, almost shattering the country in the process, as Maronite Christians, Shi'as, Sunnis and Druzes fought for positions of power and influence in the state. The Gulf War of 1991 cruelly exposed the divisions within Iraq, as Kurds in the north and Shi'as and Marsh Arabs in the south of the country tried to shake the dominance of the Sunni Arab elite, which in various forms had dominated politics since the state's creation, despite numbering some 15 per cent of the population. The Kurds and Armenians, much discussed in the aftermath of the First World War, remain nations without a homeland, their frustrated ambitions regularly haunting the Middle East's establishments. Only Syria under the firm grip of Hafiz Al-Assad seemed immune, but the events in Hama in 1982 when his secular regime turned on Orthodox Muslim challengers indicate that there, too, there were tensions only just under the surface.

Despite the unifying strength of Islam, and the great lingua franca of Arabic, at least in its literary form, overlaid as they had been by four centuries of Ottoman administration, the Middle East of the early twentieth century embraced fascinating confessional and linguistic diversity, with the potential for expression in ethnic terms. The classic analogy was that of the mosaic, though that tends to imply a greater degree of distinctiveness among the various elements than existed in everyday life. Throughout the region the predominant group were Arabs belonging to the Sunni or Orthodox branch of Islam. The other main Muslim group, the Shi'as, had their main strength outside the Ottoman empire, in Persia, but also had pockets in what are now Lebanon and Iraq, especially their holy cities of Najaf and Kerbela. Two offshoots from the Shi'as, more prone to schism than the Sunnis, came to assume considerable significance in the course of the twentieth century, the Alawis and the Druzes. Persecuted for their beliefs, each found refuge in the mountains, the former in northern Syria, the latter in Lebanon, and in the cultivation of military skills. Throughout most of the Middle East there were significant Christian minorities, holding to a variety of Monophysite, Orthodox and Western traditions, the most important of the last being the Lebanese Maronites, a vigorous community using Syrian liturgy in unity with Rome. Also identified by the Ottomans as a religious minority were the Jews who had never ceased to retain a place in the Middle East since the destruction of their national life by the Romans in the second century AD. Hence, there were significant Jewish minorities in the areas of modern Iraq, Egypt and the Levant. Pious Jews had also struggled to retain a presence in their Holy Land, most notably in the Holy Cities of Jerusalem, Safed, Tiberias and Hebron; by 1880, they probably numbered some 24,000. But the Jews of the Middle East were only a tiny fragment of world Jewry, which in the late nineteenth century still had its focus in eastern Europe, though as persecutions mounted in the Russian empire ten of thousands were making their way to the United States. The position of Jews and Christians within the Muslim polity was recognised by the *millet* system, under which they were allowed to regulate their own communities according to their religious law. While in a sense this acknowledged that they posed no threat to the Ottoman structure, it was, for the Jews, better than anything Christian Europe had accorded them. Finally, there were two important linguistic minorities, each speaking languages derived from the Indo-European group. The Muslim Kurds were located across an extensive belt of territory stretching across parts of modern Turkey, Syria, Iraq and Iran. The Christian Armenians, inhabiting lands between the Black and Caspian Seas which had once enjoyed national independence, were by the early twentieth century perhaps the most obvious candidates for independence from the Ottomans, but for the fact that they were almost everywhere outnumbered by Turks. In the case of the twentieth century, these groups were to feature in the tensions of the Middle East, some to advance, others to be confounded, but all intimately affected by the decisions taken in the years between 1914 and 1923.

The Ottoman polity, which had sustained most of the Middle East in the Turkish interest for four hundred years, almost immediately came into question with the empire's entry into the war in November 1914. There was nothing preordained about this, for Turkey's rulers were divided over the relative merits of aligning with Britain or Germany and were well aware that their armies and fleets fell below the levels of the more technically and economically advanced states of Europe. One sentiment moved them more than any other: a burning desire to avenge the humiliations recently inflicted by the Italians in Libya and the Bulgarians, Greeks and Serbs who had stripped the empire of most of its remaining European possessions in the First Balkan War. Behind this lay also an understandable anxiety about the intentions of the Russians, with whom they had a one thousand-mile frontier and who had long looked greedily upon Constantinople and the Straits. The Germans were quicker to grasp these resentments and fears than were the British and as the European crisis moved towards war, their ambassador, Baron von Wangenheim, and General Liman von Sanders, head of the German military mission in Constantinople, successfully worked on Turkish susceptibilities. Their task was immensely aided by a British *coup de main* on 28 July 1914. Fitting out in British dockyards were two Turkish vessels, the battleships *Sultan Osman I* and *Reshadieh*, vital to the empire's hopes of avenging its recent defeats. Conscious of his over-riding need to preserve Britain's naval supremacy in the North Sea, the First Lord of the Admiralty, Winston Churchill, ordered their seizure. The Turks, who had raised much of the cost of the ships through public subscription, were incensed by their loss. The Germans skilfully turned the situation to their advantage. On the outbreak of war, Admiral Souchon, with his modern battle cruiser *Goeben* and accompanying light cruiser *Breslau*, evaded a hapless British pursuit in the Mediterranean to anchor off Constantinople. The ships, with their crews, were transferred to Turkey, thus making good the empire's loss. On 28 October 1914, the *Yavuz*, as the *Goeben* now was, bombarded Odessa, triggering the diplomatic events which within days brought Turkey into the war against Russia, France and Britain.

At remarkably little cost to itself Germany had acquired an asset of considerable strategic value. The Ottoman armies might lack the technological sophistication of their German and Austro-Hungarian allies, but their soldiers were tough and well led, as their victories over the British imperial forces at Gallipoli in 1915 and General Townshend's British-Indian command at Kut the following year were to demonstrate. The ability of the Turkish soldier was to be forgotten by the peacemakers, to their ultimate discomfiture. In 1914, Turkish belligerency presented the British with an unwelcome new set of strategic problems just as they were entering the first winter of a European war for which they were almost totally unprepared. Turkey threatened the security of the Suez Canal, Britain's short route to the resources and reinforcements from India, Australia and New Zealand; in fact, the war with Turkey was to tie down much of the 'imperial' war effort, particularly that of the Indian Army. At a stroke, too, Germany's ally menaced Britain's source of oil at the head of the Persian Gulf. Although oil had not yet assumed the all-consuming importance given by the development of mechanised and aerial warfare, it featured uncomfortably in British thinking. In 1912, Churchill had made the fateful decision that the Fast Division, the five 15 inch-gun battleships of the *Queen Elizabeth* class which would form the vanguard of the fleet, would be powered not by coal, which Britain had in abundance, but by oil, which had to be secured in the Middle East through the Anglo-Persian Oil Convention. The threat was obvious. Finally, there was the religious dimension to Turkish belligerency, for war with the Caliph of Islam would inevitably stretch the loyalties of the tens of thousands of Muslims both in the Indian Army and France's North African regiments. All of this meant that the war with Turkey would have to be vigorously pursued with whatever resources Britain had to hand and with such allies as she could attract in the region.

Official British attitudes to Turkey had long been ambivalent. Probably few would have dissented from Churchill's dismissal of it as a corrupt and bankrupt entity and liberal opinion had long professed itself outraged by treatment of the Armenians and Balkan Christians, but so long as the empire served as a buffer against more vigorous powers threatening the routes to India such sentiments rarely influenced policy.[1] Now that alliance with the Central Powers brought appreciable dangers to Britain's intricate network of interests around its Indian empire things were different. As early as 9 November 1914, a speech at London's Guildhall by Prime Minister Herbert Asquith seemed to question Turkey's survival in the event of a British victory, though this was not yet official policy. Interestingly, the same day the Foreign Secretary, Sir Edward Grey, was visited by his cabinet colleague, Herbert Samuel, one of the most eminent Jews in British public life. Pointing out that the war might see an end to the Turkish empire, Samuel argued that it might then be possible to re-create a Jewish state in Palestine. In January 1915, Samuel attempted to take the idea further with a memorandum to the cabinet on 'The Future of Palestine', but at this stage in the war his idea of a Jewish state under British protection was too utopian to attract support. But the idea had been fed into thinking at the highest level, catching the attention of David Lloyd George who before too long was to assume the pre-eminent place in British political life.[2] More representative of official thinking were the deliberations of the committee set up in April 1915 under the chairmanship of Sir Maurice de Bunsen to investigate the probable consequences for Britain of victory over Turkey, not least in the light of the certain appetite of Britain's French and Russian allies. Certain interesting conclusions emerged from their analysis. One was a preference for some kind of federal structure for a reformed empire which would give expression to Turks, Arabs and Armenians. But in any partition of the empire, the future shape of probable British acquisitions began to emerge. There were two clear priorities. The first was Mesopotamia, or Iraq as it will now be called, from the Shatt al-Arab waterway to Mosul, thus safeguarding Britain's oil supplies and consolidating its position in the Gulf. This was to be connected to the second area of interest, a port at Haifa which would reinforce Britain's strategic interests in the eastern Mediterranean and keep the French at a convenient distance from the Suez Canal. It was conceded that the Russians would at long last acquire the Straits and that the French would develop their existing interests in the administrative districts around Beirut and Damascus. Palestine, in which all the Christian powers were judged to have an interest, would require special negotiations.[3] As a guide to the future shape of the Middle East, it was quite instructive.

Almost from the start of the war, the ethnic issue began to stir in parts of the Ottoman empire. Just as the Serbs were the most disaffected of the Habsburg nationalities, of all the groups in the empire, the Christian Armenians had the most uneasy relationships with the Ottomans. Their sympathy with their Russian co-religionists in the first winter of the war provoked barbarous retaliation from the Turks, which was detailed in a celebrated British state paper, compiled by the eminent historian and former ambassador to Washington, Lord Bryce, and the young Arnold Toynbee. Even this was an early indication of how the nationalities' question was to be manipulated by the powers for their own purposes, for Bryce's volume, far from being the result of altruistic sympathy with the Armenians, was orchestrated by a British government which found itself in propaganda difficulty in the United States. As Russian armies retreated in the spring of 1915, they reacted savagely against the Jews who had naturally preferred the Germans and Austrians to their habitual tormentors. Evidence of Russian atrocities came as a godsend to the German General Staff, embarrassed as it was by its own army's misdeeds in Belgium. It was in an attempt, unsuccessful as it turned out, to counter German propaganda over Russian cruelties against the Jews that the British turned to the fate of the Armenians. It did not engage their attention for long.[4]

Although the de Bunsen Committee had no immediate results, it marked a clear beginning to British official thinking about how essential positions might be safeguarded. At the same time attempts were being made to secure allies against the Turks. It was an obvious strategy for the various belligerents to try to exploit presumed discontents in the enemy camp: in the course of 1915 the Germans made a number of attempts to arm revolutionary groups in India and they had hopes of working on Muslim concerns over the Turkish caliphate. For the British the obvious partners against the Turks were the Arabs, or at least any Arab groups which could be induced to shake off their allegiance to Constantinople. Such groups and individuals were known to exist, even if Arab nationalism, which had first begun to manifest itself among intellectuals in Beirut and Damascus in the late nineteenth century, had of necessity to work in secretive and tentative ways. But the British did know that Husain, head of the Hashemite family, descendant of the Prophet, and Sharif (guardian) of Islam's Holy Places of Mecca and Medina, harboured hopes of freeing the Arab lands from the Turks. In February 1914, his son Abdullah, deputy for Mecca in the Ottoman parliament, visited Egypt to probe possible British reactions in the event of his father leading an Arab rising. The outbreak of war gave both sides every incentive to push forward. As the result of the correspondence between Husain and Sir Henry McMahon in Cairo in 1915, the former agreed to lead the Arab revolt and Britain became committed to the dismemberment of the Ottoman empire in the Arab interest, or so it seemed. It was a correspondence which has generated more heat than light, for the nature of McMahon's pledges have been endlessly picked over, chiefly as a result of the accusation that Palestine became a 'twice-promised land', first to the Arabs and then to the Jews two years later. The debate centres on the import of this passage in McMahon's letter to Husain of 24 October 1915:

> The two districts of Messina and Alexandretta and portions of Syria lying to the west of the districts of Damascus, Homs, Hama and Aleppo cannot be said to be purely Arab, and should be excluded from the limits demanded. With the above modification, and without prejudice to our existing treaties with Arab chiefs, we accept these limits. . . . Subject to the above modifications, Great Britain is prepared to recognise and support the independence of the Arabs in all regions within the limits demanded by the Sharif of Mecca.[5]

The view that Palestine was excluded from the 'limits demanded by the Sharif', which the British government asserted from 1923 onwards, rests essentially on two arguments. The first is that since Palestine was already known, as in the discussions of the de Bunsen Committee, to be an area of special concern, it would not have formed part of Britain's pledge to Husain.[6] The second rests upon the simple proposition that since the entire Turkish vilayet of Damascus, which stretched from Aqba in the south to Hama in the north, lay to the east of Palestine, then that area must have been excluded by McMahon. It is true that the British government did consider Jerusalem and Palestine to be of particular significance, but in 1915 this was for reasons unconnected with the Jews or Zionism; it was a recognition that Britain's Roman Catholic and Orthodox allies, France and Russia, had cause for concern over the Christian Holy Places in Jerusalem. If McMahon's words are interpreted as excluding the entire area to the west of the vilayet of Damascus, then his specific reference to Homs and Hama makes little sense, for neither city had an Ottoman vilayet or sanjak attached to it. More pertinent is the simple fact that McMahon, who was quite precise in his references to cities, never referred to the sanjak of Jerusalem, nor to Palestine, in his exclusions. We are then left with the inference that the 'districts to the west of Damascus, Homs, Hama and Aleppo' which were not 'purely Arab' was intended to exclude the Christian areas of Lebanon in which France had a long-standing interest; and that, in the words of the Arab historian George

Antonius, Palestine 'must be held to have formed part of the territory accepted by Great Britain as the area of Arab independence'. The crucial fact is that the Arabs thought that it did.[7]

Unknown to Husain, Britain followed up its pledges to him with a series of negotiations over the Middle East with its French and Russian allies. Largely conducted by Sir Mark Sykes and François Georges Picot, the secret Sykes–Picot Agreement concluded in May 1916, further signalled Allied intentions towards the, as yet unconquered, Ottoman territories, partitioning the Arab lands between them. France's traditional interests in the Levant were recognised by giving it the Mediterranean littoral northwards from above Acre, with a belt of territory stretching into Anatolia. Britain was to assume direct rule over most of Iraq, together with an enclave around Haifa and Acre on the Palestine coast. The Arabian peninsula went untouched, but the lands lying between the areas to come under direct British and French rule were also to be partitioned into British and French protectorates. It need hardly be said that these proposed arrangements took no account of possible Arab political aspirations, still less of any ethnic or confessional nuances. Interestingly, Palestine was to be made an international sphere, because the British wanted to block French claims to the whole of 'Syria', and to head off claims to the Christian Holy Places made by its Catholic and Orthodox allies. In retrospect, perhaps the most significant aspect of the Sykes–Picot Agreement was the emergence of a distinctive 'Palestine' entity, largely comprising the area which later became the British Mandate, but without the Negev Desert or the coastal strip from Gaza to Rafah. With its proposed lines reflecting imperial concerns and cutting across any possibility of an Arab nation, it is not surprising that Arabs have viewed the document as 'the product of greed at its worst', the more so as it had been negotiated in the knowledge of Britain's pledges to the Hashemites.

While the Sykes–Picot Agreement made some gesture towards eventual Arab independence, what it looked forward to was a partition of the Middle East on the basis of imperial 'interests'. By 1917, the war had assumed a new and, for the Allies, depressing tempo. The Russian Revolution threatened to release veteran German and Austro-Hungarian troops for other fronts; the latter's victory over the Italians at Caporetto was an uncomfortable herald of what might come elsewhere. Mutinies in the French army, the defeat of Romania and the successes of the German U-boat campaign all compounded the gloomy picture. In the Middle East British forces were stuck outside Gaza. Only America's entry into the war lightened the scene but the deployment of US forces in Europe was a long way off and in the meantime no-one could be sure that its ethnically diverse population would stand whole-heartedly behind the war effort. It was largely in the hope that the Jewish communities of Russia and the United States could be moved on the Allies' behalf that Lloyd George and his Foreign Secretary Arthur Balfour turned to the Zionists. In fact, both men, and a number of other key figures in British official life, had for some time been toying with the idea that a British-sponsored Zionist presence in Palestine might provide a useful buttress for the empire in that area, not least against the French. Their interest was engaged by two Zionist leaders of formidable persuasive powers, Nahum Sokolow and Dr Chaim Weizmann. Before the war, Weizmann, a chemistry lecturer at Manchester University, had caught the attention of Balfour and, through his friendship with C.P. Scott, editor of the *Manchester Guardian*, of influential Liberals. The significance of Balfour's intellectual and emotional commitment to zionism should not be underestimated in any analysis of the events of 1917. In 1915, Weizmann's work on acetone earned him the gratitude of Lloyd George, who, as Minister of Munitions, was wrestling to unblock the supplies of ammunition to the British forces. While these various diverse strands went into the making of the British declaration of support for zionism, 'the time and manner in which these sympathies were translated into action were determined by the exigencies of the War'.[8]

The result of intense debate within the cabinet, the Balfour Declaration, as it has passed into history, was issued on 2 November 1917, it said:

His Majesty's Government view with favour the establishment in Palestine of a National Home for the Jewish people, and will use their endeavours to facilitate the achievement of this object, it being clearly understood that nothing shall be done which may prejudice the civil and religious rights of existing non-Jewish communities in Palestine, or the rights and political status enjoyed by Jews in any other country.[9]

Despite the use of the term 'National Home', which the Zionists had adopted at their first Congress at Basle in 1897, the expectation of at least some of the Declaration's authors was that in the fullness of time a Jewish state would come into being. 'It did not necessarily involve the early establishment of an independent Jewish State', Balfour informed his colleagues, 'which was a matter for gradual development in accordance with the ordinary laws of political evolution.' Such was the expectation of the Zionist leaders, for what to the British was a wartime expedient, opened up for them the prospect of the realisation of their dream, not least because the entry of General Allenby's imperial forces into Jerusalem on 11 December 1917 meant that Palestine's future would be in Britain's hands. The importance of the Balfour Declaration cannot be overstated. No matter how British officials in the Middle East tried to reassure them, the Arab reaction was one of 'bewilderment and dismay', for they could not but sense that the future of Palestine was to be shared, if not contested, with the Jews.

It is hard to escape the conclusion that Anglo-French policy towards the Middle East had been characterised by little more than wartime expediency underpinned by post-war imperial ambition. Hence, their ringing declaration of 7 November 1918 that their goal was 'the complete and definitive liberation of the peoples so long oppressed by the Turks' was hollow.[10] Still, 'self determination' had become the fashion of the hour and it remained to be seen how the victors would apply it to the peoples of the region, if at all. At first sight it might appear that the Middle East was Britain's to dispose of, for a great imperial army occupied much of it. Although the Russian army had fought well against the Turks early in the war, the new Soviet regime was playing a very different game. The French had played a marginal part in the defeat of Turkey, the Italians and Americans none at all. But Britain's partners could not be discounted. Revolutionary Russia was very much in the mind of peacemakers of 1919–1920. Italy sought to compensate for its failure to secure extensive Austro-Hungarian territories along the Adriatic by taking bits of Turkey. Under President Wilson the Americans enjoyed great moral authority but hopes that they might take an active Middle Eastern role, especially towards the Armenians, proved false. Above all, Britain had to take into account the long-standing ambition of important pressure groups in France to assert a presence in 'Syria', something which had informed all the wartime agreements, even the McMahon–Husain correspondence. Even the Greeks, whose contribution to the defeat of the Central Powers had been marginal, were to complicate matters. In the region itself, the position was far from static. Not all Arab leaders had joined the Hashemites in their revolt but even those who had remained loyal to the Ottomans knew that the empire had gone and that they now had the chance to create new power structures. This, added to a general quickening of political awareness during the war, accounts for the force of Arab nationalism in the immediate post-war period. Arab elites were not going to acquiesce tamely in a new Anglo-French imperium, especially if the former were going to try to foster Jewish settlement in Palestine. Britain's allies the Hashemites were strangers in much of the Middle East and their Hejaz base was being steadily eroded by Ibn Saud, who was to replace them as the ruler of the new emirate of Saudi Arabia. Britain's forces in the region might look imposing but military commitments in India and Ireland, and post-war financial pressures, meant that they were a diminishing asset. None of this promised that the post-war settlement might be an improvement on the wartime agreements.

The peacemakers themselves hardly focused on the Middle East during the Paris Conference. Husain's son Feisal came to press the claims of the Arabs, and Weizmann those of the Zionists, but they were nothing more than exotic distractions from the real work of the conference. Nevertheless, Article 22 of the Covenant of the League of Nations, signed with the Treaty of Versailles on 28 June 1919, ostensibly set out the intentions and obligations of the victors towards the former Ottoman territories:

> Certain communities formerly belonging to the Turkish empire have reached a stage of development where their existence as independent nations can be provisionally recognised subject to the rendering of administrative advice and assistance by a Mandatory until such time as they are able to stand alone. The wishes of these communities must be a principal consideration in the selection of the Mandatory.[11]

It was not until December 1919 that the British and French were able to compose their thoughts on the future of the region, by which time the Americans were no longer a factor. These discussions formed the basis of the San Remo Conference in April 1920 which was followed by the Treaty of Sèvres with Turkey in August. This sought to determine the political shape of the Middle

East, and in some important respects it did, for Britain and France secured their Middle Eastern interests under the cover of Mandates from the League of Nations.

Syria, one of the entities to emerge from the San Remo Conference, had long been coveted by influential groups in France. Its brief attempt at independence between 3 October 1918, when Feisal entered Damascus at the head of his Arab army, and 25 July 1920, when he was ousted by General Gouraud, whose troops had replaced the British, still makes for uneasy reading. The British might regard the French claim on Syria as an unconvincing pot pourri of historical sentimentality, Catholic ambition and commercial greed, but they were always going to favour their European ally over Feisal and the Syrian notables who hoped that by making him their king they might sustain their country's independence. The only attempt to test the wishes of the inhabitants, the mission of the Americans Charles Crane and Henry King in the summer of 1919, was effectively suppressed. As effective a gauge of sentiment as we possess, it found a strong desire for unfettered independence with the continued unity of Syria and Palestine, and strong opposition to the French as Mandatory.[12] Neither ambition was realised. 'Do we mean', asked Balfour in a remarkably candid analysis of 11 August 1919, 'in the case of Syria to consult principally the wishes of the inhabitants? We mean nothing of the kind'.[13]

The Syria which thus emerged out of the Anglo-French partition disrupted the intricate network of commercial and family relationships which had existed among the cities of Damascus, Beirut, Jerusalem, Nablus, Aleppo, Jaffa and Acre and their surrounding towns and villages, which were split across several unwelcome jurisdictions. Alongside a rigorous policy of cultural assimilation, the French followed almost a textbook policy of divide and rule. In September 1920, Gouraud announced the creation of a 'Greater Lebanon'. This arrangement gave France's favoured allies, the Christian Maronites of Beirut and Mount Lebanon, an entity which took in Sunni and Shi'a areas, around Tripoli in the north, Tyre in the south, and the Biqa Valley in the east, creating at a stroke the country which in 1975 was to explode into one of the Middle East's bloodiest communal struggles. Truncated Syria was not much better, for here, too, French policy was to accentuate and encourage division.

The area around the port of Latakia, with its Alawi inhabitants, was given special administrative status. The country's minority communities, the Kurds, Armenians, Assyrians and Circassians, were favoured in administration and commercial life. Above all, the Alawis and Druzes formed the core of the French-officered armed forces. The tensions thus created meant that post-Second World War governments in Damascus had a difficult task in cementing national unity, an aspect of Syrian history too often forgotten.[14]

As had been foreshadowed in the work of the de Bunsen committee, Britain emerged with the Mandate for Iraq, a country whose dimensions emerged out of British imperial, commercial and strategic interests. Geographically, it stretched from Basra on the Shatt al-Arab waterway, to Mosul, taking in the area of the great ancient civilisations of the Tigris and Euphrates, but otherwise including diverse ethnic and confessional groups. The most obvious division was the inclusion of a distinctive Kurdish area in the north around Mosul, the country's second city, but the 'Marsh Arabs' in the area above Basra also had a very different way of life from the Arabs of the interior. The other potential area of friction was between the Sunnis, who predominated around Baghdad, and the Shi'as, who had been discriminated against by the Ottomans. Generally poorer than the Sunnis, they were a majority of the Arab population, though a minority in the country overall if Sunni Arabs and Kurds were grouped together. It was from the start an uneasy combination and, in fact, it was by no means inevitable that the British would group these areas under a single administration in Baghdad. That they did may be attributed in no small measure to the man who dominated the country's affairs in the period between the Turkish surrender and the summer of 1920, Arnold Wilson. A vigorous, and in his own eyes enlightened, imperialist, Wilson sought to create a new British possession in the Middle East, strongly linked with India, which would be a model of imperial rule.[15] Apparently confirmed by the award of the British Mandate at San Remo, Wilson's ambitious and imperious methods provoked a widespread uprising in July 1920, not least among the Shi'a tribes around their holy cities of Najaf and Kerbela, which led to his replacement by Sir Percy Cox. By then the shape of Iraq had been determined and under Cox it provided a useful consolation prize for Feisal after his expulsion from Syria, thus providing a facade of Arab rule. Although Feisal ruled the country with some ability between 1921 and 1933, neither he nor his Hashemite successors were ever really able to reconcile the diverse elements in the population, still less to shake off the crippling legacy of being a British import. Their end in the Iraqi revolution of 1958 was grisly.

Even more controversial was Britain's Mandate for Palestine, for that was now complicated by the Balfour Declaration. The Zionist case for Palestine was presented to the Supreme Council in Paris on 27 February 1919: it looked forward to a British Mandate which would foster the emergence of an autonomous Jewish commonwealth with some of the apparatus of self-government. If granted, a 'commonwealth', *Gemeinwesen*, would have represented an advance on 'national home', *Heimstätte*, which the original Zionist Congress of 1897 had adopted as more realistic in the immediate term, and its use provides an insight into Zionist thinking at this time. 'Commonwealth' was not officially adopted by the Zionist organisation until 1942. In fact, even the use of the term 'national home' had not gone uncontested through the cabinet, and British soldiers and administrators in the Middle East, conscious of the strength of Arab feeling on the subject, were far from happy at the implications of the Balfour Declaration. But Lloyd George and Balfour were committed to it. The essence of the latter's thinking may be found in his memorandum of 11 August 1919:

> The contradiction between the letter of the Covenant and the policy of the Allies is even more flagrant in the case of the 'independent nation' of Palestine than in that of the 'independent nation' of Syria. For in Palestine we do not propose even to go through the form of consulting the wishes of the present inhabitants of the country, though the American Commission has been going through the form of asking what they are. The four Great Powers are committed to Zionism. And Zionism, be it right or wrong, good or bad, is rooted in age-long traditions, in present needs, in future hopes, of far profounder import than the desires and prejudices of the 700,000 Arabs who now inhabit that ancient land.[16]

Although the precise terms of the Mandate continued to be much debated, when it was finally submitted to the League of Nations in December 1920, Britain was charged with putting the Balfour Declaration into effect, with the significant addition that 'recognition has thereby been given to the historical connection of

the Jewish people with Palestine and to the grounds for recon-
stituting their national home in that country'.[17] Stung by the triple
impact of the fragmentation of the region, the unwanted tutelage
of the British, and the perceived Zionist threat, the Arabs of
Palestine reacted with violent rioting in 1920 and 1921, accompanied by the formation of the Palestinian Arab Congress.
Winston Churchill, who became Colonial Secretary in February
1921, personally sympathised with Jewish aspirations but realised
the need for a move to reassure the Arabs. This emerged in his
White Paper of June 1922, the wording and tone of which were
largely inspired by the High Commissioner in Palestine, Sir
Herbert Samuel, who had first placed the Zionist issue before
the cabinet eight years before. While sustaining the Balfour
Declaration, the Arabs were assured that this did not mean the
'imposition of a Jewish nationality upon the inhabitants of
Palestine as a whole', but that Palestine would become 'a centre
in which the Jewish people as a whole may take, on grounds of
religion and race, an interest and a pride'.[18] Jewish immigration
was to be restricted to the economic capacity of the country to
absorb them. Jewish immigration had already been forbidden
from the Amirate of Transjordan east of the Jordan, which had
been created to give a home to Abdullah, and which was given its
independence in May 1923, subject to British supervision. The
wording and tone of the White Paper seemed to set important
qualifications on the Balfour Declaration.

By that time the political and ethnic shape of the non-Turkish
parts of the Middle East was largely in place. But the Treaty of
Sèvres also contemplated important developments in the Turkish
heartland of Anatolia, where three ethnic groups were to be given
forms of self-determination. Greece, which landed an army there
in May 1919, was given the district around Smyrna/Izmir with its
Greek population for an initial five years, at the end of which there
was to be a plebiscite. The Armenians were to be given 'a free and
independent State' in districts around the Black Sea. Finally, the
treaty allowed for the creation of an independent Kurdistan,
should the Kurds so decide. All of this rested on Turkish
acquiescence, but the empire's defeat triggered a new nationalism
which found its inspiration in Mustafa Kemal, the hero of
Gallipoli. In August 1922, the Turks struck at the overextended
Greek forces which were routed. In the resulting debacle,
Smyrna/Izmir was taken by the Turks on 9 September, initiating

a diplomatic crisis with Britain which led to the fall of the Lloyd George government. In that sense, the Turks put paid to the period of post-war reconstruction in the Middle East. They also solved one of the region's ethnic problems by expelling over 500,000 members of the historic Greek communities of Asia Minor. Faced with a resurgent Turkey, the Treaty of Sèvres was dead. It was given a decent burial at the Lausanne Conference in 1923, which did not touch the Arab parts of the Sèvres settlement, but which saw an end to any lingering prospects for Armenian and Kurdish statehood.[19]

In all essentials the basic elements in the future shape of the Middle East were in place by 1923. The most obvious victims at the time were the Kurds, Armenians and Anatolian Greeks, successfully thwarted by a resurgent Turkey and left to their fate by the British, French and Americans. The British and French, who had parcelled out the Arab lands to suit their interests, had little to show for their efforts, though Britain's control of the 'central bastion' of the Middle East gave it a priceless asset in the Second World War. But the age of formal empire was fast passing and the brief period of Anglo-French hegemony in the Middle East was to end in the ignominy of Suez in 1956. The Americans, who had bowed out of any responsibility in 1920, took their place. The Arab independent states which emerged out of the Mandates by the end of the Second World War were those which the British and French had set up. Despite internal tensions, Syria, Iraq and Jordan established themselves as coherent state entities. Lebanon, the most artificial creation of them all, did not though French rule disguised its problems for over two decades. Lebanon's Maronite and Sunni elite set the basis for the country's constitutional future in the unwritten National Part of 1943, the essence of which used the 1932 census which gave the Christians a majority of six to five over the Muslims and Druzes. It established the convention that the president should be a Christian, the prime minister a Sunni and the president of the chamber a Shi'a; and that cabinet posts and civil service appointments should also reflect these proportions. By the 1950s it was widely accepted in Lebanon that these proportions had ceased to reflect reality, but the warning signals were ignored by political leaders basking in the illusion that they had created the 'Switzerland of the Middle East'. Their complacency ignored the burgeoning birth-rate among the Shi'as, which underpinned the increasing communal tensions that drove the country to civil war in 1975. The country was further destabilised by the influx of an estimated 97,000 Palestinian refugees in 1948–1949, and by the growing assertiveness of the Palestinian guerrilla groups after 1970. The resulting Lebanese civil war was violent and prolonged. Lebanon's reconstruction was only possible under the effective suzerainty of Syria, a tacit reversal of General Gouraud's 1920 partition of the two states. The deepest ethnic conflict became that in Palestine, with the Jews the ultimate winners. No one in the years 1917–1923 had foreseen the rise of Adolf Hitler and his manic form of anti-semitism which was to turn one of Europe's most civilised countries on to a path for genocide. But his rise to power in 1933 and the Holocaust which followed his conquest of much of Europe set in train the events which were to result in the creation of the State of Israel in 1948. The death of over six million Jews as a deliberate act of state genocide determined those who had survived to secure a state in which Jews could live secure and recognised lives. Jewish statehood meant exile and dispossession for the Arabs of Palestine. By United Nations figures, over three-quarters of a million Palestinians became refugees.[20] The subsequent Arab–Israeli conflict was to destabilise the Middle East for over forty years until the Declaration of Principles signed by the government of Israel and the Palestine Liberation Organisation in September 1993, seventy years after the events reviewed in this chapter, seemed to offer a way forward. If modern Israelis rightly honour the memory of Balfour as the author of their charter for eventual statehood, few others in the Middle East have cause to recollect the policy-makers of these years as anything other than the latter-day imperialists they were.

ACKNOWLEDGEMENT

Crown copyright material is reproduced with the permission of the Controller of HMSO.

NOTES

1   W.S. Churchill, *The World Crisis 1911–1918*, London: Odhams, 1938, vol. 1, p.434. Churchill's account naturally seeks to defend his conduct over the seizure of the Turkish warships.

2 D. Vital, *Zionism: the crucial phase* , Oxford: Clarendon Press, 1987, pp.92–8.

3 Ibid., pp.98–102; see also I. Friedman, *The Question of Palestine 1914–1918*, London: Routledge & Kegan Paul, 1973, pp.19–21.

4 For an interesting account of the various pressures see A.J. Toynbee, *Acquaintances*, London: Oxford University Press, 1967, ch. 11, 'Lord Bryce'.

5 *Correspondence between Sir Henry McMahon and the Sherif Hussein of Mecca, July 1915–March 1916*, Cmd 5959, London: HMSO, 1939; see also E.Kedourie, *In the Anglo-Arab Labyrinth*, Cambridge: Cambridge University Press, 1976.

6 See, for example, Friedman, *op. cit.*

7 G. Antonius, *The Arab Awakening*, London: Hamish Hamilton, 1938, ch. IX, 'Great Britain's pledge: 1915', is the classic Arab analysis. A vilayet was an Ottoman province, sanjak a subdivision.

8 *Palestine Royal Commission Report*, Cmd 5479, London: HMSO, 1937, p.23; any account of these events must start with L. Stein, *The Balfour Declaration*, London: Valentine, Mitchell, 1961.

9 War Cabinet 261, PRO CAB 32/4.

10 See M. Yapp, *The Making of the Modern Near East 1792–1923*, London: Longman, 1987, p.293.

11 Quoted in Cmd 5479, *op. cit.*, p.29.

12 See H.W.V. Temperley (ed.), *A History of the Peace Conference of Paris*, London: Oxford University Press, 1924, pp.148–9.

13 'Memorandum by Mr Balfour (Paris) respecting Syria, Palestine, and Mesopotamia', 11 August 1919, in E.L. Woodward and R. Butler (eds), *Documents on British Foreign Policy 1919–1939*, London: HMSO, 1952, pp.340–9.

14 See T. Petran, *Syria*, London: Ernest Benn, 1972, pp.62–3.

15 See J. Marlowe, *The Late Victorian Life of Sir Arnold Wilson*, London: Cresset Press, 1967; Wilson's own books reward study: *Loyalties Mesopotamia 1914–1917*, London: Oxford University Press, 1930; and *Loyalties Mesopotamia 1917–1920*, London: Oxford University Press, 1931.

16 In Woodward and Butler (eds), *op. cit.*, pp.340–9.

17 Quoted in Cmd 5479, *op. cit.*, p.34.

18 M. Gilbert, *Winston S Churchill*, vol. IV, London: Heinemann, 1975, pp.647–8.

19 Yapp, *op. cit.*, pp.317–22.

20 Uno Gaor, Fourth Session, 1a to 9, doc. A/1106, First Interim Report of the United Nations Economic Survey Mission for the Middle East.

Chapter 10

Ireland

Seamus Dunn and Thomas W. Hennessey

The recent history of Northern Ireland, especially since 1969, makes it difficult to argue that the 'Irish Question' has been resolved. The purpose of this chapter is to examine the hypothesis that the political-constitutional settlement in 1922, which partitioned the country into two parts, was flawed and incomplete in both geographical and psychological terms. The fundamental causes of the problem, in particular the divided aspirations of nationalists and unionists[1] – especially those in the North – were not dealt with or solved by creating a new independent Irish state and a jurisdiction of Northern Ireland. The large Catholic minority left in Northern Ireland, most of them nationalists, did not cease to be nationalists or become converts to unionism, and so the problem was likely to re-emerge at regular intervals. The Protestant majority was left with political control over a region containing a large, recalcitrant and unhappy minority, which felt abandoned and betrayed: even had it been possible to generate structures and processes within Northern Ireland calculated to win over this minority, it is doubtful if much would have changed, at least in the short and medium term.

The outbreak of the First World War, it is generally agreed, had a starkly defining role in events[2] and its effects have since been interpreted in two essentially opposing ways. The first argues that the war interfered with and postponed an evolving political process, which, left alone, would have produced an agreed and rational, if unspecified, settlement with potential for positive evolution and development. The second view is that the situation was already close to stalemate, if not violence, and that the war only postponed for a time the inevitable physical separation of an already profoundly divided country. What is certain is that the war constituted a watershed which dramatically changed the overall pattern of events, ensuring – among other things – that the unionist threat of physical force was diverted and grounded in the mud of European battlefields, and that the physical-force tradition within nationalism was given an opportunity to change things utterly in 1916.

The discussion, however, must also take account of more recent world developments which – pessimistically – indicate the universality, obduracy and timelessness of national questions; but more optimistically indicate how current ideas about nationalism, pluralism and internationalism can inform the Irish dilemma and point to ways forward instead of back.

The fall of the Iron Curtain has allowed the question of nationalism to re-emerge as a central international and intellectual concern. Its lack of prominence during and even before the Cold War did not mean that nationalism had disappeared, or that it no longer influenced the feelings and aspirations of ethnic groups. The break-up of Eastern Europe however created political spaces which national and ethnic groups hurried to fill and the result has been both new, and the revival of many old, conflicts. Indicators of the current salience of nationalism as an explanatory force include the great range of literature, both theoretical and historical, being published on the subject and the intense debate generated by its many paradoxes and contradictions.

In Ireland the concept of nationalism is often written about in a way suggesting that the idea was born in the island and that its range of understandings and interpretations must be applied in particular to the Irish context.[3] It is true that many of the central paradoxes of nationalism – theoretical, practical and historical – can be highlighted and made plain in Ireland, both with reference to the past and to today. Words and phrases such as 'right to self-determination', 'cultural heritage and tradition', 'indigenous and settler populations', 'secession', 'assimilation', 'founding myths', and many others, are central to Irish history as well as to its current discourse. Walker Connor writes: 'It is indeed a truism that political and ethnic borders seldom coincide.'[4] Ireland, in the longevity of its quarrels and wars, is an example of this lack of coincidence. The 'right to self-determination', for example, is often paradoxical when presented in the form of simple Manichean categories: any population, with a coherent sense of national consciousness (an imagined community), that seeks self-determination, is likely to contain a minority with a similar ambition. If Ireland can secede from Britain, Ulster can secede from Ireland, Derry/Londonderry can secede from Ulster, and so on. The forces of history and strategic politics will often determine events, rather than rational argument or moral force.

It is not the purpose of this chapter to describe in any detail the conflict and violence of the last twenty-five years.[5] It is, however, necessary to try to identify the elements and attitudes that have changed, and those that have remained – especially those that continue to reflect decisions and formulations made in the crucial early years of this century, before, during and after the First World War.

Of the changes, perhaps the most significant development since 1975 is the emergence of a belief that each of the two political understandings of Northern Ireland must be taken into account in any future constitutional arrangements. This means that in some way the circle must be squared so that both Irish and British senses of identity can be accepted as valid and worthy. The refusal, or inability, to devise such a system in Northern Ireland since its creation, and the resentments that this created, finally produced an explosion that is only now, twenty-odd years later, beginning to lose its energy. The current negotiations and debates, which have followed the ceasefires of 1995, are in a sense taking up again the process which the outbreak of war in 1914 interrupted.

In 1886 and 1893 two Home Rule Bills, to establish a devolved Irish Parliament, were defeated in the London Parliament and it was not until 1910 that the possibility of Home Rule returned. Following the 1910 general elections, Herbert Asquith's Liberal Government relied upon the support of John E. Redmond's Irish Parliamentary Party (IPP) to secure a House of Commons majority. And, after the passage of the 1911 Parliament Act which restricted the ability of the House of Lords to reject Commons legislation (a power it had used previously to block Home Rule), it appeared that the final obstacle to Home Rule had been removed. It now seemed that Redmond was to secure the goal that had eluded his great predecessor Parnell. At this stage, however, it became clear that the Irish Question was in fact two questions: nationalist Ireland's relationship with the rest of the United Kingdom, and Protestant Ulster's relationship with Catholic Ireland.

Irish Nationalists, such as Redmond, thought that the distinctiveness of the island of Ireland meant that it was a 'homeland', a discrete geographical entity.[6] Nationalists rejected the argument that Irish Protestants might form a national entity within Ireland, separate from Irish Catholics. 'We claim' explained Redmond, 'that Ireland is a nation, made up of many races...We are not dealing with the case of a few counties of Britain that happen to be separated from this island [Great Britain] by a few miles of water'.[7] Of particular significance was Redmond's rejection of the charge that Irish Catholics could not be loyal to the British Crown, as many Protestants claimed. Redmondites did not therefore seek to dissolve the Union of Great Britain and Ireland, but rather to alter the relationship of Ireland to the rest of the United Kingdom. Ireland would have control of her domestic policy, but for all 'Imperial purposes the two countries would continue to be a "United Kingdom", and to constitute in the face of other nations one Imperial State'.[8] Redmondites proposed Irish Home Rule within the United Kingdom and Home Rulers sought to 'strengthen the tie between England and Ireland, to make the Union a real Union and not the sham Union that it has been up to the present time.'[9] Redmond, like Parnell before him, did not advocate republicanism but allegiance to the British Crown: the Home Rule which he aspired towards would ensure that Irish nationalists would remain British subjects of the United Kingdom.[10]

Such pronouncements, however, did little to dampen the opposition of Irish Unionists, and in particular those in Ulster, to Home Rule. Unionists, who were predominantly Protestant and wished to retain the Union with Britain, feared that a Home Rule Parliament would preside over a confessional Roman Catholic state. Presbyterianism and Roman Catholicism in particular represented an ideological schism within Christianity of fundamental proportions; the sacramental role of the priest was seen by Presbyterians as hindering the right of individuals to approach God directly through His teachings in the Bible; and the institutional Catholic church was perceived as wishing to control access to religious knowledge, and to exert a powerful influence over political and social institutions within society.[11] The pronouncement in 1908 of the Papal decree *Ne temere* – which declared that mixed Protestant–Catholic marriages not celebrated before a Catholic priest were invalid – added to these anxieties. Ulster Unionists also saw Home Rule as a threat to their Britishness and feared that the establishment of Irish self-government would lead ultimately to an Irish Republic. Unionists at that time thought of themselves as both Irish and British, and, like the Scots or Welsh, saw no contradiction in this.[12]

As the Home Rule Bill made its passage through Parliament, Ulster Unionists, led by Sir Edward Carson, began in 1911 to form themselves into an armed militia, the Ulster Volunteer Force (UVF), whose membership was eventually thought to number around 100,000 men. September 1912 saw 218,206 Ulstermen sign an 'Ulster Covenant' pledging resistance to Home Rule on the grounds that it was 'subversive of our civil and religious freedom, destructive of our citizenship, and perilous to the unity of the Empire'.[13] The political situation was transformed by the importation in 1914 of a large shipment of arms for the UVF, making the threat of civil war ever more likely. Nationalist opinion was subsequently mobilised into a rival Volunteer organisation, the Irish National Volunteers (INV), with a membership approaching 130,000 by May 1914.

By that time the Home Rule Bill had passed its third reading in the House of Commons and needed only the King's signature to become law. However, the Bill was held up as attempts to find a compromise continued. These centred around the temporary or permanent exclusion of four or six of the nine Ulster counties from the jurisdiction of an Irish parliament. Although there were Protestant majorities in four of these counties – Antrim, Armagh, Down and Londonderry – there were Catholic majorities in counties Fermanagh and Tyrone. In addition all of the counties contained substantial religious minorities; as Redmond pointed out at the Buckingham Palace Conference (called by the King in July 1914 to resolve the crisis) there were more Catholics in counties Londonderry and Armagh than there were Protestants in Fermanagh and Tyrone, and over 100,000 more Catholics in the four 'Protestant' counties than there were Protestants in the other five 'Catholic' counties.[14]

With the outbreak of the First World War in August 1914, discussion of the Irish and Ulster Questions was submerged in the British state's desire to conclude a successful peace, and it was felt that the United Kingdom should present publicly an image of unity in its attempts to cope with the developing European situation. Irish Nationalists and Unionists, however, continued to vie for political advantage. On 3 August Redmond offered the British government the use of the INV to defend Ireland's shores against a German invasion.[15] This speech appeared to give the political advantage to the IPP, and to ensure that the Home Rule Bill would become law. But on 28 August the Unionists went one stage further when Carson unconditionally put all the membership of the UVF at the War Office's disposal, with an assurance of 35,000 recruits to go abroad.[16]

On 17 September the Home Rule Bill became law, but a corresponding Suspensory Act postponed it coming into operation until the end of the war, allowing the government to defer any decision as to the precise form Home Rule would take. In effect, therefore, although the Bill was placed on the statute book, the amendment about which Ulster counties were to be excluded was left hanging until after the war; this meant that, in principle, even in 1914 partition of some kind was almost certainly assured. Despite such uncertainties and niceties, with Home Rule on the statute book Redmond took the unprecedented step, for an Irish Nationalist leader, of advocating that nationalists should join the British army and fight for Britain in a British war. In September he told members of the INV that '[your] duty is two-fold ... account yourselves as men, not only in Ireland itself, but wherever the firing line extends, in defence of right, of freedom and religion in this war'.[17] Redmond, who believed that Ulster unionists could not be coerced into a united Ireland, hoped that the sight of nationalists fighting alongside unionists for King and Country would prevent partition, by convincing unionists that nationalists could be loyal to the British Crown. He appealed to unionists 'as our soldiers are going to fight, to shed their blood, and to die at each other's side, in the same army, against the same enemy, and for the same high purpose' that 'their union in the field may lead to a union in their home [Ireland], and that their blood may be the seal that will bring all Ireland together in one nation, and in liberties equal and common to all'.[18] By December 1915, out of 75,795 Irish recruits to British forces 36,775 were Catholics and 38,121 were Protestants, of which 18,200 were members of the politicised INV and 24,628 from the UVF.[19]

The dilemma for Redmond was that, in committing himself to recruiting for the British army, he risked alienating his nationalist supporters, since his strongest card was only a promise that Home Rule (and almost certainly a partitionist form of Home Rule) would be implemented. John Dillon, his deputy, summed up the feeling of many Irish Nationalists when he said 'I am England's friend in this war...so long as she stands by that [Home Rule] Bill.'[20] But, as the war wore on, it looked increasingly unlikely that Britain would stand by the Home Rule Act. In May 1915 Asquith's Liberal administration was forced, by domestic concern with the way the war was being run, into a Coalition government which included British and Irish Unionists who had supported Ulster's paramilitary resistance to Home Rule, including Sir Edward Carson as Attorney-General. Many of the IPP's supporters came to the view that the formation of this Coalition placed the IPP in a weak bargaining position, and that Carson now had the advantage over Redmond.[21] The balance of power had shifted decisively towards the Unionists. By July 1915 the state of political feeling in nationalist Ireland was considered by John Dillon to be the worst he had known since 1900.[22] The extent of nationalist concern was illustrated, presciently, by Bishop Fogerty of Killaloe, a staunch IPP supporter, who declared 'Home Rule is dead and buried and Ireland is without a national party.... What the future has in store for us God knows...I suppose conscription, with a bloody feud between people and soldiers.'[23]

The Dublin Insurrection of Easter 1916 changed everything, and the balance of its effects on relationships in Ireland is still a matter of debate. In particular it constituted a watershed in the declining fortunes of the IPP. The Rising was led by a small elite of the Irish Republican Brotherhood (IRB), a revolutionary national- ist organisation seeking to break Ireland's link with Britain. The IRB led a small section of the Irish Volunteers, who had separated from the main Volunteer organisation in protest at Redmond's recruiting policy in 1914, against British military forces in Dublin. The rebels declared themselves the Provisional Government of the Irish Republic, with Patrick Pearse as its first president. The Rising initially met with hostility from the general population, but its quick defeat by British forces, the decision to execute the Rising's leaders and the imposition of martial law, all combined to turn public opinion against the British. In addition a great many nationalists became alienated from the IPP which was seen as having abandoned nationalist principles in favour of British imperial interests by its support for Britain's armed forces. Anti- IPP nationalists coalesced politically in a resurgent Sinn Féin, a movement originally formed in 1905 as a cultural nationalist organisation by Arthur Griffith. During 1917 the IPP's support in nationalist Ireland declined rapidly, with Sinn Féin – a coalition of physical force republicans and disaffected moderate nationalists – winning successive by-elections against the IPP in North Roscommon, Kilkenny and East Clare.

One of the advantages that the reconstituted Sinn Féin derived from the Rising's aftermath was a general sense of identification among nationalists with the rebels. It was felt that, by rebelling against British rule, the 1916 insurgents had fulfilled the traditional nationalist role of fighting for Ireland in Ireland. This was in contrast to the nationalist soldiers fighting abroad in the British army. As Augustine Birrell, Chief Secretary for Ireland until the Rising, commented

> The spirit of what to-day is called Sinn Féinism is mainly composed of the old hatred and distrust of the British connection, always noticeable in all classes and in places, varying in degree and finding different ways of expression, but always there, as the background of Irish politics and character. This dislike, hatred, disloyalty (so unintelligible to many Englishmen) is hard to define but easy to discern, though incapable of exact measurement from year to year. You must assume it is always there and always dangerous.[24]

Richard Mulcahy, later an Irish Republican Army commander in the Anglo-Irish War, did not believe that the post-Rising executions altered nationalist opinion in favour of the rebels. He explained the surge in support for the Sinn Féin movement by comparing the Rising to a detonator: 'A detonator is a small thing which detonates latent and powerful forces that are there' and the Rising 'altered and...detonated the whole strength of the people'.[25] Thus, he argued, while the majority of nationalists initially exhibited disapproval of the Rising, a latent sympathy with the rebels' ideals had always existed.

In the Rising's immediate aftermath, British cabinet member Lloyd George was given the task of producing a settlement of the Irish Question by a government fearful of the impact of nationalist alienation upon support for Britain's war effort in the United States and the Dominions. The proposal, which he persuaded Redmond and Carson to agree to, involved the 1914 Act being brought into operation as soon as possible, but not applying to the excluded six counties of Antrim, Armagh, Down, Fermanagh, Londonderry and Tyrone, which were to be administered by a Secretary of State. The Act was to remain in force during the war and for twelve months thereafter, with a final settlement to be agreed with the Dominion governments in a proposed reshaping of the administration of the empire.[26] But unknown to Redmond, who agreed to the proposals on the basis that the six counties would be temporarily excluded for the war period only, Lloyd George had promised Carson and the Ulster Unionists that the exclusion would be permanent, a decision ratified by the Cabinet when it became apparent that a number of its members were prepared to resign over the whole process.

When the terms given to the Ulster Unionists became public Redmond's influence in Ireland was irreparably broken. He was held responsible for the failure, and for committing Ireland to conciliatory gestures without any compensating concessions or practical results. Opinion grew that Redmond's whole policy since August 1914 had been disastrously misjudged. He had offered co-operation when he might have exerted pressure that would have compelled the British government to settle the Irish Question.[27] The speed with which the government sought some kind of accommodation, so soon after the Rising, was widely interpreted as being due to the efforts of the rebels, who, some felt, had acted as they did because they saw the prospect of Home Rule slipping away.[28] Sinn Féiners had consistently opposed any recruitment for the British army and many nationalists felt that conscription had not been applied to Ireland in 1916, as it had in Britain, for fear of another armed Sinn Féin rebellion. This led many nationalists to deduce that it was British fear of extremism which forced the government to negotiate.

The IPP sought to retrieve its political position in Ireland through participation in the Irish Convention, which sat from July 1917 until March 1918. It was called by the British government as an attempt to get 'representative' Irishmen to agree a form of self-government for Ireland; Sinn Féin, however, boycotted its proceedings. The majority of the Convention delegates carried a series of resolutions which together formed a complete scheme of Irish self-government. This provided for the establishment of a parliament for the whole of Ireland with an executive responsible to it, and full powers over all internal legislation, administration and direct taxation.[29] Although Ulster Unionists and a number of Nationalists dissented from the Convention's conclusions, a section of Unionists from Southern Ireland agreed to Home Rule for the first time, on the grounds that, through their participation in the war, Irish Nationalists had proved that they could be loyal to the British Crown and empire.

Any attempt to implement the Convention's conclusions was dashed by the massive German offensive on the Western Front in March 1918, which led the British government to consider extending conscription to Ireland. The conscription threat united all shades of nationalist opinion against the government and killed any chance that the Convention's conclusions would be implemented. The Mansion House Conference in Dublin in April 1918, representing all shades of nationalist opinion, produced a pledge inspired by Sinn Féin denying Britain's right to impose conscription on Ireland, and pledging 'solemnly to . . . resist conscription by the most effective means at our disposal'.[30] Joseph Devlin, IPP leader of Nationalists in Ulster, summed up the opinion of all nationalists when he denied the right of the British to decide whether 'an unemancipated race should pay its blood tax to another'. The British, he claimed, had given Irish nationalists a dual insult – the denial of self-government and the denial of the right to determine whether their nation's sons were to be conscripted.[31] The main political beneficiary of the conscription débâcle was Sinn Féin. Many nationalists believed that the British had drawn back because they feared another rebellion, and supported Sinn Féin because it had always stood against any sort of military alliance with Britain. Electorally this was demonstrated in the 1918 general election which saw Sinn Féin sweep away the IPP, winning seventy-three seats to the latter's seven.

The lesson drawn by Ulster Unionists from these developments was that nationalists were inherently disloyal. The Ulster Unionist delegation at the Irish Convention argued, in the face of increasing nationalist hostility to the war-effort, their belief that

> this war is Ireland's war, as well as England's or Scotland's, all through to the end. The blood of our sons has fallen and is falling in no stinted flow on many a field in the defence of liberty and for the securing of peace and freedom to future generations.[32]

The blood sacrifice of nationalist soldiers for king and country was forgotten by Ulster Unionists who instead contrasted their sacrifice at the Battle of the Somme with that of the Easter rebels who had appealed for support from 'gallant allies in Europe', that is to the Germans. At the Battle of the Somme the 36th (Ulster) Division, exclusively recruited in Ulster and overwhelmingly Protestant, was virtually wiped out on the morning of 1 July 1916, suffering 5,104 casualties, of which some 2,000 died.[33] The Reverend R.S. Morrison, rector of St Saviour's, Portadown, summed up the unionist sense of betrayal when he explained how

> A feeling of profound and heartfelt sorrow held chief place in their minds for their gallant and noble brothers who had made the supreme sacrifice for King and country...so willingly rendered, and involving such costly self-sacrifice to our Empire in her hour of greatest need. . . . The Sinn Féin rebellion . . . in the midst of such a national crisis...was an irrefutable impeach-ment of the Nationalist...party...which no Loyalist Britisher would ever forget. . . . To talk of a future compromise arrived at by the patriotic Irishmen who have fought side by side on the banks of the Somme, and whose forefathers fought against each other on the banks of the Boyne, was the dream of a visionary.[34]

Before 1916 Ulster Unionists had felt it possible to avoid any kind of Home Rule in Ireland, and so had not had to reflect on the implications of the reality of Home Rule for their definitions of Irishness and Britishness. But, in the aftermath of the 1916 Rising, both British Unionist and Liberal members of the government concluded that Home Rule, for at least part of Ireland, would have to be implemented to appease Irish-American and Irish-Dominion opinion. For Ulster Unionists, Ireland's exclusion from conscrip-tion, which was applied throughout Great Britain, had a deep psychological effect upon their relationship with their Irishness. In 1916 Carson asked how Ireland was to be looked at in England; he was receiving letters, daily, from Englishmen calling him a cow-ard, accusing him of preventing Irishmen from being exposed to the same dangers as they were, and reflected 'when the hour of victory comes...we who are Irishmen will feel ashamed to remember that we expected others to make sacrifices from which we provided our own exclusion'.[35] Sir James Craig, Northern Ireland's first prime minister from 1921 to 1940, told Nationalists in 1916 that 'It has always been a pride to a man, no matter what part of the country he came from, to say he was an Irishman', but if Ireland's nationalist representatives refused to accept conscription in Ireland, 'then I say for my part if this victory is gained it will be no pleasure to me to call myself an Irishman, and in future it will either have to be a Britisher or an Ulsterman'.[36] This also extended to a future Northern Ireland premier, Lord Brookeborough, who served during the war, and over fifty years later was not happy about being called an Irishman because of the 1916 Rebellion.[37] This experience was compounded when the Irish Convention recommended a Home Rule scheme. For example, one adviser to the Ulster Unionist delegation to the Irish Convention warned Nationalists and Southern Unionists, who had agreed to these proposals, that

> If the choice is forced upon them ... of saying which Union they attach more importance to, they will be bound to say that strong as the ties are which attach them to the rest of Ireland, the ties which attach them to Great Britain are stronger, and if one set of ties has to be severed they would regretfully decide that it must be the Irish ties.[38]

The war transformed the nature of the Irish and Ulster Questions. At the beginning of the war the dominant Irish nationalist political party had sought self-government within the United Kingdom and had shown itself willing to compromise over Ulster; after the war, Sinn Féin, which replaced it, sought self-government outside the United Kingdom and seemed unable to take seriously the views of the Northern unionists. Sinn Féin was not committed, as was the IPP, to Irish unity by consent, believing instead that it was in the power of the British government to legislate Ulster unionists into a united Ireland. Shaped by this belief Sinn Féin began to carve out its vision of a Catholic and Gaelic Ireland. Ulster Unionists, on the other hand, embraced Home Rule for their part of a partitioned Ireland as the best deal available to them and as a bulwark against any attempt to force them into a united Ireland. The post-war settlement ultimately was a partition of the country which created, on the one hand, an independent Irish Republic with an aspiration to be both Catholic and Gaelic, an aspiration unhindered by any substantial opposing minority; and, on the other, a jurisdiction in Northern Ireland with a clear Protestant–unionist majority, an unassailable purchase on power, and a disgruntled and ultimately discriminated-against Catholic minority.

The December 1918 General Election saw Sinn Féin win seventy-three seats to the IPP's seven. Sinn Féin's MPs refused to take their seats in the British Parliament, instead constituting themselves in Dublin as the Parliament of Ireland (Dáil Eireann) and issuing a Declaration of Independence announcing an Irish Republic in January 1919. Sinn Féin, unsuccessfully, looked to present their case for independence to the post-war Peace Conference, sending a message to the free nations of the world, calling on them to support the Irish Republic's appeal for recognition. The claim rested on the view that Ireland had never willingly surrendered its sovereign status and that Ireland, by history, culture, and language was a distinctive, individual and separate nation.[39] However, despite President Wilson's rhetoric about 'small nations', the forces of international politics, combined with the pro-German sympathies of some elements in Sinn Féin during the war, combined to ensure that the case received little support.

The new political realities caused by the election results led to a physical confrontation between the armed wing of the Sinn Féin movement, the Irish Republican Army (IRA), and the British armed forces. The result was, from 1919 to 1921, a guerrilla war fought with great brutality on both sides including what amounted to acts of sanctioned state terrorism. During this savagery, to placate Ulster Unionists, the British Parliament passed the 1920 Government of Ireland Act, partitioning Ireland into the devolved jurisdictions of Northern Ireland and Southern Ireland. The intention was that both these new entities were to remain within the monarchical state of the United Kingdom of Great Britain and Ireland.

However, the military stalemate between the British and the IRA during the period 1919–1921 led eventually to negotiations between the British and Sinn Féin and a treaty which saw the Irish delegates accept 'Dominion status' for twenty-six Irish counties. On paper this independence seemed limited: the British King was head of state, represented by a Governor-General, and all elected representatives had to take an Oath of Allegiance to the King. The terms of the treaty produced a split within Sinn Féin causing a bloody civil war during 1922–1923 and the formation of two new political parties: the pro-treaty Cumann na nGaedheal party of W.T. Cosgrave and the anti-treaty Fianna Fáil party of Eamon de Valera. Members of the Dáil had taken an oath to the Republic in 1919 to 'support and defend the Irish Republic and the Government of the Irish Republic...against all enemies, foreign and domestic'.[40] De Valera, President of the Irish Republic, believed his first duty was to secure a republic. On 25 October 1921 he had decided that if the alternative to war with Britain was making the

Irish people enter an arrangement which would 'make them subject to the Crown or demand from them allegiance to the British King', then 'If war is the alternative, we can only face it'.[41] Those opposed to the treaty argued that, as Ireland's Governor-General would be appointed by the British Crown and Ireland's constitution would be embodied in a British Act of Parliament, there could be no equality between Britain and the new Irish state; that the question was one of 'master and slave, of fealty and faithfulness', and that the Irish were going into the British empire as British subjects.[42] The rejection of the treaty was on the grounds that Irish nationalists would be doing for the first time what (they claimed) no previous generation of nationalists had ever thought of doing – wilfully admitting themselves to be British subjects, voluntarily giving allegiance to the British King.[43]

The political unity of the British Isles was therefore ended by the establishment of the Irish Free State or Saorstát Eireann (encompassing the twenty-six counties of 'Southern Ireland' as defined in the 1920 Act) as an Irish Dominion, within the British empire, or British Commonwealth of Nations, but outside what was now the United Kingdom of Great Britain and Northern Ireland. Ulster Unionists were granted their own devolved Parliament made up of the six counties of what constituted Northern Ireland, but within the United Kingdom. Unionists believed that the leaders of Saorstát Eireann were avowed Republicans who challenged the entire basis of self-government within the empire – that of loyalty to the Crown. They claimed that Saorstát Eireann intended to secede from that empire even though the legal status of British Dominions stated that they had no right to secede. Unionists none the less distinguished between the legal and the real status, arguing that if Australia decided to secede then the British fleet would not be dispatched to prevent this. Unionists argued that there was in practice an independent republic in Saorstát Eireann.[44]

Those opposed irrevocably to partition ensured that the early years of the new administrations, North and South, were characterised by violence and social disorder, a pattern that was to continue at intervals in Northern Ireland up to the present day. Political life in the South settled down fairly quickly to a peaceful contest between the competing constitutional visions of Cumann na nGaedheal and Fianna Fáil. The first government (Cumann na nGaedheal) believed that the empire had evolved into a commonwealth of nations, each with a growing sense of nationhood. They sought to restore the Kingdom of Ireland which had existed before the 1800 Anglo-Irish Union: that is a kingdom separate from the Kingdom of Great Britain before the Act of Union of 1800 merged the two kingdoms into the single United Kingdom of Great Britain and Ireland. The consequence of this would be that the people of Saorstát Eireann would be Irish subjects of the King of Ireland alone, while the people of Great Britain would be British subjects of the British King alone, although the monarch of both countries would be the same person.[45]

The succession of De Valera's Fianna Fáil party to power in 1932 ended this experiment. De Valera's vision was of a Republic of Ireland, and he proceeded to remove the Oath of Allegiance in 1932, to delete all domestic constitutional references to the King in 1936, to abolish in the same year the office of the governor-general, and to introduce in 1937 a new written constitution. The effect of these changes was to dismantle the treaty's provisions and effectively establish a republic in all but name. De Valera redefined independent Ireland's relationship with the Commonwealth by developing his concept of External Association. External Association sought to reconcile British imperial and Irish republican aspirations by proposing that Britain recognise a republic in Ireland, this to be balanced by that republic's association, from outside, with the British Commonwealth of Nations, for the advancement of their common interest.[46]

These efforts at state-making further alienated Ulster Unionists from their fellow Irishmen in the South. Unionists did not wish to become Irish citizens of an Irish republic or Irish subjects of an Irish kingdom, but to remain British subjects within a British kingdom. The creation of Saorstát Eireann alienated even those Unionists who sought some sort of ultimate Irish unity. The Government of Ireland Act 1920 had set up a Council of Ireland composed of members of the Northern Ireland and Southern Ireland parliaments to make executive decisions on an all-Ireland basis. In 1920, Sir Edward Carson, had expressed the hope that this Council would contain the germ of a united Ireland in future.[47] However, the condition under which Unionists such as Carson were prepared to accept a united Ireland was one which would see Ireland loyal to Great Britain and loyal to the empire, and within the United Kingdom.[48] By 1924, however, Carson, surveying relations between Northern Ireland and the Free State, believed

Saorstát Eireann was a republic in all but name. He resented the fact that Saorstát Eireann refused to fly the flag of the Commonwealth, the Union Jack, that the King's name was removed, as that of a foreign King, from every legal proceeding, that Britons were considered 'foreigners', and that it was compulsory for children, including Protestant children, to learn the Irish language.[49]

In Northern Ireland, the combination of a guaranteed majority in government, a sense of being under siege, and the presence of an often violent, trapped and profoundly reluctant minority, led to the creation of a state apparatus designed to ensure survival. The consequence was, almost inevitably, a society which treated the minority with, at best, suspicion and, at worst, discrimination and bias. A succession of narrow and unimaginative governments seemed unable to perceive that, with equal inevitability, the minority would remain hostile and therefore ensure instability. The problem was never constructed as a problem to be solved rather than simply a position to be defended.

One-party Unionist governments were guaranteed by the electoral system, ensuring the political dominance of one community over the other. The primary grievance of Northern Nationalists was that the partition of Ireland was unnatural and there was a general refusal to accept its legitimacy and, particularly in the early years, to participate in its institutions.[50] Northern Nationalists complained that the Northern Ireland Parliament refused to give justice to the minority and their representatives. Every attempt to have the grievances of the minority discussed at Westminster was defeated by the existence of a 'convention' which prevented discussion of matters which were within the competence of the Northern Ireland Parliament. Northern Nationalists protested at discrimination against Catholics in the civil service, the creation of a Protestant-dominated paramilitary police force, and the gerrymandering of electoral wards to produce artificial unionist majorities.[51]

In turn, Ulster Protestant Unionists, who wished to retain the union with Britain, regarded Northern Catholic Nationalists, seeking union with Saorstát Eireann, as enemies determined to destroy the state. Northern Ireland's first prime minister, Lord Craigavon (formerly Sir James Craig), believed that the employment of 'disloyalists' in the civil service was prejudicial to the safety of the state. Craigavon argued 'in the South they boasted of a Catholic State. They still boast of Southern Ireland being a

Catholic State. All I boast of is that we are a Protestant Parliament and a Protestant State.'[52] Lord Brookeborough, Northern Ireland's prime minister from 1943 to 1963, asked if discrimination against Catholics could have been eased, replied 'Yes, it could have been done, but it would have been politically difficult because of the antipathy of the Roman Catholics and the fact that they were backing the IRA. They were out to defeat Northern Ireland and shoot our people.' Asked who were the disloyalists, he replied 'Most of them Catholics.' 'I am not', he insisted, 'criticising their religion', but 'they won't do anything about the Union Jack, they won't take their hats off, they won't stand up when God Save the Queen is played.'[53] Brookeborough said that Catholics were not given positions of power because 'how can you give somebody who is your enemy a higher position in order to allow him to come and destroy you?'[54]

The new Irish state was equally unable to understand that the Northern unionists were not just posturing in their determination to remain British, and that their protestantism was an important and unbargainable part of their position. The power of the Catholic church was obvious and public and a religiously homogeneous southern Irish state was assumed and legislated for. Developments included: legislation prohibiting divorce, promoted sternly by the Roman Catholic Archbishop of Dublin;[55] De Valera's publicly expressed view that, while there would be no religious discrimination against the Protestant minority, the Irish people were 'ever firm in their allegiance to our ancestral faith and unswerving even to death' in their devotion to the Holy See; and the recognition, in Article 44 of Bunreacht na hÉireann (the Constitution of Ireland enacted in 1937), of the 'special position' of the Catholic church 'as the guardian of the Faith professed by the great majority of the citizens'.[56] All these served to confirm the Ulster Protestant fear of domination by the Catholic church.

The gaelicisation of Saorstát Eireann also alienated Unionists from their sense of Irishness. The Sinn Féin philosophy had been that to de-anglicise Ireland they had to de-anglicise themselves first.[57] To do this it was necessary, in Pearse's words, to make 'Ireland not merely free, but Gaelic as well'. One of the architects of the treaty, Michael Collins, believed that in a free Ireland 'we can fill our minds with Gaelic ideas, and our lives with Gaelic customs, until there is no room for any other'.[58] Cumann na nGaedheal decided that all instruction in the first two years of national schools should be in the Irish language, a policy which Fianna Fáil expanded to permit even greater emphasis on Irish.[59] Ulster Unionists, not surprisingly, saw 'Pro-Gaelic' as 'Anti-British'.[60]

The Great War changed the overall pattern of events and gave opportunity and power to the forces of cultural and political separation in both parts of Ireland. The need to continue with a process of consultation, discussion and compromise that events prior to the war seemed to make inevitable, was denied by the press of international events. Boundaries and demarcations – both of thought and of territory – that had seemed permeable before, became fixed and solid. Consequently, the solution to the Irish problem that emerged in the 1920s from the shadows of the Great War, the Easter Rising, the savageries of civil and internecine struggle and community violence, gave rein to much that was worst about both nationalist and unionist. In the decades that followed, suspicions, fears and prejudices were consolidated and solidified by attitudes which emphasised and accentuated difference and encouraged mutual ignorance and dislike. Two distinct forms of cultural nationalism generated what Louis MacNeice called 'morose vendettas', which characterised all social, cultural and political life. It seemed impossible for either side to attach any value, worth or esteem to the way of life of the other.

All of this might have been defensible and even viable, if regrettable, but for the large minority of Catholics in Northern Ireland, who lived unwillingly in one culture and aspired to the other. Events, including the long twenty-five years of violence since 1969, seem to demonstrate empirically that their existence – and their unexpiated sense of grievance – made the settlement of 1920 inherently unstable. The problem for the future is to devise a system that does not simply ignore these difficulties, and to create a situation where violence is less likely to reappear.

NOTES

1   Note that 'Nationalist' and 'Unionist' refer to a particular political party organisation while 'nationalist' and 'unionist' to the more general political communities.
2   R.F. Foster, for example, writes, 'The First World War should be seen as one of the most decisive events in modern Irish history', *Modern Ireland, 1690–1972*, London: Allen Lane/Penguin, 1988, p.471.

3   Ernest Gellner in *Encounters with Nationalism*, Oxford: Blackwell, 1994, refers to the 'intellectual autism' of Conor Cruise O'Brien in his writings on Irish nationalism, p.59.
4   Walker Connor, *Ethnonationalism*, Princeton: Princeton University Press, 1993, p.4.
5   For a recent set of background papers see Seamus Dunn, *Facets of the Conflict*, London: Macmillan, 1995.
6   John Bowman, *De Valera and the Ulster Question 1917–1973*, Oxford: Oxford University Press, 1982, pp.11–12.
7   *House of Commons debates*, vol. XXXIX (*Hansard*, 13/6/1912), cols 1086–7.
8   J.E. Redmond, *The Justice of Home Rule: a statement of Ireland's claim for self-government*, London: (n.p.) 1912, p.10.
9   *The Irish National Convention 1912*, London: (n.p.) 1912, p.23.
10   Redmond, *op. cit.*, p.13.
11   John Hickey, *Religion and the Northern Ireland Problem*, Dublin: Gill & Macmillan, 1984, pp.62–3.
12   Thomas Hennessey, 'Ulster Unionist territorial and national identities 1886–1893: province, island, kingdom and empire', *Irish Political Studies*, 1993, vol. 8, pp.27–32.
13   A.T.Q. Stewart, *The Ulster Crisis: resistance to Home Rule 1912–1914*, London: Faber, 1967, p.62.
14   Michael Laffan, *The Partition of Ireland 1911–1925*, Dundalk: Dundalgan Press, 1983, pp.44–5.
15   Dennis Gwynn, *The Life of John Redmond*, London: 1932, p.365.
16   Edward Marjoribanks and Ian Colvin, *The Life of Lord Carson*, vol. III, London: Gollancz, 1934, pp.32–4.
17   *Freeman's Journal*, 21/9/1914.
18   Ibid., 17/9/1914.
19   Paul Bew, Ellen Hazelkorn and Henry Patterson, *The Dynamics of Irish Politics*, London: Lawrence & Wishart, 1989, p.15.
20   *Freeman's Journal*, 6/10/1914.
21   Trinity College Dublin Manuscripts: John Dillon papers, 26/9/1916: Dillon to O'Connor.
22   Ibid., 4/7/1915: Dillon to O'Connor.
23   Gwynn, *op cit.*, pp.431–32.
24   Parliamentary Paper Cmd 8279, *Royal Commission on the Rebellion in Ireland: minutes of evidence and appendix of documents*, London: HMSO, 1916, pp.20–1.
25   University College Dublin Archives: Richard Mulcahy Papers, P7/D/30.
26   Public Record Office, London, CAB 151/39.
27   Ibid., p.524.
28   *Dungannon Democrat*, 21/6/1916.
29   *Report of the Proceedings of the Irish Convention 1918*, Parliamentary Paper Cmd 9019, London: HMSO, pp.5–6.
30   Ibid., p.83.
31   *House of Commons debates*, vol. 104 (*Hansard*, 9/4/1918), col. 1371.

32   Public Record Office of Northern Ireland: Sir Edward Carson papers, D1507/A/25/5.
33   Philip Orr, *The Road to the Somme: men of the Ulster Division tell their story*, Belfast: Blackstaff Press, 1987, pp.199–200.
34   *Belfast News-Letter*, 11/7/1916.
35   *House of Commons debates*, vol. LXXVII (*Hansard*, 11/1/1916), cols 1483–84.
36   Ibid., vol. LXXVIII (17/1/1916), col. 49.
37   *Irish News*, 1/8/1969.
38   Public Record Office of Northern Ireland: Hugh de Fellenburg Montgomery papers, D627/436/25A & B; De Fellenburg Montgomery to Mary ffolliott, 23/8/1918.
39   *Documents Relative to the Sinn Fein Movement in Ireland*, Parliamentary Paper Cmd 1108, 1921.
40   *Dáil Eireann public session*, 20/8/1919, pp.150–1.
41   *Dáil Eireann private session*, 14/12/1921 pp.101–3.
42   *Dáil Eireann public session*, 21/12/1921, pp.100–1.
43   *Dáil Eireann public session*, 7/1/1921, p.330.
44   *House of Commons debates*, vol. 151 (*Hansard*, 2/3/1922), cols 693–5.
45   *Dáil Eireann*, vol. 39 (16/12/1931), cols 1633–4.
46   *Dail Eireann private session*, 15/12/1921, cols 202–3.
47   *House of Commons debates*, vol. 134 (*Hansard*, 8/11/1920), cols 925–7.
48   Ibid. (11/11/1920), cols. 1441–42.
49   *House of Lords debates* (*Hansard*, 8/10/1924), col. 563.
50   Michael Farrell, *Northern Ireland: the Orange State*, London: Pluto Press, 1976, pp.66–7.
51   J.H. Whyte, *Interpreting Northern Ireland*, Oxford: Clarendon Press, 1990, p.166.
52   *Northern Ireland House of Commons debates* , vol. XVI (24/4/1934), col. 1090.
53   *Belfast Telegraph*, 18/2/1969.
54   *Irish News*, 1/8/1969.
55   J.J. Lee, *Ireland 1912–1985: politics and society*, Cambridge: Cambridge University Press, 1989, p.157.
56   Ibid., p.203.
57   *Sinn Féin*, 25/9/1909.
58   D.G. Boyce, *Nationalism in Ireland*, London: Croom Helm, 1982, p.354.
59   Lee, *op. cit.*, p.34.
60   Dennis Kennedy, *The Widening Gulf*, Belfast: Blackstaff Press, 1988, p.182.

Chapter 11

The enduring legacy
Reflections on Versailles

A.M. Gallagher

The First World War was to be the war that ended all wars as it demonstrated the horrifying consequences of industrialised slaughter and foreshadowed the new vulnerability of civilian populations. That it had been unlike anything experienced before can be seen also in the way people approached the construction of the peace at war's end. For Harold Nicolson the journey to the Peace Conference in Paris was not:

> merely to liquidate the war, but to found a new order in Europe. We were preparing not peace only, but Eternal Peace. There was about us the halo of divine mission. We must be alert, stern, righteous and ascetic. For we were bent on doing great, permanent and noble things.[1]

In such an atmosphere the moral attraction of Wilsonism seems obvious. Past congresses and conferences in Europe had traded people and territory in the interests of a balance of power. Wilson's Fourteen Points seemed to provide an alternative basis for settlement, which, by applying democratic ideals, would ensure the future peace.

The advocates of the older balance-of-power system felt that peace in Europe was most likely to be achieved by either a system of shifting alliances with no protagonist ever gaining predominant power, or the occasional intervention by a balancing power. In this view a plethora of little states was undesirable because it gave power to those ill-versed in statecraft, created a large number of weak states, increased the number of potential conflicts that could break out and generally heightened the fault-lines in the international system. So important was the idea of maintaining balance that friends could be abandoned and borders changed if the needs of stability so required.

The newer world-view advocated from the United States sought the same ends of peace and stability, but offered an alternative path to their achievement. From this viewpoint the balance of power system had only produced selfishness and aggression. By contrast, states based on the self-determination of their populations would be more stable because, being democratic, they were 'naturally' peaceful. Not only would they not go to war or oppress their neighbours, but they would rise to defend the gains achieved by the international community.[2] So, was the grand vision of Wilson realised?

Writing in 1929, Winston Churchill argued that the grand vision had worked. While accepting that some territorial settlements had to take geopolitical and economic considerations into account, he argued that all the remaining disputed areas were but a tiny fraction of the continent. Indeed, he went on to assert that this was the first time that the map of Europe had conformed with the general wishes of its peoples.[3]

Writing somewhat later, Birdsall was to make essentially the same point when he argued that:

> the territorial settlement contained in the various treaties negotiated at Paris is still, with all its faults, the closest approximation to an ethnographic map that has ever been achieved.[4]

A more recent, and contrasting view, is offered by Hobsbawm. The primary aim of achieving peace in Europe had collapsed within twenty years. More particularly Hobsbawm felt that the attempt to promote stable states and reduce interstate and interethnic conflict also failed: 'The national conflicts tearing the continent apart in the 1990s were the old chickens of Versailles once again coming home to roost'.[5] In fact he goes further to suggest that not only did the treaty not solve problems of the time, but by creating new, artificial, multi-ethnic states, it actually made the future worse than it might have been.

In his chapter in this volume, Sharp provides us with a more balanced assessment. On one level the territorial arrangements of Versailles resulted in the number of people living as ethnic minorities being halved, as was the proportion of people living as minorities in east and central Europe. It may be, as he suggests, that this was about the best that could have been achieved given the ethnic mix that existed on the ground. Sharp also reminds us that the peacemakers recognised that minority communities remained in post-Versailles Europe, but that they sought to legitimise the rights of minorities and their protection through the League of Nations. However, the basis for the protection of minorities was not on the pluralist grounds of celebrating diversity, but rather in order to make the conditions of minorities so reasonable that they would quickly assimilate into the national communities within which they lived.

Before drawing some general lessons from the case studies of this volume, let us briefly remind ourselves of some of the main territorial rearrangements that occurred after the end of the First World War. Under the Treaty of Versailles (1919), Germany surrendered Alsace–Lorraine, Posen (Poznan), west Prussia, the Hultschin (Hlusin) district and the Memel district. Danzig (Gdańsk)became a free city and the Saar Basin was placed under the administration of the League of Nations for fifteen years. In addition, plebiscites were planned for Eupen-Malmedy, northern Schleswig, parts of east Prussia and Upper Silesia. Under the Treaty of St-Germain (1919), Austria ceded South Tyrol to Italy. In further territorial concessions Austria was to give up Trieste, Istria, Dalmatia, and parts of Carinthia and Carniola. In addition, Austria was obliged to recognise the independence of Hungary, Czechoslovakia, Poland and Yugoslavia, and was prohibited from considering *Anschluss* with Germany.

In November 1919, the Treaty of Beuilly was signed by Bulgaria. Under the treaty Bulgaria ceded south-western areas of Trace along the Mediterranean coast to Greece, but retained access to the sea. In June 1920, the Treaty of Trianon was signed with Hungary. As one of the successor states to the Austro-Hungarian empire, Hungary was considered to be, and treated as one of the powers responsible for the outbreak of war. Thus Slovakia and Carparto-Ukraine were ceded to Czechoslovakia; Croatia-Slavonia and parts of Banat were ceded to Yugoslavia; Transylvania and parts of Banat to Romania; and Burgenland to Austria.

Under the Treaty of Sèvres, signed in August 1920 by the Turkish government but not ratified by the Turkish parliament, Turkey ceded eastern Trace, some of the Aegean islands and Smyrna to Greece; Syria and Cilicia to France; Iraq and Palestine to Britain; the Dodecanese and Rhodes to Italy; and Armenia received autonomy. Between 1920 and 1922 many of these territorial losses were regained. Turkey's eastern border was confirmed in a series of treaties with the USSR while in the rest of the country the territorial arrangements were ratified in the Treaty of Lausanne (1923), after which 1.3 million Greeks and 0.4 million Turks were resettled.

Within this broad pattern of territorial arrangements, the cases considered in this volume cover a range of circumstances. These include situations such as Northern Ireland and the South Tyrol where the territorial situation in the 1920s remains essentially the same today. Another case where the basic framework remains similar is Hungary, albeit that this context altered considerably during the war years. In most of the remaining cases considered, the territorial conditions have changed over time: thus in the Middle East there has been the partition of Palestine, the creation of Israel, and alteration of territorial control following the fortunes of war. In Czechoslovakia we have seen the rise, fall, restoration and separation of the state. In Yugoslavia the state imploded in the 1990s and in Ukraine national independence has been achieved. What do these cases tell us about the hopes invested in Versailles and beyond? To what extent has ethnic politics played a role in these situations, or have any changes been consequent on other factors?

Dunn and Hennessey highlight the role that the rhetoric of Versailles played in the dispute over Ireland's future. On the one hand Irish nationalists argued that the island was a 'discrete geographical entity' while, on the other hand, the idea of a confessional Roman Catholic state held few attractions for the Protestant minority on the island. That this minority was geographically concentrated in the north-east of the island only complicated matters still further. The nationalist Rising in 1916 illustrates well the capacity for unforeseen circumstances to disrupt the apparent flow of events and send them careering off into another direction. One immediate consequence was to elevate Sinn Féin as the main nationalist political voice and it tried to promote the cause of an independent Ireland on the basis of national self-determination. The actual settlement in the 1920s created two jurisdictions on the island: an independent Irish state and a largely self-governing province of the United Kingdom. Both came to be characterised to an extent by mono-ethnic symbolism and the smaller entity, Northern Ireland, was afflicted also by political instability because of the continuing presence of a nationalist minority.

The Protestant unionists in 1920 saw little economic sense in going into the Irish state while the Catholic nationalists in Northern Ireland saw little emotional virtue in not going into the Irish state. In time, the Catholic minority viewpoint in Northern Ireland would become reinforced by material factors. The circumstances of the birth of Northern Ireland did not encourage the unionists to display magnanimity. That they did not do so discouraged the nationalist minority for playing the role of loyal opposition and this in turn reinforced the unionist perception that they were dealing with an irredentist fifth column in their midst. Three-quarters of a century after Versailles this dispute remains unresolved.

A similar framework, if somewhat different consequences, can be seen in Alcock's chapter on South Tyrol. This territory was ceded from Austria to Italy in 1919 and remains there today. The key issues in South Tyrol have concerned the treatment of the territory and people by the Italian state, which itself changed over time as well, and the extent to which the German-speaking community in the territory pursued the objective of reintegration with Austria. As Alcock's discussion makes clear, the territory never became Italian in the sense that the autonomous identity of the German-speaking community did not change or disappear. In the period after the Second World War the failure to achieve an agreed level of autonomy for the region provided an opportunity for violent opponents of the Italian state to operate for a time. However, agreement was eventually reached and material circumstances have worked to the relative advantage of the South Tyrolese. This combination of relative wealth and autonomy appears to have reconciled the German-speaking community in South Tyrol to a future in the Italian state even though they appear to be considering new ways of developing that autonomy through the EU, as we shall see below.

Wallace's chapter details the account of the birth, death, rebirth and divorce of the Czech and Slovak states. A key feature of the discussion lies in the fragility of the unity between the two peoples. This was compounded by the fact that approaches which may have helped to ameliorate differences between them were restricted by the impact such measures might have had on other communities living within the territory. Thus Wallace reminds us that even though Czech representatives at the 1919 Peace Conference outlined a vision of the new state as the Switzerland of the east, once independence was achieved there was no question of cantonisation because of the autonomy this might have devolved to the Sudeten Germans, among others.

Is this sufficient to explain why the differences within Czechoslovakia persisted? Another factor appears to have been material differences between the two communities, or perhaps more accurately between the regions within which each community predominated. Wallace's account reminds us again how easy it is to translate such material differences into ethnic discourses, even if it takes a special confluence of circumstances for the ethnic activists to begin to set new agendas. And this remains the final paradox of the Czechoslovakian experience: with all the persisting differences and the retrospective ease with which we can see the flaws of unity, when the split occurred it happened peacefully. Perhaps Wallace is completely right when he suggests that no perfect solution to their relationship ever existed, but that the solution adopted at different times was the best that might have been hoped for at those times. And just as circumstances changed, so too did the solution they followed.

A fragile unity between communities is a theme also of Lane's account of Yugoslavia. The conflict in Yugoslavia in recent years has prompted many to question why the state collapsed so suddenly and in such violence. Lane, on the other hand, indicates that the more appropriate question may be to ask why Yugoslavia survived as long as it did. At birth the state seemed to be based on a loose compromise which was not to be resolved in the ensuing years. Lane suggests, in fact, that as the state became increasingly centralised and autocratic the problems did not so much go away, rather, conditions were created to minimise their expression. After the Second World War the compromise continued, now based on both a fictive account of Yugoslav resistance to the Nazis and the drawing of a veil over the collaborationist approach of some Yugoslavs. The ideological unity which this twin-track approach aimed to reinforce might have worked had it not been for the destabilising effects of economic decline, the rise of ethnic politicians and consequent inter-community rivalry. Indeed it seems clear now that the compromise upon which the state was based has not so much been addressed as abandoned, in favour of strategies of ethnic dominance.

In Wallace's discussion of Czechoslovakia, a persistent theme lies in the role of external powers. Whatever the differences between the two main communities, a crucial role in bringing matters to a head was played by external powers. This was true of Germany in the 1930s, the USSR in 1968 and, by contrast, the impact of the disappearance of the USSR towards the end of the 1980s. In Lane's account we also see the important role of external bodies, but on this occasion the role is somewhat different. Whereas in the case of Czechoslovakia external powers were a destabilising force which brought internal contradictions to a head, in Yugoslavia it would appear that external threats helped to reinforce internal cohesion. In the inter-war years, for example, Lane suggests that for most of the constituent nations of Yugoslavia the attraction of the state was less in its positive merits and more in the perceived negative consequences of separation. Similarly, Tito achieved a degree of internal cohesion because of the isolation of Yugoslavia from both the socialist and the capitalist camps. The strength of this explanation is reinforced still further by Lane's suggestion that by the end of the 1980s this external threat no longer existed: Yugoslavia was no longer isolated or under threat, but this external stabilisation ironically appears to have prompted internal destabilisation. It would seem that the alternatives to unity no longer appeared to some Yugoslav politicians to be so bad. The fragility of Yugoslavia was revealed by the fact that once some started to follow particularistic agendas then others were encouraged or felt obliged to follow similar paths. Not only was no-one left to speak for Yugoslavia, but the voices that were heard were the siren voices of ethnic essentialism.

So far we have considered four examples. Two of the examples, Northern Ireland and the South Tyrol, are regions within a larger state, created in the post-Versailles period and containing communities with irredentist ambitions. By the 1990s the regions remained within the larger units, the irredentist communities had not been assimilated even though the extent of their irredentism had perhaps reduced. The other two cases concerned multi-ethnic states which were brought into existence at the end of the First World War but which did not survive the 1990s. In both cases the collapse of the states was on ethnic grounds, although only one collapsed in violence. Now we turn to a different type of example. Hungary offers a case where the legacy of Versailles is not a multi-ethnic population, but the fact that a significant proportion of the

Hungarian 'nation' lives outside the territory of the Hungarian 'state'. Furthermore, an important component of the Hungarian diaspora is a 'near-diaspora' in adjoining states. As Pearson puts it, Hungary is 'a territorial heartland politically detached from, but in tantalisingly close physical proximity to, about one-quarter of all the people who identify themselves as Hungarian'.

In its post-war attempts to hold the territory together, the Hungarian leadership, like the Czechoslovaks, declared the goal of an eastern Switzerland. Unlike the Czechoslovaks, the Hungarians were not to get the opportunity to try the experiment. Indeed, as Pearson also points out, the short-lived Communist regime of Bela Kun perhaps only reinforced the Allied concern for punitive conditions to be imposed on Hungary. Notwithstanding these terms it is clear that the dream of restoring territory was not readily given up. That Turkey successfully replaced the measures contained in the Treaty of Sèvres with the more acceptable measures in the Treaty of Lusanne demonstrated that change was possible. In addition, support from a great power was needed to move it from possible to probable. Hence the 'marriage of convenience' between Hungary and Nazi Germany, that was in time to prove to the detriment of Hungary yet again. Not only was Hungary reduced back to its Trianon borders, but, in 1947, lost a little more to Czechoslovakia. And so it remains today.

The basic tenets of the Hungarian problem remain as they emerged after the First World War, despite changes consequent on the Second World War and the Cold War. At worst, Pearson suggests, the legacy of Trianon maintains the opportunity for ethnic fanatics to promote their cause and destabilise any or all of the seven neighbouring states. At best, the legacy of Trianon continues to scar Hungarian politics and render problematic its relationship with its neighbours. That said, these problems are not currently manifest, perhaps because Hungary is seeking to be the first Eastern entrant to the EU.

If the case of Hungary illustrates a situation where the basic parameters of the problem have remained the same since Versailles, the chapter by Wilson on Ukraine highlights the extent to which circumstances have changed. At the beginning of the century the Ukraine was a multi-ethnic mosaic, with a largely rural ethnic Ukrainian peasantry and a largely urbanised mix of German, Jewish and Polish populations. By the end of the century the extent of ethnic pluralism has dropped considerably. In large part this is explained by Ukraine's strategic location as a battle-ground. In particular, the Second World War had particularly dramatic consequences for Ukraine, not least being the post-war expulsion of the German and Polish populations, and the wartime extermination of Ukrainian Jews. Thus the ethnic crucible in Ukraine has changed considerably in the years since Versailles, and the changes have been largely consequent on forces outside Ukraine itself. A second point highlighted by the Ukrainian case concerns the non-inevitability of ethnic politics. In Ukraine the ethnic mix has reduced so that the contemporary context mainly involves ethnic Ukrainians and Russian speakers. However, not all Ukrainians follow a nationalist agenda or support nationalist political parties.

The final case we examine here concerns Fraser's assessment of the consequences following the reorganisation of the Ottoman empire after the First World War. Fraser argues that here too the promise of Versailles has not been realised in that there has been a history of ethnic disputes based on religious, cultural, linguistic and other divisions. It may be that Wilsonianism was not applied to this region. Fraser points to the example of Britain's attitude to the Ottoman empire's treatment of Armenian and Balkan Chris-tians: they could be outraged at what was happening without actually doing anything about it, until such time as Ottoman action seemed to threaten supply lines from within the British empire. If this reflects the balance of power world-view which Wilson sought to displace, Fraser suggests that essentially the same approach may have been applied after Versailles. Balance of power considerations, he argues, seemed to loom larger in the minds of the Great Powers than any consideration of the wishes of the indigenous populations: 'It need hardly be said that these proposed arrangements took no account of possible Arab political aspirations, still less of any ethnic or confessional nuances.' Later Fraser notes that 'It is hard to escape the conclusion that Anglo-French policy towards the Middle East has been characterised by little more than wartime expediency underpinned by post-war imperial ambition.' While their declaration that self-determina-tion of the peoples oppressed by the Turks rings hollow to the historian, '"self-determination" has become the fashion of the hour and it remained to be seen how the victors would apply it to the peoples of the region, if at all'.

Fraser highlights the particular case of Greater Lebanon, the establishment of which was announced in 1920 and which, in 1975, was to explode into one of the Middle East's bloodiest communal struggles. This conflict itself resulted from the collapse of a complex political compromise between the various ethnic communities which was based on population proportions of 1932, but which, once established, was too fragile to be developed even though everyone knew, unofficially, that the population proportions were changing. In an interesting echo of the discussions on Czechoslovakia and Hungary, Lebanon was to be the Switzerland of the Middle East. Its relative longevity is not to be lightly dismissed, but nor should the lesson from its unpreparedness to change with circumstances, or its use of a solution that had a built-in self-destruct facility because it militated against change or development. And then, of course, there was the dispute between the Jews of Israel and the Palestinians, only recently mitigated by a political settlement that itself has yet to pass the test of history.

So where do these case studies leave the promise of Versailles? Sharp suggests that Wilson himself did not really understand the implications of what he said, and even the American delegation were unsure of the unit that was to form the basis of self-determination. In any case, there were numerous examples where the new principled approach to international relations was abandoned in favour of the older balance-of-power approach. Indeed, Sharp argues that the wartime protagonists had toyed with the notion of promoting nationalism prior to Wilson's intervention, although as he also points out, for any multi-ethnic, imperialist or autocratic power this was a double-edged sword. The British, for example, could encourage the Arabs to revolt for independence, but only make clear after the war that their understanding of independence was that the Arabs would be independent of any European power save Britain. It is also possible that the principled position was one developed for tactical reasons rather than as a result of a grander strategic vision. The alternatives of breaking up or maintaining the Habsburg empire, for example, remained as options, suggested Sharp, even up to and almost beyond the point where the empire ceased to exist. Also, and in a further illustration of this point, Sharp can quote the words of Gilbert Murray when he declared that 'It was quite late in the war when we discovered that we were fighting for the independence of the Czecho-Slovaks and General Smuts confessed that it came to him as a surprise.'

In the event balance-of-power considerations did clearly influence the final decisions and minorities were left in various states. The Allies might claim that 'Every territorial settlement of the Treaty of Peace has been determined upon after most careful and laboured consideration of all the religious, racial and linguistic factors in each particular country', but one does not have to search too hard to find examples of where these grand words were not matched by the reality on the ground.

Viewed from another direction, however, Wilsonianism may have been based on something quite new and different, albeit that it was confused in its exposition and fitful in its application. The balance-of-power view was based on a notion of sovereignty that reflected a pre-liberal, or early liberal view of the state. Wilson, by contrast, was offering a more radical conception of sovereignty based on the people. As Sharp suggests, Wilson may not have intended to promote a multiplicity of ethnic communities, but rather to promote state communities where the state had been freely chosen, and hence legitimised, by the people. The experience of active citizenship would, for Wilson, provide the stabilising glue of the new societies and the new Europe. In the event active citizenship did not create a new band of loyalties to displace more traditional identities. In societies like Northern Ireland, South Tyrol, Czechoslovakia and Yugoslavia, the older ethnic identities did not disappear through processes of assimilation. Similarly, in Hungary the exploitation of territorial issues for ethnic ends remains possible, if unlikely.

But perhaps, in asking whether or not the Versailles settlement solved the problem of ethnic conflict, we are asking the wrong question. It may be that ethnic problems are never resolved in the sense that mathematical problems are resolved. In some cases the terms of the problem changes, for good and bad reasons. In other cases the problem in the past remains the basic problem today. In some cases the problems have resulted in war and violence, while in others they have been managed or dealt with by other means. If we recognise the dynamic nature of any human society and the actual extent of territorial reorganisation that has occurred over a longer time span, then we might lay aside the unattainable goal of ethnically pure states. All societies are, to some degree, ethnically plural, and problems typically arise when this reality is actively denied. The best that we can hope for is the peaceful management of relations between groups, where disputes exist. And in circumstances where territorial boundaries look set to change, the best hope is that the changes occur by agreement, even if reluctant as in Czechoslovakia, rather than through war, as in Yugoslavia.

As a final thought, however, perhaps there is another path prefigured in some of the case studies. More recent developments in the European Union, allied to new ideas on regional organisation, open the intriguing possibility of a conception of sovereignty different from the autarkic model implicit in the idea of state sovereignty over defined territory, and in so much of social theory. In the South Tyrol, for example, we see the possibility of a mix of administrative authority at the level of the province, region, state and continent. The regional basis of organisation can be enabled by the overarching framework of the EU. At the same time it can provide a focus of identity that cuts across state identities and helps to ameliorate the statist myth of national homogeneity. The twentieth century has seen the end of three wars in Europe: the First and Second World Wars, and the Cold War. At the end of each the political map of Europe has changed and, less clearly, but no less profoundly, the way in which we understand the fabric of our own societies has changed. All we can be sure of in the future is that these processes of change will continue.

NOTES

1   H. Nicolson, *Peacemaking 1919*, London: Constable, 1933.
2   Henry Kissinger gives a good account of the contrasting principles in both positions: H. Kissinger, *Diplomacy*, London: Simon & Schuster, 1994.
3   W.S. Churchill, *The World Crisis: the Aftermath*, London: Odhams Press, 1929.
4   P. Birdsall, *Versailles Twenty Years After*, London: Allen & Unwin, 1941.
5   E. Hobsbawm, *Age of Extremes: the short twentieth century 1914–1991*, London: Michael Joseph, 1994.

Index